FREEDOM OF INFORMATION

LAW IN CONTEXT

Editors: Robert Stevens (University of California, Santa Cruz),
William Twining (University College, London) and
Christopher McCrudden (Lincoln College, Oxford)

ALREADY PUBLISHED

Freedom of Information

The Law, the Practice and the Ideal

PATRICK BIRKINSHAW
Lecturer in Law, University of Hull

WEIDENFELD AND NICOLSON
London

For my family

George Weidenfeld and Nicolson Ltd
91 Clapham High Street, London SW4 7TA

ISBN 0 297 79344 6 cased
ISBN 0 297 79386 1 paperback

Photoset by Deltatype Ltd, Ellesmere Port, Cheshire
Printed in Great Britain by Butler & Tanner, Frome and London

CONTENTS

PREFACE AND
ACKNOWLEDGMENTS

The final stages of this book were written amid a virtually un-precedented frenzy of litigation involving the press and media, and Government attempts to restrain what they could publish or broadcast. It also ended with a promise by the Home Secretary to 'reform' section 2 of the Official Secrets Act, and apprehension over intrusive information gathering associated with Poll Tax registers. These events, important as they are, are but a part of the information debate – a point which I hope this book will clarify.

Maurice Frankel of the Freedom of Information Campaign has been a constant source of assistance, and so too has Ron Bailey of the Community Rights Campaign. Harold Relyea of the Library of Congress has been an invaluable aid in his instruction on the operation of American laws. I would like to thank the Canadian Information and Privacy Commissioners for their help, as well as Professor John McCamus of Osgoode Hall. Denis O'Brien and Ron Fraser of the Australian Administrative Review Council helped me with the Australian dimension, as did the office of the Australian Commonwealth Ombudsman.

Norman Lewis read the typescript and he was generous in his time and criticism. I would like to thank the Centre for Criminological and Socio-Legal Studies at Sheffield University for inviting me to talk on the subject, as well as the Socio-Legal Group. William Twining and Chris McCrudden were exemplary in their help and constructive criticism on style and content. I benefitted enormously from their advice. Helen Forrester word-processed the manuscript with extra-ordinary competence and diligence. Needless to say any errors or oversights – *mea culpa*.

Patrick Birkinshaw
January, 1988

STATUTES

CASES

Introduction: Setting the Agenda

'Freedom of Information' has the ability to generate more controversy and heated debate than virtually any other aspect of contemporary government and administration. Press and media make daily references to the Official Secrets Acts, the confidentiality of state secrets, access to files, and protection of information collected by public or private bodies. 'Freedom of Information' has become a rallying cry of libertarians, if not quite the contemporary equivalent of 'Wilkes and Liberty' in eighteenth-century London or 'Reform' in nineteenth-century England.

But what does Freedom of Information mean? For most of those who employ the phrase it means having access to files, or to information in any form, in order to know what government is up to. Or it means access by individuals to files containing information about themselves – and an assurance that the information is not being used for improper or unauthorised purposes. Though it covers individual access to information, and the protection of information upon individuals from unjustified use, the scope of this book is much broader. Much of the information which this book covers is of little or no *direct* concern to individuals as individuals. But it will all, to a greater or lesser degree, constitute data on which decisions affecting the collective welfare, or someone's perception of that welfare, will be taken or influenced.

If individual access to such information is too costly, or too sensitive, or not worth the effort because of public apathy, or because there is little public feedback of views or ideas to inform specialists or decision-makers, is this an argument against freedom of information? Or is it an argument in favour of the provision of essential and unadulterated information to bodies whom we trust, so that they may check the policy-making process, render that process accountable, and report on their findings? One can imagine a departmental claim that a request by me to see all the files on the Channel Tunnel project is unreasonable, but that does not mean that nobody outside the department should have access to them in order to assess the project's viability and feasibility. The Freedom of Information debate tends less to promote this latter aspect but rather the question of individual entitlement and punitive governmental reaction to a sensational leak.

The collective aspect, as well as the individual one, is a central feature of the information debate; its analysis, at all levels of government, pervades the following pages. It makes little sense to be given access to government information when there is no independent method of checking its accuracy and reliability and no way of ensuring that government has given a full account of what it has been up to, and of knowing what alternatives to preferred options there are.

Government, it might be claimed, is the official regulation of human affairs for the greater good. What of government by unofficial means? Does the duty to inform end when regulation of essential interests or decisions affecting the collective welfare are taken by private bodies? Does the bartering between government and organised interests, in the private sphere, over the delivery of services to the public or for the public escape from scrutiny – scrutiny which is performed by the public or on behalf of the public? Is the market a suitable accountability device in itself? No responsible government has accepted such a stark conclusion, though it has accepted that constitutional controls will be much attenuated where the primary actors are private and not public. What place is there for freedom of information in this way of arranging the public interest? Where does the theme of freedom of information stand in relation to the belief that government is also the organisation of information for the use, effective or otherwise, of power in the public interest?

Freedom of information naturally flows into topics such as freedom of speech, censorship, the right to remain silent and not to answer incriminating questions, freedom of assembly, and so on. These themes form part of the information debate, but any allusion to them in greater detail than I have allowed would have altered the nature of the work. They are topics which have attracted a considerable amount of critical attention from informed sources. Freedom of information in a British framework has attracted much polemical and political attention. There is, however, little sustained analysis by a lawyer of the subject *de profundis*. What follows can only be an introduction to this vast subject.

The Audience

The primary audience for this book will be students of constitutional, administrative or public law. They are concerned with the relationship between law and politics, between law and political choice, political institutions and administration on behalf of the public interest. What sort of questions one poses about the relationship is often a matter of personal or political preference. The provision of information has always been at the centre of the relationships between government and society; provision of information has always been instrumental in the way governmental institutions have been created or allowed to develop. Such developments have occurred to fulfil public expectations in oversight, accountability, explanation or legitimacy for the exercise of power.

The use of the courts by individuals to extract information from political and administrative institutions as part of, or to mount, an attack on the exercise or non-exercise of public power depends upon the law. Much of this law, as we shall see in Chapter 6, is created or controlled by judges. It has been characteristic of the 1980s that we have seen the emergence of a variety of statutory duties to allow access to information in the possession of public and, in the case of the Data Protection Act 1984, private bodies, and this is likely to continue into the 1990s. In the concluding chapter, I shall present proposals for a Freedom of Information Act for central government and its agencies. As I write in mid-1987, the Government does not accept the need for such an Act. By the time this book has been published, or has acquired some birthdays, the position may be very different. Lawyers and administrators will find increasing demands placed upon their services in the 'Information Society' into which we have moved. This book attempts to examine the public law implications of such a movement. Interest in the subject ought to extend well beyond the field of public law.

I

Persistent Themes and Novel Problems

The popular phrase 'Information Society' was coined to describe the essence of the advanced computerised world. From financial markets to government, from national security to education, from multi-national corporations to small employers, from police to social welfare, medical treatment and social services, we are confronted by information repositories and retrieval systems whose capacity to store information is staggering. A moment's thought should make us appreciate that we have always been an information society. Anyone who has studied the constitutional history of Britain will appreciate that a major factor in the struggle between Crown and Parliament was the latter's desire to be informed about who counselled and advised the Monarch in the formulation of policy. That monumental work in the history of our public administration, the Domesday Book, was basically an information exercise to assess the wealth and stock of the nation. Our process of trial by law constitutes an attempt to exclude unreliable evidence and to establish by rules of evidence a more reliably informed basis of fact on which to establish guilt or innocence. Law-making itself 'confessedly needs to be based on an informed judgment' requiring 'the widest access to information'.[1] The spread of information in the form of fact, opinion or ideas has variously been repressed, exhorted, victimised or applauded to advance the ideologies of those whose moment of power is in the ascendant. In this general sense, we can see previous societies as information societies. What is novel in our society, however, is the heightened awareness of the use, collection, dissemination or with-holding of information. Such functions are facilitated by artificial intelligence systems, advanced information technology and the opportunities which exist to influence public opinion through ever more sophisticated broadcasting and telecommunications networks.

Many recent *causes célèbres* have involved information in the form of the giving or keeping of confidences. Socrates would have been in his element in discussing the case of a civil servant deliberately leaking information to 'advance' the public interest; the nature of informed consent before medical treatment;[2] the extent of the duty to inform parents of advice by doctors to their children;[3] a leak of a difference of opinion between the Head of State and the Prime Minister on government policies;[4] the failure to inform those affected of the extent of nuclear accident and disaster; abuse of information stored in computerised retrieval systems. For a Socrates, the details would be novel; there would, however, be a persistence in the nature of the problems they pose. The 'problems' surround the 'use' and 'abuse' of information. 'Use' and 'abuse' in this context are evaluative terms, and ones which I hope will be clarified in the course of this book. They are also relative terms. We may consider that a government abuses information when, without apparent justification, it refuses individuals access to information in its possession. This would not be the case in a system geared towards representative democracy. It would certainly not be the case where government is absolutist and is accepted as such by those whom it governs.

A further comparative aspect of the terms 'use' and 'abuse' is present in two other features. One concerns the changing nature of the role of government not simply as an agent protecting and defending the realm from external and internal strife, but as a shaper of people's lives in almost every conceivable way. Government intervenes more and more in our society, whatever its political hue. Different roles require different sorts and amounts of information. The administrative regulatory state is the most acquisitive. In addition, the sophistication of information technology has made the collection, storage and retrieval of information not simply a national and corporate preoccupation, but a global one. The speed and ease with which information may be transferred across national boundaries, by governments or private concerns, or matched by computers for different purposes from those for which the information was collected, is seen by many as an abuse in itself. The 'abuse' would be in the creation of information systems which are incapable of effective regulation at a price that treasuries would be prepared to tolerate. Privacy is not given a high priority in the United Kingdom; the developments which I have referred to diminish it even further.

Things must be seen in perspective. The UK Government is a holder of vast amounts of manual (i.e. documentary) information, much of it on individuals. For instance the Department of Health and Society Security holds 75 million personal social security files; the Immigration Department has 3.75 million personal files, 'many over a foot thick'; there were in 1987 8.7 million files on current schoolchildren, 11 million on public sector tenants, 1 million social work records.[5] But the movement towards a 'paperless environment', as IBM's administration was described during the passage of the Access to Personal Files Act, is a distinct characteristic of our age. The characteristics of Information Technology, however, require further elaboration.

Computers and Information

Information technology is often described in exceptional and dramatic terms. The following is a vivid example:

In the last hundred years, we see the rapidly accelerating advent of a technology so powerful, novel, widespread, and influential that we may indeed call it the Second Industrial Revolution. Its basis is electromagnetic, in many interconnected forms: photography, photocopying, cinematography, and holography; telegraphy, telephony, radio communication, radar, sonar, and telemetry; sound and video recording and reproduction; vacuum tubes, transistors, printed circuits, masers, lasers, fiber optics, and (in rapid succession) integrated circuits (IC), large-scale integration (LSI), and very large-scale integration (VLSI) of circuitry on a tiny semiconducting 'chip'; and, finally, the bewildering variety of electronic digital computers. All these devices are intimately interrelated, and any advance in one tends to generate advances in all of them.

The progress has been truly amazing. In only about 40 years, electronic communications and news media have become commonplace and indispensable; computers have proliferated, becoming increasingly fast, powerful, small and cheap, so that now there is scarcely a human activity in which they are not to be found, bearing an increasing share of the burden of repetitive information processing, just as the machines of the First Industrial Revolution have taken over the majority of heavy and unpleasant physical labor (we may say, energy processing).

Now, information can not only be stored, retrieved, communicated, and broadcast in enormous quantities and at phenomenal speeds; but it can also be rearranged, selected, marshalled, and transformed.[6]

A decade ago, the Lindop Committee[7] offered a thoughtful and informative account of the problems posed by data accumulation and protection. It noted that the electronic computer was 'only a part of any information system' and that the rest of the system will perform 'the functions of collecting and preparing the data for the computer, devising its instructions, and transferring the information produced to those who need it'. All of this would require human control and 'often human intervention' and the creation of 'at least some manual records'. In 1978, the system dealing with National Insurance, Pensions and child allowances held some 48 million records. The Department of Education and Science held, at that time, 3.5 million data records of students for the Further Education Statistics Record.

The report spoke quite correctly of the dangers of abuse of information that would come with centralisation of information on computerised systems. Since 1931, for instance, the Driving and Vehicle Licensing Centre had informed the Inland Revenue of the addresses of individuals. More recent examples include the report that MI5 – the security service – had access to data on 20 million people by linking its computer, under Prime Ministerial approval, with a growing network of other government computer data banks.[8] Computer network contracts have specified how a free flow of information can pass between the major government departments contrary to existing legislative requirements.[9] A more authoritative source has warned that police officers should be issued with strict guidelines about the use and misuse of the Police National Computer to which police forces are, or will be, linked, together with the Scottish Criminal Record Office.[10] The Police Complaints Authority had found 529 potential causes of complaint on one subject alone concerning misuse of computerised information.[11] In another case, secret guidelines from the DHSS had encouraged legal aid officials to pass on useful information to officials in other departments in spite of the Legal Aid Act, which stipulates that information must not be released without the donor's consent.[12]

In his research Lindop was not given all the detailed information he wanted from the Metropolitan Police.[13] At the time of his investigation the extensive scope and use of their computer was widely reported, especially by the Special Branch, who were expected to be allocated almost half the computer's capacity by 1985.[14]

The use of such information technology (IT) can have a potent impact on centralising and co-ordinating information, facilitating centripetal administrative tendencies within organisations and between hierarchical levels of bureaucracy, but there are dangers in over-sensationalising. It is naive to believe that Government in whatever form will not exploit new technology. The Treasury has established a Central Computer and Telecommunications Agency which publishes booklets, one of which concerns appropriate levels of security.[15] No less a figure than the Comptroller and Auditor-General has voiced his misgivings about the lack of appropriate security for Government-held data.[16] Data with a comparatively high security rating will 'generate a considerable volume of traffic'. Security procedures for handling classified information are laid down separately for all departments to follow and implementation of IT security procedures is the responsibility of individual departments. For every 100 administrative staff there are now two workstations – word processors, personal computers – or advanced workstations. By 1992, the agency predicts there will be 20. An increasing interface between government officials and their dependence upon private company experts for the installation, operation and management of computer systems is foreseen. In November 1987, a contract to establish and operate the biggest and most advanced computer network in Whitehall was to be put out to tenders from private organisations. The successful tenderer was to implement the Government Data Network, it was hoped, ambitiously.

The importance of governmental control over information technology has been dramatically evidenced by the US Department of Commerce's refusal to grant licences to companies to export computers to British universities unless they sign documents giving America control over their use. Ostensibly this is to ensure that the technology and information obtained from such computers are not shared with proscribed Communist countries while the USA maintains its technological supremacy in this field. Sir Michael Havers, the former Attorney-General and Lord Chancellor, has stated his opinion that such a restriction is unlawful.[17] CIA involvement in gathering information on companies such as British Nuclear Fuels and Amersham International whetted the appetite of conspiracy theorists but nonetheless brought home the importance attached at the highest levels to information technology.

More beneficial features of the brave new world of the computerisation of governmental administration were recently highlighted in the evidence of a Permanent Secretary before the Select Committee on the Parliamentary Commissioner for Administration. He described how aspects of the social security administration would be simplified by use of computers which the DHSS had already introduced.[18] The Inland Revenue are computerising their whole network,[19] but were reluctant to use systems in the private sector, contrary to US practice, because of the risks of breaches of confidentiality.[20] This reluctance may, however, be overtaken by events if this system is linked to a Government Data Network. The Treasury Model of the British economy has been available since Schedule 5 of the Industry Act 1975 came into effect. The Economic and Social Research Council in conjunction with the Bank of England and the Treasury has announced a programme of study to link micro-economic models of companies and local authorities with the macro-economic model of the Treasury in an effort to achieve better understanding between the Government, industry, unions, local authorities and financial centres. One police force has claimed that its own computer has released its officers from 'mountains of paper-work', putting them back on the beat.

On police computers in particular, the Lindop Report expressed concern at the secrecy attaching to their operation, the classification of information upon, for example, 'political activists', and their potential abuse. He recommended a Data Protection Authority which would oversee the operation of data systems and which would liaise with the police in setting appropriate standards, as in the case of Sweden.[21] For 'national security' data the Authority should have an officer with a security clearance sufficiently high to enable him to operate in effect as a consultant to the Home Office and the security services and to establish with them the appropriate rules and safeguards for their systems. None of these recommendations was accepted. Versions of such a scheme are operational in Sweden and France.

We will return to the provisions of the Data Protection Act 1984 in a later chapter when we will examine the extent to which government and private data holders have been forced to open up their 'files' on individuals to those individuals.

At this stage the primary focus will be upon a theoretical analysis of information, its importance in human relationships and its treatment in State/civil society compacts. I wish to advance the argument that citizens have a right to expect more information from their government than is currently the case in the United Kingdom. Legislation, it will be argued later in the book, can go some way to redressing the current imbalance. It can help to a certain extent in creating a better-informed public and establishing the basis of fuller participation of individuals and groups in the process of rule. But we need to understand why information is limited. Are there justifications for limiting it? Does current practice represent an implicit theory of State/individual relationships which the overwhelming majority are happy to accept? If so, are they misguided? Claims and counterclaims about freedom of information are couched in terms of a theory of democracy by their respective proponents, often unwittingly. An attempt must be made to unpack and analyse these claims. Ironically, freedom of information could make us a very undemocratic society.

The Importance of Information

Our capacity as human beings to acquire, use and store information is essential for our survival. This might appear a tall claim for something which in English law cannot be the object of theft.[22] At a practical level, disasters are avoided, accidents prevented and sustenance provided by our use of information. Hamlet's tragedy was that he was accurately informed; Othello's that he was not. While information itself is important, our ability to discern the degree of the reliability of the information provided is essential in the exploitation of resources or relationships, or in the exposure of sham. Information acquired through scientific inquiry establishes that it is irrational to believe that consulting the auspices, the stars or the tea leaves is a reliable indication of future events. Information is necessary to make sensible choice or wise judgment. Moral and ethical evaluation depends upon information acquired through our own and our predecessors' experience. Information in the form of facts constitutes the basis of order in our lives, of community, regularity and knowledge. Are 'facts' nothing more than the haphazard ascription of names or categories to phenomena impinging on our consciousness, however? And if there are no facts, is it possible to know anything? In order to think or make decisions we apply categories of thought such as quantity, substance and causality, or 'a priori intuitions' such as space and time, to myriad phenomena which we encounter. These are categories or intuitions which, according to Kant, inhere in the working of the mind itself. They are the starting-point, he argued, of our organisation of confused data. They are the most basic forms of information. Their existence, Kant reasoned, is a basic fact.

Without the application of these categories and intuitions we would be incapable of achieving judgment or making decisions. We would be incapable of existence beyond that of a vegetable. Such intuitions and categories, Kant believed, are inescapable in the human predicament. But the information to which we apply our faculties of judgment and decision-making is far from immutable. It is subject to change, historical development, inaccuracy, distortion or imprecision, and so on. This is why we normally set a high premium on telling the truth, faithful and accurate recording of events, care in the provision of information; and why we punish cheats and frauds or censure liars, or hold as culpable the negligent transmission of information that causes harm. These examples illustrate the importance of the mutual and implicit acceptance of certain ground rules in the use of information and its employment in human communication. Rather like the categories of thought, they are an inescapable feature of existence, in particular of communication.

These are commonsensical observations. Can they be given a theoretical, explanatory framework? A theory of communication that might assist has its most recent expression in the work of Jürgen Habermas.[23] He has sought to establish that the process of communication between human beings, of which information is an essential if not exclusive component, is only possible on the basis that certain ground rules representing an underlying consensus are accepted. These will cover such obvious features as that assertions are made on the basis that they are believed to be true, or that the facts that we allude to in our speech are correct. Rational discourse is premised upon norms such as these. Even if we rejected the norms, we would still have to accept them implicitly to communicate. If I operate on the basis that deception is the fundamental truth of communication, I will set out to deceive. But a corollary of what I accept as a fundamental truth is that others may operate on the same basis. If they are attempting to deceive me, how can I assume that what they are uttering is not in fact the truth? – for they will deceive me by telling the truth, which I will not believe since I will accept it as lies. More importantly, in order to deceive, I must have an idea of the concept of truth. Deception implies truth or the concept of truth. If the consensus of the claims inherent in communicative competence is challenged, then its validity, correctness or acceptability can only be tested by debate and argument.[24]

Habermas argues that through discourse, as he calls it, the only form of pressure that is allowed to operate is the force of the better argument. Discourse is a 'special form of communication', but all communicative action implies that those 'interacting in it are discursively justifying their beliefs and norms through the giving of reasons'. As a practical reality, this is very often not the case; but communication must take place on the basis that the 'conditions constituting communicative competence are true'. If not, communication would be impossible. What discourse presupposes, Habermas believes, is 'an ideal speech situation'. In this situation all participants must be given the same opportunity to debate and justify according to reasoned argument without external pressure or domination. All assertions and norms and claims are subject to examination and appraisal in discussion. By this method, norms will only be found to be justified when grounded in 'generalisable interests' and not simply on the power of those asserting the norms. The 'ideal speech situation' is precisely that – an ideal, although it is a fulfilment of the conditions which enable meaningful communication. It is forever frustrated as a matter of practice by 'systematically distorted communication' – by, for instance, manipulation of public opinion, misinformation, a lack of full information on which to exercise a proper freedom of choice, or ideologies legitimating class, economic or political domination. Habermas argues that a fundamental question of practical philosophy today 'has been ... a question of the procedures and presuppositions under which justifications can have the power to produce consensus'.[25] This will be a point to which I shall return.

The attempt to convey correct information is the basis on which communication is premised. We are all regular providers of information, and we know the consequences of providing false information if we are caught out. There is a converse side to the provision of information. This is the control of information: that pursuit of secrecy or confidentiality which is essential to our full development as human beings. How can this be reconciled with the 'ideal speech situation' advanced by Habermas?

It can be reconciled by accepting that there are spheres of our personal and public lives that are a legitimate object of secrecy. Without adequate protection for justifiable secrets our integrity can be compromised, our identity shaken, our security shattered. Details of legitimate intimate relationships, medical facts, of prolonged sensitive negotiations, investigations in the public interest, development of strategic or commercial plans, often require secrecy. Likewise the long-term development of products requiring constant experimentation and creative thought or the protection of ideas. Without the guarantee of secrecy, there would be no protection for their development. The law has come to recognise this by the enactment of copyright and patent laws, the burgeoning area of intellectual property law, the law of confidentiality and specific privacy laws such as those that have been enacted in America and parts of the Commonwealth and Europe.[26] Some American states have gone further and made unauthorised appropriation of industrial secrets a crime.

In other respects secrecy is essential for and between participants to make sense of a situation; there would be little point in playing cards or chess if one constantly revealed one's future plans. This illustrates a deeper theme. 'What is at issue', argues Bok, 'is not secrecy alone but rather the control over secrecy and openness.'[27] It is very often a question of the timing of the release of information so as not to prejudice legitimate interests. Financial information or examination papers are obvious examples. But with information comes power, and with the exclusive control and use of information power is augmented. The problem then becomes one of establishing when secrecy operates not only to protect or advance the interests of those possessing or sharing secrets, but to subvert the interests of those not privy to such secrets. To a lawyer this is familiar territory: a balancing of interests, protection of proprietorial or quasi-proprietorial rights, reasonable behaviour. But the law can only play a minimal role in opening up closed societies or secret relationships given the strength of the attraction of secrecy and confidentiality in business relationships, professional associations, bureaucracy whether private or public, political groups, government, police and Freemasonry. The problem concerning the exclusive use of information is at its most acute when we have a state or an official institution speaking on behalf of the collective or public interest which accumulates unimaginable amounts of information and which carries out its operations, whether by design, stealth or accident, in secrecy.

Information and the State

The position that a ruling body adopts towards the provision of information about its activities to a representative chamber or the civil society at large will inevitably be coloured by considerations about the proper role of government, as well as sheer political expedience.

When government was in the personal household of the Monarch, the words of James I of England expressed the 'private nature' and arcane mysteries of state business by warning that 'None shall presume henceforth to meddle with anything concerning our government or deep matters of state'.[28] Francis Bacon was more subtle in his justification of state secrecy and in his presaging of a Leviathan, an almighty State:

Concerning government, it is a part of knowledge secret and retired in both these respects in which things are deemed secret; for some things are secret because they are hard to know, and some because they are not fit to utter. We see all governments as obscure and invisible.

In Leviathan, the all-powerful State, citizens have no need of governmental information and nor do those who purport to speak on their behalf. Government is absolute. It is absolute because it needs absolute power to defend society.

When Government is limited, however, in the nature of a trust on behalf of the community, such assumptions of absolutism which inform the relationship between State and society, Government and the community, can no longer prevail. The nature of the bond between the State and its citizens, and between citizens *inter se*, is formulated in an implied contract, not an unalterable status. Breach by the Government justifies its removal. John Locke saw the supreme power of the State residing in a legislature, and behind the legislature the people. The people governed, but they were not government. Nor were they the legislature, although they were represented in it. In matters of government, claims for information could not be made by the community directly, but via their representatives. Part of Locke's philosophy also justified acquisitive individualism and the rights of citizens to own what 'they have mixed their labour with' deriving from a natural right of property antecedent to the existence of government. When property is extended to information we have the joinder of issue with which we are still engaged – the conflict between a representative democracy and a democratically elected government and its preserve upon information on the people's behalf. The force of the argument posed on behalf of society is political not legal.

The growth of governmental power, quite simply, necessitated greater safeguards against abuse. 'Secrecy, being an instrument of conspiracy', said Bentham, 'ought never to be the system of a regular government.'[29] His appeal is to a political morality which government must adhere to and which, for all Bentham's apprehensions on extending the franchise,[30] is sympathetic to representative democracy, and especially publicity 'in matters of government'. 'Without publicity, no good is permanent; under the auspices of publicity no evil can continue.' Secrecy was the climate in which, at worst, those placed in government would abuse the power which had been given to them. It protected misrule. Publicity, regular elections and a free press were needed to safeguard the electorate from their chosen governors. The risk that mistake or perversity in the electors' choice would increase as the franchise was extended was the dilemma Bentham found. Much has been made of this dilemma in present-day analysis.[31] But elsewhere Bentham represented that rational impulse which insisted on the goodness of publicity, of knowing. He quoted enthusiastically from Pope's *Essays on Man*: 'What can we reason but from what we know?' It was a theme that was to be developed in the liberal tradition.

With the extension of the franchise, liberal democracy proclaimed its strength as a political system in which individuals were given the greatest opportunity for self-development and self-fulfilment, especially under the influence of John Stuart Mill. The author of *On Liberty* would have approved of the words of Adam Smith, who in postulating the example of the 'ideal observer', said it was one who could infer that a moral principle for human guidance was correct after pursuing a mental procedure that was dependent upon such valuable human characteristics as being 'fully informed, free, imaginative, sympathetic, calm, impartial, fair, willing to universalise, acting on principle, considering the good of everyone alike, and so forth'.[32] The emphasis is upon being fully informed and rational. Within limits, modern pleas for freedom of information would have struck a chord of sympathy in Mill's breast, and later liberal philosophers came to realise more keenly that sharing of information was an essential component of democracy itself. Democracy had to be extended to ensure the greater informed participation of citizens in the process of government. It was a representative participation. The questions would be put by elected representatives, and information would filter through the system to the citizens. In spite of Mill's desire for an informed society in which maximum opportunity was available for self-improvement and the development of individuals, he prevaricated upon the extension of the franchise. Freedom was one thing, irresponsibility another. Other notes of caution must be sounded.

Bentham, however, would have seen it as proper for government to have restricted a free flow of information about its activities. Bentham argued for three exceptions to a prohibition on government secrecy: where publicity would assist an enemy of the State, where it would harm the innocent, or where it would inflict unduly harsh punishment on convicted persons. I cannot envisage arguments which would establish and successfully support the need for no restriction on freedom of information. The difficulty lies in allowing government prerogative alone to call the tune.

Secondly, liberal philosophers of a different school have frequently urged caution in so far as the well-informed individual wishes to use information, or to keep information secret, not only to advance his own position but to distort equality of opportunity or a like liberty for all. In administering a state, Kant argued, there is a problem in knowing how 'to organise a group of rational beings who together require universal laws for their survival, but of whom each separate individual is secretly inclined to exempt himself from them'. Possibly the most influential of present-day liberal theorists, John Rawls, has argued that a fully informed individual *cannot* make the decision to deduce what principles *ought* to govern the operation of social institutions and government. Rawls argues for a method whereby individuals will achieve a state of 'reflective equilibrium' to establish through consensus the basic principles of justice that will be applied in their relationships as individuals and collectively.[33] He imagines rational men and women coming together in a temporary state of ignorance of their own personal strengths and weaknesses to form a compact in which the 'principles of justice', as he calls them, will be arrived at. The individuals will be rational – they will know how to reason and they will have information allowing them to argue on a general rather than a personal level. They will also be self-interested. They will be equipped to assess what their reaction as rational human beings would be to particular situations and what principles justify their decisions. The principles would allow them to assess moral priorities; they are 'constitutive of justice'.[34] As Rawls sees it, the temporary lack of information by each individual of their personal abilities, strengths and weaknesses is an essential ontological feature of the method of establishing 'principles with independent moral appeal'. If they knew of their strengths and weaknesses, they would load the dice to achieve an outcome that would be in their individual interest and not in the collective interest of all or of the whole in which they have an equal part. Rawls's device is a fiction; it is a method to capture an objective analysis required in moral philosophy. Apart from establishing the principles of justice, Rawls would not argue that a lack of information is a good thing *per se*; the principles of justice would be given full publicity in their existence, interpretation and application so that individuals would not misunderstand how they work.[35] But this does not tell us how much they are entitled to know.

It is one aspiration, that social and ethical relations should not essentially rest on ignorance and misunderstanding of what they are, and quite another that all the beliefs and principles involved in them should be explicitly stated. That these are two different things is obvious with personal relations, where to hope that they do not rest on deceit and error is merely decent, but to think that their basis can be made totally explicit is idiocy.[36]

It is ironic that Rawls chose for his tableau individuals in a 'veil of ignorance'. To simplify a Marxist critique of liberal philosophy and practice one need only address a Marxist belief that liberalism as an ideology perpetuates a veil of ignorance inasmuch as it is a legitimating device for capitalist accumulation and exploitation. The class structure is not seen for what it is: an organised enterprise bent on the exploitation of the economically weak by the economically powerful who manage to cloak the partial nature of the exercise of power with the ideologies of equality and liberty emanating from and supporting the material relations of production. The true nature of liberal society will be concealed by providing no information, disinformation or misinformation. Even in its more humane manifestations, the critique continues, it is elitist. In liberal society, information given by the Government only serves to mystify because it is either intentionally false or it is part of a matrix in which systemic distortion is generated.

The last note of caution on democracy and information concerns power groups which are not ostensibly governmental, but which may be private and professional or trade associations and unions, and which are often protected by oaths, duties, or a culture, of confidentiality. There are arguable reasons why confidentiality must be maintained or not maintained in various relationships. These relate to individual respect and integrity. A problem arises when the private body in question exercises considerable influence in public life but insists on confidentiality in its operations to such an extent that it is effectively its own master. A lack of information facilitates a lack of accountability for the exercise of power and influence and the impact these forces have upon the public interest where democratic controls are absent.

Information and Communication

It will be recalled that Habermas maintained that an 'ideal speech situation' is one where there is no distortion of discourse by contained inequalities or ideologies concealing inequality and that the 'ideal speech situation' was nothing more than the fulfilment of what is presumed in the effort of communication.[37] At the political level, he continues, legitimacy – justification for the exercise or non-exercise of power on the public behalf – can only properly be achieved under certain conditions. These are satisfied where decision-making processes are organised in such a way that arrangements can be found in which the institutions and political decisions would meet with the unforced consensus, if not approval, of the members of society *if they had been allowed* to participate as free and equal in policy-making.[38] The issue then becomes one of organising decision-making processes that provide information about their operations in as full and timeous a manner as possible as well as establishing the most appropriate procedures, organisations and mechanisms which 'are in each case better suited to bring about procedurally legitimate decisions and institutions'. Attempts to arrange a society democratically can only be perceived as 'a self-controlled learning process'[39] for all its members, not simply governmental or other elites.

One response to Habermas's attempt to extend his theory of communicative competence to political institutions and collective decision-making is to assert that it is all visionary and idealistic, that the world does not and cannot work like that. On the other hand, there is a link with the liberal tradition which has argued for liberalism as *the* system for the encouragement of individual development and achievement for all. Participation in government and publicity about the working of government have been consistent themes in the liberal tradition. Where Habermas differs fundamentally is in insisting upon an assessment and reassessment of the procedures and the information which are available so that legitimation can be achieved only after a participation of all as free and equal, or most importantly, who *would agree as such persons* if they had participated in policy and decision-making, i.e. if the process were seen to be even-handed and above-board. Habermas here accepts, it seems, certain realities of governmental decision-making. The decisions are made by government or elected chambers or elsewhere, and the 'elsewhere' poses particular problems. We cannot all be there in the chamber, in the Cabinet, in the department. But what does go on in those places we would agree to, if not in terms of the substantive outcome, then at least on the basis that decisions were made on a rational assessment of the information which was not perverted by ideology, or distorted by influence and domination which is tangible or subliminal.

But if we are not in the chamber or elsewhere, how do we know the debate was rational? Experience may lead us to believe it is anything but. The point is that the more irrational the process, the more governors will want to conceal, the more they pervert the conditions of legitimacy. It must be accepted, however, that we cannot know everything about a government's operations and decision-making whenever we want. Such a restriction is consistent with Habermas's theory. The reasons for not imparting information, however, must satisfy the test that would justify an unforced consensus which would constitute a sure basis for legitimation. As long as we accept as inescapable that people exercise power on our behalf, then the exercise of power in whatever form must satisfy those ultimate criteria. Where I find strength in Habermas's analysis, which is lacking in the work of much of liberal theory, is his attempt to establish the ontology, the pure conditions of legitimation for the exercise of power through institutional frameworks whose arrangement is only justified to the extent that it facilitates discussion, information, reasoned decisions and supporting evidence. It is not a liberalism which assumes the inherent inequality of the social condition around which the agenda is set. Nor is the *tabula rasa* of Habermas contingent upon material forces of production distorting the information which shapes its inscriptions, as Marxists believe. Economic inequality is a distorting feature of domination preventing true consensus. It must be seen for what it is, and the interests of the economically weaker must be equally represented, *and represented with equal efficacy*, as other interests. When a government does not wish to publish its Cabinet proposals for changes in child benefit[40] or when it makes 19 changes in the formula for calculating the number of unemployed,[41] or provides information on the increase of poverty and its effects in a manner designed to attract as little attention as possible,[42] or in a form which is incomprehensible,[43] one can see the forces of domination perverting the discussion.

Freedom of Information – The Good, the Bad and the Ugly

The 'Information Society', or its members, are making increasing claims for Freedom of Information and Open Government (the two are not the same although they are very closely related).[44] Freedom of Information does not mean access to brute information alone such as documents or records in whatever form, as we shall see. It leads into Open Government in so far as it necessitates access to governmental decision-making in a more public and participatory form. The claims for such are couched in terms of a right to know, a democratic right. Such claims are easily made, but more difficult to justify if one has not established what theory of democracy one accepts. Information is inherently a feature of power. So too is its control, use and regulation. Government, to repeat, is the organisation of information for the use, effective or otherwise, of power in the public interest. Take away a government's preserve on information, and its preserve of when and what to release, then take away a fundamental bulwark of its power. This may be desirable or it may not. It is undeniable, however, that its impact is potentially profound. Such developments could establish new centres of power and organisation outside of government, where 'government' would be 'all inside and no outside', to rearrange Woodrow Wilson's snappy phrase. It could facilitate an even more acquisitive and inquisitive and captious society, or an oppressive one. One has only to remember that the President who coined the phrase 'executive privilege' in 1958 to circumscribe Congressional investigations was the same President who refused to hand over executive documents to Senator McCarthy in his witch-hunt of Un-American 'activists'. An investigative press or lightly regulated broadcasting system could do untold damage to individuals in a Freedom of Information state. Any responsible advocate for open government and freedom of information must accept that there are subjects which we do not all need to know and be informed on and which we cannot insist on knowing as of right. The question then becomes: what kind of information is this, and if I do not know, is someone entitled to know on my behalf?

Information and Institutional Structure

This leads us to the question of institutional structure. How do we best organise our institutions which are responsible for making decisions affecting the public and the public interest? How can they be structured to ensure that the debate is carried on in as informed a manner as possible? What allows unjustifiable domination in present institutions? On what, if any, issues should information be the preserve of the Prime Minister and one or two others? Is it wrong that it is so restricted, and why? When should information be exclusive to the Cabinet? When should it go to an assembly of elected members and how should it go – to the whole chamber or to specific committees? When is there a need for wider public debate at either inquiries or other public meetings, and how well informed will the public be? When is a subject appropriate for a judicial body or tribunal, and how widely should such bodies, especially courts, range in seeking information? Should there be a difference between litigation between private individuals according to law, which is therefore a matter of public interest, and litigation about the public interest itself? When do we need to present information for the assessment of outside experts who will assist either Ministers, the elected and representative chambers or the nation at large? The reaction of British governments to such questions as these has been a tinkering at the edges and an insistence on the maintenance of the status quo. This is not simply because of the power of tradition and confidentiality. It is because in the British tradition, unlike the American or Scandinavian traditions which provided the prototype of freedom of information legislation, political power and survival are inextricably bound up with control of information.[45] This point can be more conveniently discussed in the following chapter, but it is interesting to speculate on the implications of proposed 'hiving off' of departmental responsibilities to 'independent' governmental agencies.

It is now time to move from the general and fairly abstract to the particular and to examine a problematic area which poses significant political, legal and practical difficulties in relation to information control and its regulation.

Information and National Security

National security poses the most difficult of practical problems in respect of information. It concerns what many regard as *the* quintessential function of the State. National security involves the most developed form of information technology – much of it highly secret. The area covers the most intrusive of information-gathering exercises conducted on behalf of government agencies. National security is also a virtually unanswerable plea to immunity, preventing access by individuals to information upon those individuals, and confidentiality. As we shall see in Chapter 6, the courts have long shown themselves sensitive to executive assertions of national security precluding judicial investigation of an individual grievance.[46] Many of the most controversial cases concerning information in recent years have related to national security. The peculiar potency of the subject must be fully realised. It is not characteristic of all areas of government activity. However, it will provide an interesting area of human activity in which some of the theoretical points may be tested. This is because the subject poses the most difficult of questions about executive action and its relationship with effective accountability and informed public opinion. The culture of government secrecy which will occupy our attention in later chapters owes much of its inspiration to this responsibility of government.

Is distortion allowable for the greater public good? Is this an area which is appropriately colonised by the powers of 'democratisation', as Habermas advocated? If so, with what necessary concessions to the claims of responsible and efficient government?

On national security, the United Kingdom approach has meant that the assessment of such an important matter is for the Executive alone.[47] What ought we to know about decisions on national security, the security services, their general operations and those of the police in security work? What should we know of their techniques for obtaining and dealing with information, and what safeguards exist, and should exist, to prevent abuse?

From the many points which arouse interest and controversy on the subject of security, two are particularly pertinent for this study. The first concerns our information, or lack of it, about the security and intelligence services themselves and their activities. The second concerns the methods the services adopt to extract information from individuals or institutions. In so far as security involves the police it will be pertinent to examine recent developments augmenting police powers while maintaining a suspect's right to silence.

Despite the 'covert' ethos of the security services, they still manage to present an extraordinary picture of botched amateurism and eccentricity.[48] The whole question of accountability of these services in a democratic state was given dramatic not to say sensational prominence by the events in a Sydney court-room, and later in English courts, when the British Government sought to restrict publication of the memoirs of the former MI5[49] agent Peter Wright. There were allegations of the infiltration by foreign spies at the highest level in the service, and the catalogue of 'dirty tricks' regularly practised by security officials, which involved their role in the resignation of a Prime Minister and the undermining of British governments in the past. Suppressing Wright's memoirs became a world-wide drama. It was an extraordinary episode in which the public caught a glimpse of the working of British government at the highest level. One of the most dramatic moments was the rare scenario of a Cabinet Secretary upon oath under hostile cross-examination in a court of law. The case precipitated further calls for reform of the security services in the UK, which have been not only distant but isolated from any form of democratic oversight or accountability commensurate with their power and influence. Only one statute, Cook has claimed, names the Secret Service: the Civil List and Secret Service Money Act of 1782, which restricted the issue of public money to the service to £10,000 per annum. When the statute was repealed in 1977 expenditure was estimated at £30 million per annum, and by 1983–4 expenditure was £71 million per annum.[50] Unofficial estimates vastly exceed this amount. The service owes its origin and operations to the murkier side of the Crown Prerogative. Nor should we forget that the Crown possesses a Prerogative power not to prosecute charges, and to stop criminal proceedings.[51]

In spite of the Prime Minister's claim that she had, if anything, been 'too forthcoming' in her disclosure on security matters,[52] the public has witnessed a growing body of information and speculation about the security services and its operations. Scandals and revelations throughout the late 1970s and the 1980s coincided with the prolonged dispute surrounding the introduction of polygraph 'lie detectors' at General Communications Headquarters,[53] the subsequent banning of trade unions at GCHQ, and the Peter Wright affair.

The Security Commission makes intermittent appearances to examine breaches of security and advise on security procedures. This body was established in 1964 following the Denning Report on the Profumo scandal.[54] Its chairman is a senior judge (in 1987, Lord Griffiths, a Law Lord). The Prime Minister, traditionally, after consulting the Leader of the Opposition,[55] refers cases to the Commission. In 1982, the Commission, then under Lord Diplock, recommended a relaxation of positive vetting[56] in the civil service, and a relaxation of the rules governing release of classified inform-ation especially where it was held back to prevent possible political embarrassment. A report in 1985, however, recommended an extension of positive vetting in the security service following the case of the spy in the service, Michael Bettaney. The Commission found faults in the management of the services, but the Prime Minister ruled out any Parliamentary oversight, a stance recently repeated by the Home Secretary when Parliament rejected a motion calling for a special commission of Privy Counsellors to monitor the security services.[57] Internal reforms had, the Home Secretary asserted, led to a 'more open style of management and improved vetting'. The essential position of the security services in the defence of the realm means that neither the Prime Minister nor the Home Secretary will answer detailed questions about them in Parliament. In the 1985 report which the Home Secretary referred to, the two appendices covering detailed recommendations on the internal structure of the security services were not published.

At present, 'national interest' demands that operations relating to the services are not discussed in Parliament.[58] Harold Macmillan described how such matters were for discussion between the Prime Minister and the Leader of the Opposition[59] – a convention which Mrs Thatcher threatened not to follow in 1986. The House of Commons is told as little as possible. The Denning Report revealed in 1963 that responsibility for security had rested with the Prime Minister until 1952. A recommendation from Sir Norman Brooke, the Cabinet Secretary, resulted in a directive from the Home Secretary of that year to the director-general of the security service – MI5. This stated:

in your appointment . . . you will be responsible to the Home Secretary personally. The Security Service is not, however, a part of the Home Office. On appropriate occasions you will have the right of direct access to the Prime Minister.[60]

The Prime Minister continues to answer questions on 'broad issues of security', but as Drewry suggests,[61] formal ministerial responsibility is rendered largely irrelevant by keeping Parliament uninformed. Indeed, the question of how far the Prime Minister is informed by the services is a major imponderable.[62] Apart from the inner caucus, 'Ministers do not concern themselves with the detailed information which may be obtained by the Security Service' and receive only such information as is necessary for them to provide guidance. Parliamentary Questions on 'matters, of their nature secret, relating to the secret services and to security' are not in order,[63] and ministerial prerogative has allowed them to decline to answer.[64]

Select Committees of the House of Commons are unlikely to fare any better. The Employment Committee was not allowed to question certain officials when it investigated the background to the Government's decision to ban trade union membership at GCHQ. D Notices[65] and Positive Vetting[66] have been examined by the Defence Committee, and the Home Affairs Committee has investigated aspects of the administration and accountability of the Special Branch. The Speaker of the House has even ruled that MPs could not see in the confines of Parliament a proposed TV programme allegedly endangering national security.[67] The House of Commons Committee of Privileges upheld the temporary ban until a full debate in the Commons could be held. The Committee rejected any removal of MPs' existing immunity from prosecution under the Official Secrets Act, or any restraint upon MPs by court injunction from disclosing information damaging to national security in the course of Parliamentary proceedings.[68] It further rejected any prohibition by Ministers (through the Speaker) of an MP's right to publicise information in the House which he or she believed should be available.

In December 1987, the BBC was prevented by injunction, drafted in the widest terms, from broadcasting a Radio 4 programme discussing the security services. The programme included politicians who had held the highest offices of State and former members of the services. Information from the latter, and indeed their very identity, was a confidential matter.[69]

The potential for abuse by security service officials has been exemplified by accounts of former officials which support the claims of informed, speculative or privileged 'outsiders'. As we shall see in Chapter 6, the Government successfully obtained an interim injunction in the Court of Appeal and House of Lords against the reporting of a former security official's allegations of abuse by officials, on the basis that a breach of confidence to the Crown would be perpetrated, even though a similar publication of the information had been made.[70] The court believed that the confidentiality owed to the Crown by employees and former employees of the service outweighed any public right to know of alleged shortcomings in the security service, whose papers are never put into the Public Records Office and whose activities were of the 'highest sensitivity'. These arguments did not prevail before Mr Justice Powell in the Supreme Court of New South Wales, nor when the Government sought to restrict publication of the same book in New Zealand. Indeed the Powell judgment was devastating in its critique of the Government's behaviour and actions.[71] They were also rejected in the English High Court by Scott J. when the Government sought a permanent injunction. In spite of repeated Opposition requests for an inquiry into the allegations of treasonable and criminal conduct of MI5 agents, the Prime Minister categorically refused to authorise such an inquiry, stating that she was content with the *internal* review by the head of MI5.

In November 1987, the Prime Minister announced that a former head of the Northern Ireland Office was to be appointed as a 'staff counsellor' to security and intelligence personnel where their disquiet or grievances about their work could not be assuaged through 'conventional ways', i.e. an interview with superiors. He is to have access to all documents and all levels of management and the Cabinet Secretary. He is to report not less than once a year to the Home Secretary, the Foreign Secretary and the Prime Minister. In all, an estimated 12,000 officials in MI5, MI6 – secret intelligence – and GCHQ will be covered. The counsellor can make recommendations to heads of MI5 and MI6, but the Prime Minister refused to accede to a request that he be allowed to sit on meetings of the Directorate.[72]

It is a fact that we live in a security-conscious world. Confrontation between world powers and the continuing presence of terrorism dictate the necessity. The existence of a security and intelligence service is not the point. The point is to what extent should they be rendered accountable? Who should know of their activities and responsibilities and call them to account? It is frequently claimed that simply leaving the information as a preserve of the Prime Minister and a few trusted Ministers and aides is inadequate. This can allow improper influence on a Prime Minister,[73] or pressure upon the security services only to provide the information the Government wishes to hear. In the 1960s, GCHQ and MI6 informed the Government of how Rhodesia was able to break trade sanctions after its unilateral declaration of independence, only to be told by the Government that it did not want to know.[74] Who should know of the activities of the security services in order to vouchsafe to the public that those activities are conducted according to proper mandates and the law? Who should know of the degree of interrelationship between GCHQ and the US National Security Council[75] or the Central Intelligence Agency? The Americans appear to know more about our intelligence and security services than we do ourselves, since Congressional Committees are in existence to survey the Executive in this sphere of activity[76] and formal investigations by the Justice Department may be set in motion.

Do we need to know whether MI6 have plotted to kill Colonel Gaddafi or President Nasser or of the 'dirty tricks' of our agents?[77] The answer is 'we do'; if not directly then there should certainly be a more extensive report and oversight than exists within the present privileged circle of communication. By insisting on too much secrecy the Government will invariably engage in efforts which are counter-productive or destructive of democratic values themselves. For example, GCHQ after the union-banning fracas was raised from 'useful obscurity' to become the most notorious government HQ outside Whitehall.[78] The frequency of catastrophe within the services, from spies to internal mismanagement, makes the public expect the worst in the absence of appropriate accountability mechanisms. The brevity of past Security Commission investigations does not enhance their reports. The investigation by Lord Bridge into telephone tapping[79] considered 'all relevant documents' and the 'merits' of 6,129 tapping warrants issued between 1970 and 1984.[80] He was asked by the Home Secretary to investigate on 28 February 1985. He reported to the Minister on 6 March. During that period two full days were spent by the chairman sitting as a Law Lord in the House of Lords. Not one 'tap' examined was unauthorised or used improperly, the Commission found. The Home Secretary declared that he knew no tap had ever been made *without* authority, in spite of the fact that a previous Home Secretary had stated that he found it impossible to know everything that the services did, let alone what they did not do.[81] What safeguards are there for the practices of the services?

Interception of Communications

Interception of communications has been performed by the Executive since correspondence began, although until 1985 there was no legislative basis for such action. The Birkett Report of 1957 thought that the position of the law could be stated to recognise the power to intercept letters and telegrams, and 'it is wide enough to cover telephone communications as well'.[82] In *Malone* v. *Commissioner of the Metropolitan Police*[83] the power of the Secretary of State to authorise telephone taps was judicially recognised absent any other tort or criminal act. Birkett described the authority of the Secretary of State as 'absolute', although authorisations were in practice issued to a limited number of listed agencies. When the European Court of Human Rights held that the British Government's guidelines on tapping were in contravention of Article 8 of the European Convention on Human Rights,[84] the Government produced a Bill intending to secure compliance with our obligations under the Convention. *The Times* spoke of the Bill as an act of 'dumb insolence' attempting to achieve the absolute minimum to comply with the Court of Human Rights ruling in *Malone*.[85]

The Interception of Communications Act 1985 only covers interception of communications by post or telecommunications systems. It does not apply to other means of surveillance, although guidelines were tightened up on surveillance techniques. These guidelines extended the range of cases on which the Commissioner's or Chief Constable's personal authority is required.[86] The Act makes unauthorised interception a criminal offence. Authority can be given by the consent of the person who made or received the communication, or where reasonable grounds exist to believe consent has been given, or by the warrant of the Secretary of State.[87] The Government rejected the need for prior judicial approval for a warrant. A warrant must not be issued unless necessary for one of three specified grounds: the interests of national security; preventing or detecting serious crime; or safeguarding the economic wellbeing of the UK. Consideration must be given to whether the information could be obtained by other means before a warrant is issued, and there are limits set for the duration and premises and persons intercepted.[88] The Secretary of State has to make arrangements to secure that disclosure of information obtained and copying of the information is limited to the minimum necessary to comply with the three criteria given above, and that uncertified material obtained on an interception is not regarded or examined.

The Act establishes a Tribunal which is appointed by the Crown to hear complaints from those who believe they are the victims of interception of a communication either by or to them. It investigates whether a 'relevant warrant' has or does exist, and if so whether there has been a breach of the relevant conditions of the Act. If there has been a contravention, it notifies the complainant of such; it reports its conclusions to the Prime Minister and it can make an order quashing the warrant as well as ordering destruction of intercepted material and payment of compensation. The Tribunal's conclusions are not subject to approval or question in any court. A Commissioner of 'high judicial office'[89] will be appointed by the Prime Minister to review the Secretary of State's exercise of his powers under the Act and to assist the Tribunal. He may require documents and information from relevant persons to perform his duties and he receives copies of the Tribunal's reports. He makes annual reports to the Prime Minister and reports on contraventions of the Act or inadequate protection of information received after interception.[90] An amendment to report to a Select Committee of the House of Commons or a 'Board of five Privy Councillors' failed, as did the proposal for a Complaints Commissioner to hear complaints from members of the security services of misconduct or abuse by other colleagues in interception, though reference was made above to the 'counsellor' appointed in 1987.

It has to be clearly realised that the Act only allows examination by the Tribunal of whether a warrant or certificate exists or has existed; if it does not or has not, the Tribunal inquires no further. It can only examine authorised interceptions, not unauthorised ones, and then only to the extent that the authorisation specification procedures have been met. It is not a body effectively to examine improper motive for an authorisation or to investigate unauthorised leaks.[91] In other words, the most contentious issue has been avoided – a point brought home by unsuccessful complaints made to the Tribunal by the CND alleging unauthorised and/or improper motive.[92] If the Tribunal establishes no breach it does not have to give reasons for its decisions; nor does the Tribunals and Inquiries Act apply to the Tribunal.

The Act is an insult, and a cynical insult. Unauthorised interceptions will be a crime and therefore investigable by the police. With the best will in the world – and it must be remembered that the 'criminals' may well be an elite group within the police or the security service – detection is likely to be an impossibility. The Act secures that there is no likelihood, apart from the Tribunal, of civil redress against a Secretary of State who is in breach of the authorisation provision or against an official who has conducted an unauthorised interception.[93] Unlike in West Germany, the victim of an interception is not informed of the fact as soon after the interception has terminated as can reasonably be done so as not to prejudice the purpose(s) of the interception. Further, the practice of metering – i.e. recording the numbers dialled, dates, times and duration of telephone calls from any phone – by British Telecommunications is insufficiently safeguarded. The details can be provided to the police for the prevention or detection of crime – any crime – in conjunction with criminal proceedings, under a court order or in the interests of national security. It is alleged that BT allows the police access on request.[94] The Act gives no protection to innocent third parties who, for example, have not given consent to be intercepted or who are not the 'target' of an interception.[95] A further factor is that GCHQ has the capacity to eavesdrop indiscriminately. Finally, it has been alleged that a new computer-run telephone exchange, System X, will allow monitoring of calls and automatic call tracing without the protection of the Act as no 'interception' is necessary.[96]

Obtaining Information by Other Means

One reason why the number of interceptions has been surprisingly small, it has been suggested, is that the security services and the police use other surveillance techniques far more frequently than is acknowledged. The security services rely upon the police, both civil and military, and police powers to conduct the more 'conventional' forms of search and interrogation, although security services may train police in techniques such as those which were challenged in *Ireland* v. *United Kingdom* and which concerned the interrogation of IRA suspects.[97] In the 1985 trial for offences under the Official Secrets Act, section 1, of seven servicemen who had been serving in a Signals Regiment engaged in crucial intelligence-gathering work, the jury acquitted the defendants because, one supposes, of the unreliability of the confessions extracted from them by Special Branch and service police.[98] The case, and the subsequent inquiry based upon the procedure of, but not actually under, the Tribunals of Inquiry (Evidence) Act 1921, raised the relationship of the 'rules of criminal justice that protect suspects against oppressive investigation' and the extent to which they should be waived in 'the interests of national security'.[99] What rules of 'criminal justice' apply when police obtain information? It must be emphasised that these are rules of general applicability and are not restricted to national security.[100]

The Police and Criminal Evidence Act substantially altered the rules of 'criminal justice' to augment police powers of entry, search and seizure. This is especially so in relation to evidence which previously may have been privileged but which is now obtainable on a warrant or order from a circuit judge and includes 'excluded material' and 'special procedure' material under the Act. The former covers personal, trade, professional and other records held in confidence, or human tissue or tissue fluid taken for diagnosis or medical treatment and held in confidence, or 'journalistic material'[101] held in confidence. Special procedure material is material 'acquired or created in the course of any trade or other occupation or for the purpose of any paid or unpaid office' and held *inter alia* subject to an express or implied undertaking to hold it in confidence.[102] Police forces have successfully used these powers to obtain a journalist's photographs of a riot.[103]

Under section 19 of the Act the law of seizure of articles has been extended to allow evidence to be seized when it might implicate virtually 'anyone in any crime'.[104] The right of seizure of computerised information is extended so that the police may require information from a computer and 'accessible from the premises' to be produced 'in a form in which it can be taken away and in which it is visible and legible'.[105]

The powers to obtain intimate body samples and fingerprints, to detain and question persons, and to tape-record the interviews constitute, on one interpretation, a serious infringement of civil liberties. The Government and police chiefs regarded the changes as a necessary measure to combat increasing crime and increasingly professional and well-advised criminals. The Act was to operate under strict safeguards, some of which have had little effect.[106] The increased record-keeping, form-filling and bureaucratic detail accompanying the Act and Codes of Guidance are all meeting with increasing criticism from the police. Their complaint is that the cost of the 'safeguards' in the Act in man hours is too high. Cost is a theme I wish to return to at the end of this chapter. From the perspective of judicial safeguards the Act is pusillanimous. Section 76 concerns the admissibility of confessions at trial. Confessions are not to be admitted where they have been obtained as a result of 'oppression', which includes 'torture, inhuman or degrading treatment, and the use of threat or violence (whether or not amounting to torture)' or 'in consequence of anything said or done which was likely, in the circumstances existing at the time, to render [it] unreliable'. It is true that the prosecution must prove 'beyond reasonable doubt' that the confession was not obtained in such a manner and the court may require the prosecution to establish as much on its own motion, even if the defence has not raised the point. This loosely follows the recommendation of the Eleventh Report of the Criminal Law Revision Committee, which recommended a relaxation of the common law. The common law test was that a confession was only admissible if the prosecution could show that it was voluntary: that is, not induced by 'fear of prejudice or *hope of advantage* exercised or held out by a person in authority', nor obtained by oppression.[107] The Government rejected the test for admissibility of 'unfair' evidence proposed by Lord Scarman and accepted by the Lords, which provided a greater safeguard against unfair police practice. Under section 78, the court is only to exclude prosecution evidence if, regarding all the circumstances, including the manner in which it was obtained, its admission would so adversely affect the fairness of proceedings that the court ought not to admit it. The Court of Appeal has ruled, surprisingly, that section 78 also covers confessions.[108] British courts have generally favoured the admission of relevant evidence, even if obtained unlawfully and unfairly, on the grounds that its probative value invariably, if not inevitably, outweighs other factors. The existence of the Police Complaints Authority to deal with complaints against police action, or the right of redress through the courts for civil remedies, has to be seen in the context of the police maintaining the records of investigations and interviews – which they can use but which the complainant or litigant invariably cannot.[109] The chairman of the Authority complained in his Annual Report for 1985[110] that the police used information gathered for complaints unfairly and improperly, and he considered it unfair that the statute did not grant him the same liberty of publication.

Reform – Some Food for Thought

In Chapter 2 we will examine the relationship between law and freedom of information overseas. Here it is pertinent to note that a 1981 Canadian report from the Commission of Inquiry Concerning Certain Activities of the Royal Canadian Mounted Police[111] (the McDonald Commission) has affirmed that the principle 'of the Rule of Law and of responsible government in a liberal democracy' should govern the organisation of security intelligence work and policing generally.[112] The report is voluminous, and exhaustive in its investigations, which took place over a three-and-a-half-year period. It found numerous breaches of the law by security officers and deliberate withholding of 'relevant or significant information' from the Ministers who were responsible. A crucial recommendation of the McDonald Commission was that a security agency's mandate must be 'clear and public' and must be stated in the legislation which would establish the agency. The agency's activities in relation to security and its reponsibilities should be defined in statute and not 'diffuse and ambiguous' sources arising as they did from a 'melange of Cabinet directives, ministerial correspondence and unstated RCMP assumptions'. As well as arguing for more ministerial and judicial involvement in surveillance and information acquisition, the report also proposed an independent review body with complete access to the new agency's records, and a Security Appeals Tribunal to hear appeals against decisions in security screening procedures. The review body would be advisory, not executive, and would report to the Solicitor-General and to a Parliamentary Joint Standing Committee on security and intelligence.

The Canadian Security Intelligence Services Act 1984 created the Canadian Security Intelligence Service. The Director is 'under the direction of the Minister'. The Minister has power to give written directions to the Director, copies of which are given to the Security Intelligence Review Committee (SIRC) which was established under the Act. It has been argued that the Act falls short of the McDonald Commission's recommendations, though the Service's mandate is spelt out in statute[113] and it has to report to and advise the Canadian Government. Members of the SIRC are Privy Councillors (but not current senators and MPs). A complaints procedure is established for individuals concerning the activities of the Security Intelligence Service, together with an Inspector-General (IG) who has powers of monitoring and review, though not as wide-ranging as the SIRC's. Cabinet secrets are precluded from investigation by either the IG or the SIRC. The SIRC differs markedly from the McDonald proposals as it is not a Joint Parliamentary Committee. It nevertheless has full powers of access to agency records, reports annually to Parliament, and reports to the Minister.

The Commission under Mr Justice McDonald reported that while the security services of other liberal democracies are not a matter of public record, he doubted whether they were completely innocent of the kind of excesses the Commission recorded in the Canadian security service. Britain is a case in point. In December 1986, the Home Secretary refused to accept the need for a special commission to scrutinise the work of the security services more effectively.[114]

Serious thought does need to be given to the following points. Should intrusive surveillance only be authorised after the approval of a senior Minister and judge, excluding the Lord Chancellor because of his political proximity to the Prime Minister? Should the security services become the creature of statute and should their powers and objectives be defined and clarified? Should subjects of security investigation and monitoring only be those who fall within the definition 'subversive'?[115] A security commission would be an advance, and while Privy Councillors would form the membership, surely there is no reason to exclude MPs unless cause is shown.[116] Few citizens would accept that they as individuals have a need to know the details of security operations. But that does not mean that knowledge and oversight would not be more effective, and thereby a greater safeguard for civil liberties, if they were more widely established as suggested. Such a development has taken place in Australia.[117] This followed a Royal Commission under Mr Justice Hope. Australia has a Joint Parliamentary Committee to oversee the activities of the security and intelligence organisation, and an Inspector-General to hear complaints from officers. A charter spells out the powers and responsibilities of the organisation, and its Director-General reports to the Minister, and has to obtain the approval of the Attorney-General for phone taps and the other sensitive operations.

The Cost of Freedom of Information

National security, and the activities and oversight of those responsible for national security, is a difficult but instructive testing ground for problems associated with freedom of information. It is an area where Government has made very few concessions to openness. Cutting through the variety of arguments supporting or undermining the existing state of operations, there is one factor implicit in this or any government's reckoning. That is cost. The cost of opening up the world of security operations, it argues, even on the scale suggested above, would be destructive of our security. Giving more information, even to limited numbers of elected representatives, would increase the risk of leaks and treasonable use of information. The consequences would affect all of us. The Canadian security service is reported to be suffering a lack of morale because of the publicity given to its operations. This, the service believes, will reduce its efficacy.

In other areas of freedom of information, as we shall see, the cost factor is used as a leading argument against introduction. 'Cost' may take a variety of forms. There is the sheer financial cost. Allow access and everyone will want to see everything. This will entail indexing, and staff to deal with requests, to provide reviews, to check that exempt material is not included, to deal with litigation, to check that filing is carried out correctly. There is the cost of a loss of candour in advice when the giver or the referee knows that it may be published or shown to the subject. There is the fear of perpetual intervention when policy-makers are constantly exposed or challenged and have to justify their every move. In such a situation individuals may not wish to take risks or make innovative decisions. The cost could be a reduction in professionalism. There is the cost of inertia. There is also the possible cost of creating greater secrecy: the spectre of the file behind the file, the meeting behind the meeting, the state behind the state. There is the possible cost of 'the paperless environment' where record-keeping is minimised. As we shall see in the next chapter, overseas experience shows that the financial costs are inevitably exaggerated. The other costs are factors to consider, and will be considered throughout the book.

2

Freedom of Information – Overseas Experience

In the previous chapter, the attempt was made to draw out some persistent themes and problems concerning control over and freedom of information. These themes were then examined in the light of one difficult area concerned with the regulation, dissemination, use and obtaining of information. This chapter will focus upon the role of legislation in other countries, as well as their political practice, in providing and protecting information, whether to or about individuals or, in the case of the USA, committees of the legislature overseeing the operation of legislation and expenditure. I will concentrate on the USA, Canada, Australia and New Zealand.[1] These are countries which in spite of their enormous differences both between themselves and with Britain, nonetheless possess certain legal cultural similarities with the British system, either through common law inheritance or through direct or indirect constitutional influence. I will also look briefly at Swedish and French practices. This examination will allow us to assess the contribution which overseas practice has made to opening up government, and will also act as a benchmark for our own practice. While it will be argued in the next chapter that the secret state in Britain has a long and virtually unbroken tradition which legislation of itself will not remedy, the shortcomings and difficulties of overseas practice will not be overlooked. Picking up the theme of cost in the last chapter, we should note the impact of overseas legislation upon the administrative systems in which they operate.

USA

The USA has possessed a Freedom of Information Act (FOIA) since 1966. Previous statutes had only allowed public access to government documents if a 'need to know' was established,[2] and they allowed agencies to withhold information for 'good cause'. All agencies in the executive branch of the Federal Government, including administrative regulatory agencies, are subject to FOIA. Excluded from the operation of the Act are the judicial and legislative branches of government. So too are members of the President's *immediate personal staff*, whose sole function is to give advice and assistance to the President. State government and local and city government are not included in this legislation.[3]

The aim of the Act, as amended in 1974, is to provide public access to an agency's records if it is covered by the Act. An applicant does not have to demonstrate a specific interest in a matter to view relevant documents – an idle curiosity suffices.

Exemptions

Although the basic thrust of the Act is positive and supportive of openness, there are nine exemptions from the FOIA which include national defence or foreign policy information that is properly classified. An executive order of 1982[4] reversed the trend of relaxation of security classifications and 'broadened the discretion to create official secrets' since any form of unspecified damage may be used to justify exemption. Mandatory secrecy requirements rather than permissive ones have become more common, the 'balancing test' requiring the weighing of public access against the government need for secrecy has been eliminated, and systematic declassification has been cancelled.[5] The order allows for its own mandatory 'Review Requests' of classified information as an alternative to FOIA actions.[6] Internal rules and practices of an agency will be exempt but not the manuals and instructions on the interpretation of regulations. Other important exemptions include: trade secrets; commercial and financial information obtained by the Government that is privileged or confidential; inter- or intra-agency memoranda or letters which are not available by law; information protected by other statutes; personnel or medical files disclosure of which would constitute an invasion of privacy; and investigatory records compiled for law enforcement purposes if disclosure would result in certain types of harm. Reliance by an agency on an exemption is discretionary and not mandatory.[7]

Challenging a Refusal

Where there is a refusal to supply information, appeal procedures are specifically provided in each agency's FOIA regulations. A denial letter will inform the applicant of a right of appeal – usually within 30 days.[8] The official refusing the appeal must be identified, and the exemption and reasons for refusal must be given. The requester must be informed of his or her right to apply to the federal court where there is a complete rehearing with the burden of proof on the agency. Attorney fees are recoverable where an applicant 'substantially succeeds' and FOIA cases receive automatic priority in federal court dockets.

After a Federal Court of Appeals decision,[9] trial courts may, on a motion by a plaintiff, require the Government to itemise the documents, to provide a detailed justification of claimed exemptions, and to index by cross-reference the itemisation to the justification. A justification requires 'a relatively detailed analysis in manageable segments'. An itemisation must 'specify in detail' which parts the agency believes to be exempt. An index cross-references the itemisation and the justification, allowing easier identification of the information required.[10] This is particularly helpful where the applicant does not know what the content of the documents is, where classification is obscure, or where it is difficult to meet a government claim without a clearer description of the documents.

The court can engage in *in camera* inspection of documents. If a third party wishes to stop an agency handing over information concerning him to a requestor, he may seek judicial review of an agency's decision. This is known as a reverse FOIA suit.[11]

Basic Requirements

Each agency covered by FOIA has to publish in the *Federal Register* details of its organisation; the employees from whom and the methods whereby information may be obtained; details of its procedures *including* informal ones; rules, policies or interpretations of general applicability; and rules of procedure and instructions as to the scope and contents of all papers, reports, or examinations. The agency cannot rely in legal proceedings upon any matter which it is bound by law to publish and which it has not, and on which the litigant has not had 'actual and timely notice'. One point that awaits final clarification is that the federal FOIA, as opposed to some state and city FOIA laws, does not spell out the types of information sources, other than documents, which are covered by the Act.

General Impact of the FOIA

The FOIA is often hailed as the great initiator of open government. We should not be blind to the fact that there is considerable opposition to it in the USA. In 1979, Dresner[12] spoke highly of the FOIA's impact upon government accountability, scrutiny and improved decision-making, as well as on inhibiting corruption. Since 1980, however, the Executive has presented repeated proposals for reform of the FOIA because of the cost of its administration, the quantity of case law, and because the Act was being used in ways which Congress never intended.[13] The business community has long lobbied for reform which would facilitate businesses' opportunity to challenge requests for information about them. The law enforcement agencies were not satisfied with the exemption which covers their operations, and in 1986, 'after years of deliberation',[14] Congress passed a major FOIA reform which extends the exemption available to law enforcement practices. In fact, the 1986 Act actually *excludes* certain categories of documents from the FOIA.[15] Further, the records or information no longer have to be investigatory, and may be withheld when they *could* (not would) reasonably be expected to interfere with enforcement proceedings; could deprive a person of a fair trial; could reasonably be expected to constitute an unwarranted invasion of privacy; could reveal the identity of a confidential source which furnished information; could disclose techniques and procedures for law enforcement investigations or prosecutions; or disclosure could reasonably be expected to endanger the life or physical safety of *any individual* (not only law enforcement personnel).

The exemption which has been the subject of most litigation concerns inter- and intra-agency memoranda and letters not available by law. The exemption is meant to cover advisory opinions, not factual information, although 'pre-decisional memoranda expressly incorporated by reference in a final decision must be disclosed'.[16] The 1986 Act was a major success for the Executive, and other reforms include the Paperwork Reduction Act 1980 which seeks to minimise the extent and cost of the 'paperwork burden' on small businesses and state and local government. Reference has already been made to Executive Order 12356, which facilitates the classification of material to render it exempt under FOIA as well as adding new categories of information, e.g. crypotology (secret codes).[17] Further, the Federal Government has employed the Espionage Act to punish unauthorised disclosure of information even though the cases did not concern spying. The Executive has also taken steps to placate the British Government since Crown documents not available in the UK may well be available in the USA under FOIA. UK departments mark such documents 'UK Confidential', although this, by itself, would not ensure exemption in the USA.[18]

Looking on the positive side, Relyea has described how a civil service acceptance of the Act has been fostered within the agencies. Specialists are responsible for FOIA requests and 'brokerage' thereon.[19] However, charging fees without justification, refusing to act until money is 'up-front', intentionally understaffing FOI departments, forcing litigation, indiscriminate censorship, and other unhelpful practices are all known occurrences. So too is ignoring time responses which should take 10 days for an initial response. One FOIA suit has taken 11 years to resolve through the courts.[20]

Many agencies have established procedures giving third parties notice and allowing opportunity for challenge when documents relating to them are sought. The Executive is keen to obtain legislation on this matter, and the business and commercial community are anxious for such a right. The 1986 FOIA has amended the basis for charging fees for complying with duties under the legislation. Requests for commercial purposes will be charged the actual cost of document review, though requesters may still be entitled to a fee waiver if, for instance, their request is for information which it is in the public interest to disclose 'because it is likely to contribute significantly to public understanding of the operations of Government'. Search fees will be waived for educational, non-commercial scientific organisations and requesters from the news media.

The FOIA has generated a vast industry in the USA among the business community.[21] Approximately 50–60 per cent of requesters are from commercial bodies seeking information on business competitors. Next comes the public, accounting for 20–25 per cent of requests. The press accounts for only 5–8 per cent. In 1983, there were 262,265 requests for FOI; in 1984, 281,102 of which approximately 60 per cent were processed by the Department of Defense and the Department of Health and Human Services. About 80 per cent of all requests are fully granted.[22]

Relyea has estimated that the cost of administering FOIA runs to about $50 million per annum. In 1983, the US General Accounting Office estimated the cost of the Act in 1981 at $61 million, 'although costs cannot currently be measured with any precision'.[23] This is comparable with the price of maintaining armed services marching bands or golf courses on military bases. Estimates of the cost of government self-promotion and public relations exercises run to about $1 billion per annum. 'Thus, it is considerably less expensive to provide the public with the information it seeks via the FOIA than it is for the Executive to provide what it determines the public should know about agency activities and operations'.[24]

The FOIA is one of four major statutes facilitating open government in the USA. The FOIA is primarily concerned with individuals gaining access to agency records. Since its inception, however, a large number of professional organisations, known *inter alia* as 'data brokers or 'surrogate requesters', use FOIA to gain information which they can market and sell to those with an interest.

Federal Advisory Committees Act (FACA)[25]

FACA is within the FOI mould but has its rights set more firmly on the real target of bureaucratic decision-making. The Act, enacted in 1972, has six basic objectives: to establish standards and uniform procedures to govern the creation, operation and termination of federal advisory committees; to ensure that whenever possible advisory committee meetings are open to the public and accessible; to reduce their cost; to avoid specific interest group domination and rubber-stamping of prior decisions; to keep the public and Congress advised on all aspects of advisory committees; and to ensure they remain advisory and not executive. In 1970, it was estimated that as many as 3,200 such committees existed with a membership of 22,000[26] and that subjective preferences of organised interests could easily influence official decision-makers.[27] An early indication of its potential utility was given in *FCN, Inc.* v. *Davis*,[28] when a newspaper editor wished to be present at meetings between Treasury officials and consumer groups which were recommending whether labelling should be required for chemical additives in liquor. He obtained a court order prohibiting the closure of future meetings.

FACA gives a broad definition to the advisory committees, or their sub-committees or sub-groups, of agencies and departments whose members are not full-time officers or employees of the agency.[29] The Act covers such bodies if they have a fixed membership; they have a defined purpose of providing advice to a federal agency; they have regular or periodic meetings; they have an organisational structure.

Committees have a two-year lifespan and those rendered otiose are terminated. A designated official will chair the meetings or attend, and FACA requires a 'balanced representation of points of view'.

Adequate advance notice of the meetings must be given in the *Federal Register*, and subject to reasonable regulations any member of the public is given the right to attend, file a written statement or make an appearance. Detailed minutes with a complete description of the discussion must be kept, along with conclusions, and they must be available for inspection and copying.

The FOIA exemptions apply with some modifications. The Agency head to whom the committee reports determines whether an exemption will apply in writing, and these have to be explained in detail. Reports have to be made out by the Agency head on the extent to which he has accepted committee recommendations as well as on the latter's activities, status and membership.

It will be appreciated that on paper the FACA could go to the nerve centre of many of the essential decisions in the interface of public/private relationships and state regulation of private interest groups. That being the case, it is not surprising that its reception was marked by 'non-administration, non-use and ingenious bureaucratic techniques of evasion'.[30] In the first year of its operation there was widespread closure of meetings, often without citation of the exemption, or with citation of exemptions which courts had ruled did not apply. Setting up of 'informal ad hoc groups' has been resorted to, although in *Aviation Consumer Action Project* v. *Yoke*[31] the District Court ruled that an ad hoc Civil Aviation Bureau meeting with airline representatives was covered by the FACA, though not where the President consulted informally with various groups as part of a publicity exercise.[32] Other evasive tactics have included holding meetings abroad, even on a private yacht! Domination by private interest groups was not uncommon, e.g. the National Petroleum Council carried out much of its work in sub-committees convened without public notice and often in oil company offices.

Recommendations to strengthen the safeguards – including oversight of FACA by an agency other than the Office of Manpower and Budget,[33] effective enforcement sanctions, quick and informal appellate procedures to challenge closure, and a verbatim transcript of meetings which are closed for subsequent judicial review purposes – have not been accepted.

The Sunshine Act

The Sunshine Act (SA) is an 'open meeting' law allowing access to the meetings of those agencies within its scope. Its aim is to open up to the public portions of the 'deliberative processes' of certain agencies. It does not provide a right to participate in decision-making, nor can it be invoked to insist that a meeting be held.[34]

The Act applies to all multi-headed agencies, that is 'agencies headed by a collegial body composed of two or more individual members, a majority of whom are appointed by the President, and sub-divisions of agencies appointed to act on its behalf'. Certain internal advisory meetings are not covered, nor are departments headed by a single person.[35] The Act covers the deliberations of the requisite number of agency officials 'where such deliberations determine or result in the joint conduct or disposition of official agency business'.

One week's public notice of the date, time, place and topic of the meeting must be given. A named official with a publicised telephone number must be appointed to answer queries. The law requires more than notice in the *Federal Register*. The federal law does not, however, require the keeping of minutes or verbatim transcripts – unlike many state sunshine laws, though regulations adopted by an agency may themselves require minutes. Records do have to be kept of closed meetings. To close a meeting a majority of agency members must agree, not simply a majority of the quorum of a meeting. The FOIA exemptions, with modification, apply.

Where judicial review of a closure of a meeting is sought, the burden of proof is upon the agency concerned. A failure to exhaust domestic remedies does not preclude the opportunity for relief via the courts. The courts will usually only interfere with a failure to pursue the procedures under the law if the breach was intentional, repetitive or prejudicial. The courts have, however, been reluctant to allow parties under the Act to use their transcript of an agency proceedings under the Act to supplement the record of other agencies' decisions or rule-making in judicial proceedings. The Act provides for 'reasonable attorney fees and other litigation costs reasonably incurred' against any party (not simply the Government as in FOIA) where the requesting party substantially prevails in the application.

As under the FOIA, agencies submit annual reports to Congress on the SA and the Congressional Research Service compiles an overview to discern trends for Congress.

The Privacy Act

The Privacy Act (PA) was passed in 1974, and it regulates the collection, control, content, dissemination and use of certain categories of government information.[36] It allows individuals on whom executive federal agencies have documents, files or data to examine the documentation after a written application. A *Citizens' Guide*[37] describes in detail the procedures to follow to obtain information about oneself, and it spells out in simple terms the kinds of information that agencies are likely to possess on individuals, adding that this was 'just a fraction of the information held on individual citizens'. An individual may write to an agency head or PA official, who both have a duty to inform the individual whether files are held on him or her. Or a more thorough check may be made by consulting the compilation of PA Notices published annually by the *Federal Register*. This contains details of all federal records systems, the kinds of data included, and the categories of individuals on whom the information is held. Retrieval procedures and relevant officials are identified, and the volumes are available in reference, law and university libraries. The compilation is, however, poorly indexed and difficult to use.

Unlike FOIA, only the subject of the data or records can apply for sight of them. The subject can seek amendment of the records which he or she believes to be inaccurate, irrelevant, untimely or un- complete. Copies of the record, in a form comprehensible to the applicant, must be provided and he or she must be told who, outside the agency, has had access. The Act provides criminal and a variety of civil sanctions.[38] There is no standard procedure for retrieval, unlike FOIA, but agency regulations prescribing procedures are common: rejections must be accompanied by a letter specifying the appeal procedures. If appeal is refused, the agency must refer to the exemption it is invoking and must also state why it is not available under FOIA. The authority for the collection of information must be specified, as must the use to which it is to be put. Information should only be collected where it is relevant or necessary for carrying out lawful duties. Information must be accurate, timely, relevant and complete, an obligation which does not apply to FOIA.

Disclosure of any record covered by the PA to a third party without the written consent or request of the subject is prohibited unless the third-party request falls under one of 11 exemptions.[39]

If an agency seeks to rely upon an exemption, however, and is challenged, a *de novo* review can take place in the courts with the burden of proof on the agency to establish one of the exemptions. These fall into two categories: 'general' and 'specific'.

General exemptions cover CIA systems of records and criminal law enforcement systems of records, though the latter only cover criminal investigation records, records compiled to identify criminal offenders or alleged offenders, or compiled at any stage of law enforcement after arrest. This information is only exempt if rules state the reasons for exemption of a system of records from each provision of the PA. If an individual challenges the exemption before the courts, the courts must determine that a system of records properly falls under the exemption and that all exemption procedures have been followed.[40]

Specific exemptions cover: information classified by Executive Order as under the FOIA; law enforcement material not falling under the general exemption; Secret Service material; civil or military service employment or promotional suitability information relating to suitability for federal contracts. The exemptions are discretionary, and for an agency to invoke them all necessary procedures must be followed. Under specific exemptions, an agency head may exempt his agency's records from fewer of the provisions of the Act than under general exemptions, and challenge through the courts is allowed.

The PA is one of a number of statutes protecting the privacy of personal information, including the disclosure of information identifying certain US intelligence officers, agents and sources/informants.[41] In the 98th Congress over 30 Bills on privacy-related matters were introduced into Congress.[42] Such a frenzied activity may suggest that all is not well with the PA, and certainly there are apparent incompatibilities between the PA and FOIA.[43]

In 1983 Congressional *Oversight Hearings* of the PA, it was stated that the current US federal system for data protection was seriously deficient because it lacked an adequate monitoring mechanism to ensure compliance and enforcement.[44] Our own Data Protection Registrar might come to mind in this context. There was no overall regulatory body for privacy laws in the USA. Serious malpractices such as computer matching were common, it was felt. This is where whole categories of people may have their records screened to see if they belong to a separate, supposedly incompatible category such as 'welfare recipient'.[45]

The USA has a constitutional background which takes privacy

seriously. The First, Fourth and Fifth Amendments to the Constitution protect freedom of speech, security of property, protection against self-incrimination, and due process of law and have all been regularly invoked to protect the inviolability of an individual's privacy. The Privacy Protection Act 1980 prohibits government agents from making unannounced searches of press offices and files if no one in the press office is suspected of a crime. As befits a privacy-conscious society, many complaints are made to the Office of Management and Budget – which compiles the annual reports on PA from agencies – about agency breaches of PA provisions. It is a little surprising, therefore, that only 179 copies of the 1979 edition of the PA Information Manual were sold.[46]

FOI and Constitutional and Administrative Practice

The constitutional culture of the USA is more jealous in its protection of freedom of speech, its insistence upon informed debate and freedom of information, than our own.[47] This was evidenced when the President bowed to public pressure to allow the investigation of the Executive and the National Security Council and their roles in illegal arms sales to Iran and unauthorised payments of sums received to Nicaraguan rebels. Within days a Senate hearing was called to investigate[48] and to replace the internal Presidential executive inquiry. There followed investigations by Congressional Committee and the appointment of a Special Prosecutor. The President did not raise the plea of 'executive privilege' in these proceedings, but it has been frequently invoked.

'Executive privilege' as a term was only coined in 1958, although feuds concerning the 'President's claim of constitutional authority to withhold information from Congress' go back to the eighteenth century.[49] In *US* v. *Nixon*[50] the Supreme Court rejected an absolute claim to executive privilege by the President although the case concerned the investigation of serious *criminal* charges against senior executive officials. The courts are the final arbiters in judicial proceedings and law enforcement on what the President and his officials must produce in the interests of justice.[51]

The position is not paralleled *vis-à-vis* Congressional Committee demands for information. They do not have the same power as courts. Because Congress has no specific power to demand information, and because of the separation of powers doctrine as well as the equality and independence of each branch of government, Presidents have sought to refuse Congress the right to control and demand executive information. *Per contra* 'Congress as the arm of the Government responsible for making and overseeing the operation of the nation's laws, has the power to inquire into and review the methods by which those laws are enforced'.[52] Claims to such a privilege for the Executive increased markedly after 1954.[53] The courts have not supported an unqualified Congressional right to demand information from the President, and Congress would have to establish a strong need to fulfil its constitutional responsibilities of oversight, and that such fulfilment was only possible with access to the President's papers, before the courts ordered access. Where it was sought in 1973 by a Senate Committee – in the Watergate episode – the need was not established,[54] although at that time the House Judiciary Committee possessed most of the relevant information and was about to make available its findings on impeachment proceedings against the President. A statute giving Congress the right to demand information in global terms would, in all probability, be ruled unconstitutional.[55]

In November 1982, a White House memorandum for the Heads of Executive Departments and Agencies stated that executive privilege could only be claimed 'in the most compelling of circumstances' where after 'careful review' an assertion of privilege was necessary. Brokerage between Congress and the White House would minimise the need for the invoking of executive privilege. Within a month, there was an explosive clash between the Environmental Protection Agency (EPA) and a Congressional Committee when the head of the EPA's hazardous waste programme was holding back information on toxic waste sites and their clean-up. She was cited for contempt of Congress. The Justice Department unsuccessfully sought judicial exoneration of the head as she was acting under the direction of the President in refusing to hand over information. The court pressed the parties for a friendly settlement without further judicial inter-vention.[56] The Committee eventually obtained its information.[57] Sauce was added to the fare when it was disclosed that the head of the EPA's hazardous waste programme had frequently met, informally and socially, with representatives of companies whose activities she was regulating, although similar opportunities were not offered to environmental lobby groups.

It would take another book to describe the interrelationship between administrative process and law, the requirement of a full record of administrative hearings and rule-making proceedings, the opportunities for interested parties to participate in policy formulation and to be adequately informed about the subject matter, and the resort to courts for 'hard-look', or a very probing, judicial review of an agency's decisions or regulations in order to establish an adequate evidentiary basis for such decisions and regulations. These combine together to put administrative policy-making through a series of tests and justifications based upon informed criticism that are largely unparalleled in the UK, although one must be careful not to exaggerate. For instance, in the desire of the White House to deregulate wherever possible, the Executive has set a cost-benefit analysis which has to be satisfied before new regulations can be passed. Executive Order 12498 instructs agencies to notify the Office of Manpower and Budget of *all* agency research with links to possible regulation. The desire to deregulate is meeting with some counter-productive consequences.[58]

Canada

The Canadian constitution is a written federal constitution, but it has within its operation many features of the Westminster model of government, most notably a developed sense of ministerial responsibility and Parliamentary government. FOIA in America saw a hostile Executive, and direct advisers to the President are exempt from the Act. The American law was generated by law reformers, good-government advocates, journalists and Congress. In Canada, Crown privilege and Cabinet confidentiality had to be expressly incorporated into the legislation; the legislation was far from independent of executive influence, and the press impact for reform was minimal.[59] In the USA, FOIA was developed largely without executive assistance, frequently in the face of executive opposition; in Canada, the Access to Information Act (AIA) was 'drafted by the administration and developed through amendments it perfected'.[60] The AIA has eight or nine times as many exemptions as FOIA. Unlike the AIA, the FOIA did not provide for an information ombudsman. Congressmen were jealous of their role as citizens' representatives and Americans like litigation.[61]

The AIA was passed in 1982 and is part of a broad constitutional package reflecting a wish for a new constitutional structure as Canada sloughs off the last vestige of control from Westminster.[62] Access is allowed to Federal Government records and includes: 'letters, memos, books, plans, maps, photographs, films, microfilms, sound recordings, computerised data and any other documentary material regardless of physical form or characteristics or any copy thereof '. It is specific in a way FOIA is not. An Access Register exists which contains descriptions of government records, their probable locations, and other information which 'will likely assist you in identifying precisely which records you wish to see'. Instructions are provided on how to identify, as precisely as possible, the information an applicant is looking for, how to get assistance and how to apply for access. Government departments have Access Co-ordinators who assist free of charge. A request must be in writing, and there is an application fee of $5 with additional fees for time in excess of five hours spent on a request and for computer processing and copying time. An applicant must be a citizen of Canada or a permanent resident.[63] An agency has 30 days to respond to the initial request, though this may be extended where a request is complicated. The head of each government institution covered by the Act must submit an annual report to Parliament on the administration of the Act. If a body claims that information is exempt, it has to justify that it is exempt. The Act does not apply to Crown commercial organisations.

Excluded Material

Excluded material includes Cabinet secrets or confidences of the Queen's Privy Council covering such items as policy proposals, background options and discussions, agenda of Privy Council meetings and Minister/Adviser discussions on policy briefings and draft legislation. Discussion papers may be released if *inter alia* the decision to which they relate has been made public.[64] The Information Commissioner (IC) believes she has a right to determine whether they have become public, although her decisions cannot be enforced. The Standing Committee on Justice and Solicitor-General described this blanket exclusion as unjustified. It has not been followed in all provincial access statutes.

Exemptions

The Act provides for mandatory and discretionary exemptions. The former include: information from foreign, provincial or municipal governments; certain confidential information from the Royal Canadian Mounted Police; personal information and information supplied by outside sources (*sic*).[65] The discretionary exemptions are extensive and include those which might harm federal/provincial affairs, international affairs, Canadian defence or the detection or prevention of 'subversive or hostile activities', lawful investigations, or which might facilitate the committing of a criminal offence if released. If release would threaten trade secrets, legal privilege or personal safety it may be exempted. Also exempt is the 'advice or recommendations developed by or for an institution or a Minister' which would disclose accounts of their deliberations and consultations apropos of negotiating plans or positions – an exemption which has the 'greatest potential for routine misuse'. Third-party information covering trade secrets, competitive ability, contractual matters or other confidential information may be waived from exemption without consent where 'the disclosure would be in the public interest and it relates to health, public safety or the protection of the environment'. Safeguards ensure third-party notice and right of challenge.

Basic Provisions

Citizens are urged to use 'existing informal channels' to obtain information and access. This may be a way of institutionalising brokerage as the Access Coordinator has responsibility for all internal aspects of the administration of the Act and he has to be informed of all direct requests from the public.

Departments must introduce reading-room facilities within two years of the introduction of the Act. An Access Register, available in approximately 700 libraries and 2,700 post offices, is constantly checked to ensure accuracy and that it is up to date. The Register is organised in chapters, one covering each federal institution and related agencies, and each chapter contains:

1. A description of the organisation and responsibilities of the institution, including details on the programmes and functions of each division or branch.
2. A description of all classes of records under the control of the institution in sufficient detail to facilitate the exercise of the right of access under the Act.
3. All working manuals.
4. Titles and addresses of appropriate officials.

The Information Commissioner (IC)

An Ombudsman to deal with complaints concerning access has been established and she has access to information which is exempt under the Act. She has declared her intention to construe the exemptions as narrowly as possible. Complaints must be made within a year of the initial request, and they must be in writing unless this requirement is waived. Her decision cannot be enforced against departments although she may select for judicial scrutiny points which require judicial interpretation, even when the applicant cannot afford the cost of litigation and where she has consented to the suit's proceeding after a department's refusal. Individuals have access to the courts following refusal. The Commissioner may participate in proceedings brought by others, receive information which the complainant will not – unless successful – and may be heard *ex parte* by the court.[66]

It must be said, however, that examination of the Commissioner's Annual Reports produces a less sanguine perspective of the Act's operation. The IC has criticised the absence of publicity or explanations of the Act. Indeed, no clause was incorporated providing for public education and enlightenment on the Act and no funds are provided for such. The IC has reported that the 'FOIA cannot be improved upon nor can it serve a country well if its very existence is kept secret'. In the 1984–5 Report, the IC remarked that Access Co-ordinators were becoming demoralised and isolated and were subject to criticism from colleagues when they pursued the objectives of the Act too vigorously. Where a Co-ordinator was absent, there are no temporary fill-ins, so phones and correspondence are not answered. The 1985–6 Report was even gloomier in its tone, and it noted how the most frequent users were journalists, academics and researchers.[67]

Where the IC supports a complaint but a remedy is not negotiated, a report is made to the Minister. Investigations are conducted in private.

The Canadian Parliament is reviewing the operation of the Act and it is studying the operation and possible reform of certain of the exempt categories.[68]

The Privacy Act

One of the most commonly invoked exemptions under AIA is that relating to personal information. A Privacy Act was assented to in 1982 which allows access to personal individual records of scheduled government departments by the individual subjects concerned where these records are held by the department. It does not cover private sector bodies. A Privacy Commissioner (PC) shares premises and general staff with the IC, although they are different individuals and they have different legal advisers because the interests of the two may clash, e.g. access to personal information may be sought by a 'client' of the IC and challenged by a 'client' of the PC. Personal information is given a wide interpretation and safeguards are imposed on the use, purposes, collection and dissemination of material. Personal Information Banks and a Personal Information Index are published, setting out all personal information held, who has control of it, the purposes for which it is used, etc. The same criteria apply to applicants for access as obtain under the AIA. They can request correction and notice of unsuccessful requests for correction. The general scheme of the Act, including exclusions, exemptions and reviews of indexes, is similar to those under the AIA.

Conclusion

In 1981, a commentator upon the FOI movement in Canada noted:[69]

It has been the experience of public interest interveners such as the Consumers Association of Canada that regulated companies have tended to overwhelm them with information, and as a result the challenge has been to build up expertise so as to be able to interpret this mass of information. . . . Is the information coming in a digestible form or in an uncontrollable manner?

This raises a general problem about obtaining information. Raw information can be next to useless. What information do we want? In what form is it most useful? Who is going to use it? For what purpose is it going to be used and how is it going to be most usable? To these points we will return.

The Canadian statute is less biased towards disclosure than the American one and is more mindful of past practices of confidentiality.[70] In fact, the original proponents of the FOI Bill were the Canadian Bar Association, whose Bill was far more adventurous and forthright than that which the Government accepted.[71] A recent review of the two Acts by the House of Commons Standing Committee on Justice and Solicitor-General has made some important recommendations on the legislation.[71a] In particular, it recommended that Cabinet confidences be brought into the exempt categories and that they should no longer be excluded.

Australia

Official reports in Australia, prior to their FOIA, placed the blame for excessive secrecy in government on the residue of the influence of the English tradition and its association with Crown prerogative.[72] Any such residue may well have been expunged by Mr Justice Powell in the New South Wales Supreme Court when he ordered the British Government to produce details of MI5 activities in proceedings brought by the Crown against Peter Wright.[73] The FOIA enacted in 1982 has to be set against an ostensibly impressive range of reforms in Australian administrative law which straddle the Administrative Review Council, the Administrative Appeals Tribunal (AAT), the establishment of a Federal Ombudsman, and a reformed basis of judicial review of administrative action.[74] In 1983, an FOI Amendment Act was passed to cover certain deficiences in the 1982 legislation, including access to documents up to five years old at the time of the commencement of the 1983 Act.

In a 1983 Report on the Act by the Federal Attorney-General in Australia he spoke in hopeful tones about the benefits of the Act, which included the improvement of official decision-making, a better-informed public and a truer democratic political process as well as giving individuals information held on themselves or influencing the decisions 'fundamentally affecting their lives'. He was a little surprised, therefore, that much less use of the Act had been made than anticipated.[75]

The Legislation
The 1982 Act places a duty on the responsible Minister to publish, not later than twelve months after commencement of the Act, particulars of the organisation, its functions and powers; arrangements allowing public participation for non-official persons or groups in whatever form in the formulation of policy; the organisation's administration; the categories of its documents and details on access procedures and officers. Ministers have to publish in the *Federal Gazette* all documents – including computerised records – which may be used to make decisions or recommendations affecting rights, privileges, benefits, obligations, penalties or other 'detriments'. Every person has a legally enforceable right to agency and ministerial documents which are not exempt. A decision on access has to be given within 60 days, and

refusal must be accompanied with reasons. As with Canadian legislation, there is a third-party notification procedure.

Exemptions[76]

Documents are exempt where 'disclosure . . . would be contrary to the public interest', viz. it 'could reasonably be expected to cause damage to: the security or defence of the Commonwealth; international relations; Federal–State relations'. Cabinet and Executive Council documents are exempt, as are internal working documents where disclosure would reveal advice or deliberations relating to the 'deliberative functions of an agency or Minister or of the Commonwealth Government' and would be against the public interest. A certificate from the Minister is conclusive evidence on the public interest. The Administrative Appeals Tribunal has held that it would be cautious about entering into an unfinished course of policy-making and negotiation and the benefit of the doubt, even in cases where there were very strong grounds in favour of disclosure, would lie with the Minister where he had a 'relevant reasonable ground for non-disclosure'.[77] This exemption does not apply to purely factual information, reports on scientific or technical experts expressing an opinion on technical matters, nor to reports of a prescribed body or organisation *within* an agency. Other exemptions cover familiar territory: law enforcement; public safety; Commonwealth financial interests; documents the disclosure of which would involve unreasonable disclosure of personal information; legal privilege; trade secrets; disclosure which would deleteriously affect the national economy; or which would constitute a breach of confidence. This last exemption would seem to be very wide in scope.

In addition to the above exemptions, information may be refused where it relates to 'all documents, or all documents of a specified class, that contain information of a specified kind or relate to a specified subject matter' and would 'substantially and unnecessarily interfere' with the other functions of the agency or Minister. Reasons must be given for refusal, but again this exemption seems to allow ample scope for refusal.

Amendment and Review

Part V of the Act allows the subject of personal documents to apply to have the records amended. Part VI covers the review of the agency's or Minister's decision.

An internal review will take place within 14 days after the day of notification of refusal upon request. Three months is not an unknown period. Alternatively, an application may be made to the AAT if no decision is notified within 30 days.[78] Another route is via the Commonwealth Ombudsman, although he cannot investigate decisions taken by Ministers. The AAT has power to make any decision that could be made by the agency or Minister and can, in some cases, review whether disclosure would be contrary to the public interest.[79] *In camera* proceedings are possible for inspection of 'exempt' documents by the AAT if it is not satisfied with the Minister's certificate. If a Minister does not accept a finding of the AAT which is adverse to his classification, it is not binding upon him, but he must notify the applicant of his reasons and place a copy of these before both Houses of Parliament.[80] From the AAT there is an appeal on a point of law to the Federal Court.

The 1983 Act allows the Ombudsman to represent individuals before the AAT, though he must have especial regard to the importance of the principle involved, the potential success of the challenge and the reasonableness of the decision challenged along with the financial means of the applicant.[81]

The Ombudsman

The Annual Reports of the Ombudsman are notable for his own complaints that he receives inadequate funding to perform his responsibilities under the FOIA. Several persons who wished to be represented before the AAT were turned down because of a lack of funding.[82] He received no additional staff for his FOIA responsibilities. The 1983 legislation not only added the representational role to his responsibilities: he now has to monitor the Act and recommend improvements in access. He claimed that his treatment by the Government was both 'unfair and demonstrably discriminatory' and that lack of resources meant that he had been unable to monitor the Act as required. In 1984–5, the position had not improved.[83]

The Ombudsman is beset by other problems. It has been decided that his records of complaints investigations are not exempt, under section 38[84] of the Act, from an FOIA request. All Ombudsmen would invoke the protection of complete confidentiality for their investigations – a confidentiality usually protected by law, so the decision does appear anomalous.[85] To gain exemption, the

Ombudsman may well have to rely upon the general confidentiality provision in the 1982 Act and other exemptions.

The Ombudsman has access to disputed documents, including those for which exemption is claimed.[86] In 1984–5 he received 142 FOI complaints, virtually double the figure for 1983–4. The Administrative Review Council has noted that the Ombudsman has not played as significant a role in FOI as anticipated.[87]

Some Reaction to the Legislation
The courts have ruled that the legislation is applicable to some private institutions carrying out functions in the public interest, for example a Law Society and universities, although documents of University Council meetings have been held to be properly classified as exempt by the AAT as they were compared with Cabinet documents.[88] Boldness in some areas is not reflected in others. The High Court of Australia has held that there is no general rule of common law or principle of natural justice that required the giving of reasons for administrative decisions.[89] Another judge, however, adverting to this issue and FOIA generally, spoke of the need for legislation to 'deal with the real problems and not the symbols and to preserve democratic values' of society.[90] Information rights, he argued, must extend from the public sector to the private one – a point to which I shall return.

The Act has precipitated an increasing number of applications to the AAT, and in the years 1984–5 and 1985–6 FOI applications constituted the second and third largest items respectively. In the first full year of the FOIA's operation, there were almost 20,000 requests involving 152 agencies; of these 1,105 were refused, 500 were reviewed internally and 27 formed the subject of a complaint to the Ombudsman; 168 were referred to the AAT.

It is interesting to observe that departments are differing in their attitudes towards FOIA. Such differences seemed to be anticipated by the Attorney-General, who wrote to all relevant agencies in 1983 asking them to inform his secretariat of FOIA requests which were being taken to the AAT, so that *consistency* in approach could be achieved. There is also some evidence of informal bartering by federal and provincial government to secure opposition to a federal agency's liberal attitude to disclosing information.[91]

New Zealand

New Zealand enacted an FOIA – the Official Information Act – in 1982, which bears some resemblances to the Australian legislation, although it makes provision for the publication of internal rules and has many distinct characteristics. It would be pointless running through similar provisions once more, but it is worth pointing out that an Information Ombudsman has been created, the New Zealand Ombudsman in fact, to deal with information complaints. His decisions *are* mandatory on the Minister or department concerned and take effect from the commencement of the twenty-second day after the day on which his *recommendation* is made to the department, unless the responsible Minister otherwise directs or decides.

The Act also creates an Information Authority. Its duties are:

(I)   To review, as a first priority, the protection accorded to official information by any Act with a view to seeing whether that protection is both reasonable and compatible with the purposes of FOIA;
(II) To define and review categories of official information with a view to enlarging the categories of official information to which access is given as a matter of right;
(III) To recommend the making of regulations prescribing:
    (a) Categories of official information to which access is given as a matter of right;
    (b) Such conditions, if any, as it considers appropriate in relation to the giving of access to any category of official information.

Further duties of the Authority include reviewing of the Act and of access practices and changes in such practices; inviting public as well as official comment about the Act; making suggestions for extension of the Act; and seeking advice from and conducting investigations into all appropriate authorities. For this latter duty, access to necessary documents is given subject to veto on account of national security and to prevent crime. The Information Authority can meet in public or in private, and it reports to Parliament. It has a life-span of five years.

In 1983–4, 435 requests for investigation were made to the Ombudsman. No additional staff or resources were provided. The two areas causing most difficulty were those relating to personal and private information and to competitive commercial contracts. Exemptions most commonly relied upon were the protection of confidentiality of advice and the internal working documents exemption protecting the 'free and frank' opinions of officials. The Ombudsman has found the former exemption too expansive and has sought to restrict its scope. He heard evidence that a failure to maintain full and frank discussion neutered or hindered the civil service, and similar views had emerged from Australia.[92] Tendering for government contracts had been kept confidential, and the Ombudsman has suggested that commercially confidential information should be separated from other information in tendering.

An Official Information Amendment Bill was introduced into Parliament in June 1986.

Sweden

Outside the common law world, freedom of information took root much earlier than the mid-1960s. Sweden has had a Freedom of the Press Act as part of its constitution since 1766, and all 'official' documents are now available for inspection and copying, although public corporations, defined as commercial organisations, are excluded. Further, internal memoranda are not available until filed, i.e. the matter to which they refer has been finally resolved. Documents received by, or dispatched by, the authority are within the terms of the Act. There are four areas of exempt information: national security and foreign affairs; suppression of crime and illegality; protection of legitimate economic interests; and personal privacy. The statutory details concerning exempt items are contained in the Secrecy Act and refer to classes of documents and not their contents. The Secrecy Act specifies a period for which a document will be secret: from two years to seventy years. Since 1981 the emphasis has been on increasing secrecy.[93] Internal review may follow a refusal, followed by an appeal to the administrative courts. Appeal is cheap and readily available. A Data Act of 1973 is administered by a Data Inspection Board.[94]

The making of important decisions affecting the public is generally a secret affair, though organised interests may seek to influence membership of commissions of inquiry, administrative and even quasi-judicial bodies, or sponsored MPs may press for membership. The views of civil servants and advisers do not, however, remain concealed. A very large degree of Swedish public administration is depoliticised in so far as many, sometimes important, decisions are not taken by political overlords, or at least they bear no formal responsibility for such decisions. They are taken by and are the responsibility of administrators who must place pre-eminence upon rationality and correctness, not their political survival. This has caused one author to suggest that secrecy lies at the troubled boundary between politics and reason: 'Secrecy will cease at the point at which politics ends and reason begins. . . . Politics is the art of defining what the problems are and reason the act of solving them.'[95] How far secrecy goes depends on how widely the ambit of politics is allowed freedom to range. The distinction is too pat. However, the author quoted above suggests that in Britain, the most secret of the countries which he examined, election manifestos of political parties were the clearest and most detailed of those he studied.[96]

France

The final example comes from France. The French law on access to administrative documents was approved in July 1978 and has been in force since December 1978. Those served by the French administration have access to non-'name-linked' documents. Like the French Data Processing and Liberties Act, the 1978 Act applies to private organisations charged by the State with operating a public service. The Act has been criticised for its vagueness and for the terms of its exemptions. A special commission was established to supervise the implementation of the law. It is a purely consultative body. The general feeling was that the Act required clarification.

It has to be explained that French administrative law, the *droit administratif,* has a very good fact-finding procedure involving officials of the Conseil d'État, or local courts, and the Commissaire du Gouvernement, who represents the public interest when there is a dispute between the State and a citizen – the public interest is not equiparated with that of the State. These officials have access to documents and files, and refusal to hand over information or to give reasons for an adverse decision will be interpreted *against* the public body and will be taken as evidence of bad faith or improper motive.[97]

Conclusion

All the above examples reveal the different approaches adopted by countries operating in a liberal-democratic tradition and at broadly similar stages of economic development. The different socio-cultural and political backgrounds of the countries have ensured variations in their approaches to FOI, although all have reacted to the growth of government and bureaucracy, the escalation of information-gathering and control by executive agencies – and in some cases private bodies – and the inability of democratic institutions of representative government to oversee these developments effectively, albeit in different ways.

It might be pertinent to ask whether the legislative developments constitute an acknowledgement of the failure of representative government and the first faltering steps towards a more substantial participatory form of government. If this is claimed, then the legislation we have examined has a long way to go. One might say that public disquiet has been bought off rather cheaply in the countries we have examined. The legislation can only operate within a framework which is already in existence – a governmental attitude which *might* have to undergo change as the legislation works inwardly upon it, and a public attitude which is unknowing and unfamiliar with the use of information to challenge governmental presumptions. Expectations that the legislation by itself will achieve the goals which many FOI advocates hope for are pie in the sky. Different public attitudes and different governmental institutions are necessary for the success of FOIA legislation.

But we are running ahead of ourselves. We have seen how far progress has been made in other highly developed states. Some have been directly inspired by the Westminster style of government. It is now time to account for the reasons or forces which have prevailed against such developments in the United Kingdom, and to query how much longer such attitudes can prevail.

3
Government and Information – An Historical Development

Government control of information in Britain did not first emerge as a problem for government shortly before 1889, when the first Official Secrets Act was passed.[1] Control of information had been a central preoccupation of government since government first assumed responsibility for defence, taxation and administration, and even before. The King's household, until the Tudor monarchy, was characterised by personal government on the advice of trusted counsellors who remained bound by allegiance and confidence to the Crown. Serious breaches of confidence might involve treason in the form of adhering to the King's enemies under the Act of 1352, which was extended well beyond the terms of the statute by judicial decisions.[2] High treason 'was regarded as a final denial of the divine order of things as established in the body politic and defined in the oath of allegiance'.[3]

Breaches of confidence were not always problematic in the absence of widespread printing and publishing facilities. More pressing for the power in existence was the control of the spread of seditious ideas or movements which could threaten its position. This point is vividly illustrated by the breach with the Church of Rome and the accumulation of statutes extending treason to punish *inter alia* those who 'shall by writing, printing, preaching, speech, express words or sayings, maliciously, advisedly and directly publish, set forth, and affirm that the Queen our said sovereign lady Queen Elizabeth is an heretic, schismatic, tyrant, infidel or an usurper of the Crown of the said realms or any of them. . . .'[4] Even before the advent of the Tudor dynasty, the procedure for treason trials was weighted heavily in favour of the Crown.[5] What was novel about the Tudor dynasty was the revolution in government which took place.[6]

After 1530, there 'was a rejection of the medieval conception of the kingdom as the King's estate, his private concern properly administered by his private organisation; it conceived its task to be national, its support and scope to be nationwide, and its administrative needs, therefore, divorced from the King's household'.[7] On governmental administration, the change is characterised by the individual assertion of King's advisers as opposed to the 'anonymity' of the medieval period. Almost all the available state papers from 1530–40 are those of Thomas Cromwell, Henry VIII's Minister of State. A fastidious keeper of records, he also presided over an Act of 1536 'concerning the Clerkes of the Signet and Privie Seale' which enacted that no manner of writing was to pass the great seals[8] of England, Ireland, the Duchy of Lancester and the Principality of Wales, or 'by process out of the Exchequer', unless it had first been examined by the King's principal secretary or a clerk of the signet.[9]

From the mid-1530s onwards, the Privy Council developed as an institution whose name signified 'the special "secretness" or closeness to the King of his more intimate advisers', a 'special and more important branch of the Council' based upon the exclusiveness of its 19 or so members.[10] Nevertheless, although the Council established its right to information, particularly on foreign affairs, Cromwell 'knew and insisted that serious business should be transacted in conversations with the King and himself '.[11] He acted, according to Elton, 'in practice like a somewhat despotic Prime Minister presiding over a cabinet of comparative mediocrities'. The period witnessed the emergence of national departments of state, bureaucratically organised and independent of the King's household, but responsible to the Crown. Responsibility to Parliament had yet to come, but we should note that proceedings in Parliament itself were secret, breach of secrecy constituting a serious contempt. By Elizabethan times, Parliamentary affairs were 'the common talk of tavern life',[12] however, in spite of the injunction that 'Every person of the Parliament ought to keep secret, and not to disclose, the secrets and things done and spoken in the Parliament house'.[13] Freedom of debate, and freedom from the Monarch's intervention, required secrecy. In 1628, it was confirmed that speeches would not be printed in the *Journal*, but by 1641 the House decided to print various notes and minutes of its proceedings to gain support in the City against Charles I.[14] In 1771, the House commenced proceedings against John Wilkes, who had published details of Parliamentary proceedings.[15] The House of Commons won its legal case, but press reporting developed informally in ensuing years. And yet, over two hundred years after Wilkes's battles to open up Parliament, the Speaker of the House ruled that there was information which not even MPs *in* Parliament could be apprised of.[16]

Crown, Mace and Information

Parliament saw secrecy for its proceedings as a necessary protection against the Crown's absolutist tendencies. An astute monarch had other ways of rendering Parliament compliant. His advisers, by courtesy of sympathetic MPs, would know what was what.

In 1641, Pym's Ten Propositions to the Lords included as number 3 that the King commit 'his own business, and the affairs of the Kingdom, to such councillors and officers as the Parliament may have cause to confide in'. The Nineteen Propositions of Parliament of 1 June 1642 proposed that Privy Councillors and Ministers be approved by both Houses of Parliament. Further, 'the great affairs of the Kingdom may not be concluded or transacted by the advice of private men, or by any unknown or unsworn councillors, but that such matters as concern the public, and *are proper for the High Court of Parliament* ... may be debated, resolved and transacted only in Parliament, and not elsewhere',[17] and the King should act only on the public behalf on the advice of a majority of Privy Councillors. Parliament wanted to know who advised the King, so that they could be made accountable to Parliament. How had this come to pass?

Information and Accountability – The Struggle

In a system of government that is monistic – that is, one which is assembled around one power base – accountability is achieved by protection of the status quo through the power of tradition, the force of custom, the influence of an unquestioned hierarchy reflecting a naturally ordained harmony: 'Take but degree away, untune that string / And, hark! what discord follows.'[18] When government is arranged around pluralistic forces, any assertion of a status quo maintaining the natural supremacy of one branch of public power over another is less readily justified by appeals to tradition. The emerging conflict between competing forces inevitably centres around the *nature* of accountability itself – what form does it take, to whom and by what process? Accountability is impossible in any real sense unless the body exercising power accounts to whoever asserts the right to expect an explanation, a justification for action or inaction, for acts of prerogative and for policy. Knowing who did what, and why, is the first step to rendering accountable.

In the English tradition, the King escaped personal liability in law – the King can do no wrong.[19] Five important factors emerge on the route to constitutional monarchy: the Crown must act through a servant; a servant cannot plead in defence an unlawful command of the King; the King must be advised by councillors acceptable to Parliament; the King's will must be a matter of record; and the Commons has the power of inquiry as a necessary prelude to impeachment of the Crown's Ministers.[20] Honoured as much in the breach as in the observance, these principles, their development and scope taxed the minds of the finest constitutional and legal experts of the seventeenth century as well as their counterparts in America today.[21]

By the beginning of the seventeenth century the problem facing Parliament in controlling the King was the control over his policies; which meant, in turn, the problem of who should advise on those policies. The claim that the Crown had a prerogative right to choose its own advisers without Parliamentary interference fell increasingly on deaf ears when the Commons from 1604 'sought to superintend a public, not a personal, administration' of the Crown.[22]

Equally important was the emergence of the Commons as *the* force in Parliament with an established political and corporate identity. The English Revolution began in a constitutional, if not material, sense when the Commons insisted on being informed of who advised the Crown so that they could be made accountable for any 'unlawful, injurious or hateful' advice and policies. Unlike the Barons of previous centuries, who were content to bloody the King's nose on individual occasions by punishing his high advisers, the Commons was embarking on a process that would lead to oversight of public administration. On the eve of the Civil War in 1642, what most members wished for was 'the right to vote impeachments against Ministers whose faults they could declare to be crimes, and the right to vote censures against counsellors whose advice to the King they could read in Council books'.[23] Parliamentarians and pamphleteers realised that it was of cardinal importance to discover who provided the King with 'evil counsel', not simply to punish those who followed his 'tyrannous' orders. Publicity of advice was the universal desideratum. Its realisation, of course, would run counter to every tradition of government.

The Commons wanted to know, not necessarily to nominate. The interregnum of 1649–60 brought home to many the undesirability of placing the Executive within the legislature so that both were part of an indiscriminate whole. In that period, however, there were

[by] the right of inquiry, of the right of interrogation, of the right of surveillance, of the right of criticism, and of the right of censure inculcated in M.P.s habits not even the Restoration could erase. [MPs] . . . questioned ministers of state. They clamoured for information. They objected to oaths of secrecy taken by their own committees. They sent committees of inquiry into the counties. They examined accounts and appropriated revenues. They investigated military failures and criticised naval designs. They opposed, condemned, criticised and censured those whom they found remiss in the performance of their duties.[24]

By 1667, Charles II had to accept a statutory commission with power to subpoena any royal servant and cross-examine him under oath and with access to all records *vis-à-vis* the public accounts. There was a regal reaction. Increasing use was made of special committees of the Privy Council to deal with confidential matters, e.g. the Committee of Intelligence and the 'Cabinet Council'. Charles promised to discuss affairs of public importance with the Privy Council at all times. A small group of confidential Ministers acted as 'an informal quorum' of the Council, a trend which James II enforced:

Throughout this century, behind the formal apparatus of councils, cabinets, committees and camarillas lay the simple, usually quite easy, relationship between the King and one or two trusted ministers. . . . The really important decisions were taken in complete privacy, without surviving records.[25]

A royal proclamation of 1674 forbade Charles's subjects to 'intermeddle in private discourse with state affairs, or the persons of the King's ministers'. By that date, however, the Commons had questioned his ministers on 'the innermost secrets of state', and had voted Addresses to the Crown for their removal, refusing to grant supply until they were. To extract advice given to the King in his Cabinet Council, his advisers had to be brought before the Commons and intimidated. If that failed, the Commons had to resort to Common Fame: if a Minister was known to be a party to the Council which advised the King and of which the Commons disapproved, this could form the basis of an Address from the Commons that he be removed from office – but it could not form the basis of an impeachment. The enduring legacy of Court and Parliamentary battles between the years 1674 and 1681 was the voting of Addresses against the King's Ministers, not the voting of impeachments, which were dilatory and clumsy affairs. Having secured freedom of speech, debate and proceedings in 1689,[26] Parliament, in the Act of Settlement of 1701, insisted that important business was to be conducted in the Privy Council and Councillors were to sign all resolutions to which they assented. This solved the problem of identity, but it was unworkable and was repealed in 1706.

Also repealed in 1706 was the clause of the 1701 Act which stipulated that 'no person who has an office or place of profit under the King . . . shall be capable of serving as a member of the House of Commons'. As the eighteenth century unfolded, it became increasingly obvious that a most commodious partnership between Crown and Parliament could be built around an arrangement whereby the King appointed as leading Ministers those who could control the Commons, but the Commons knew who they were. That did not mean they were entitled to know what Ministers knew. Ministers might be forced to resign because of a lack of confidence among Members of Parliament, but the Commons has rarely questioned Ministers' right to keep confidential the innermost secrets of the Cabinet, the Closet or even, in the absence of an untoward event, the Department of State. The Commons in its collective identity might not expect this, but others, including individual MPs, the press, the public, have. The Commons is generally content to be informed on terms laid down by the Executive. At that moment when the power of the Commons to inquire into Crown business was unequivocally established, it was only operable to the extent that the power of a Minister controlling a majority party in the Commons allowed it. The implications for his own position should an inquiry cause embarrassment were obvious enough. In a Parliamentary system of government, the genesis of collective and individual responsibility of Ministers seemed inescapable. The irony is that the doctrines our forebears chanced upon to gain information on who was responsible for what, came to constitute the greatest barrier to a wider Parliamentary and public access to information.

By the early 1700s it was established that Parliament could inquire, investigate and criticise; but Ministers initiated. And what is more, they selected the materials for investigation:

'this enquiry, Sir, will produce no great information if those whose conduct is examined, are allowed to select the evidence.'[27]

Throughout the later stages of the eighteenth century and into the nineteenth century there was a growth of interest among ordinary MPs in every aspect of executive activity, initiated by concern over expenditure. With an increasing interest in social and economic problems it was inevitable that the Grand Inquest of the Nation would:

'inquire into everything which it concerns the public well to know; and *they themselves* I think, are entrusted with the determination of what falls within that category.'[28]

As we shall see, this is a high-water mark, for they may inquire into what they want but they do not always get what they want. We should not think that the desire for a greater dissemination of information was restricted to Parliament, however.

Information and Censorship

Although the demands for information and accountability formed the constitutional centrepiece of the seventeenth century, a wider audience was also involved. It was a period of prevalent censorship, although this had existed since 1408 and Archbishop Arundel's *Constitutions*. Henry VIII imposed religious censorship in 1530 before the breach with Rome, and this was augumented by royal proclamations, injunctions, Privy Council orders and Star Chamber decrees. The Star Chamber decree of 11 July 1637 was 'the most elaborate instrument in English history for the suppression of undesired publication; nothing was unforeseen except the determination with which it was defied'.[29] It became a general offence to print, import or sell 'any seditious, scismaticall or offensive Bookes or Pamphlets', and no book could be printed unless licensed, or relicensed if previously printed, and entered into the Stationers' Register.[30] The abolition of Star Chamber in 1641 left the press virtually without regulation, confirming Selden's remarks that there is 'no Law to prevent the printing of any Bookes in England, only a decree in Star Chamber'. The control over printing had been an exercise of royal prerogative. The public might write of the benefits on the alternatives of who should counsel the King in a way they had never done before, but such publication was shortlived. By June 1643, Parliament passed an order which Milton described as the 'immediate image' of the decree of 1637. This order stimulated his *Areopagitica* and his famous defence of freedom of the press and, excluding Catholics, religious toleration. The order established 'licensing, registration, signature, copyright, import control, search and seizure, arrest, imprisonment by order of Parliamentary committee and association of the Stationers in administering the order'.[31] Except for short periods in the Commonwealth, the Puritan Revolution maintained a continuous licensing in England. The preoccupation of censors turned more and more to the prohibition of obscene, scandalous or scurrilous literature, which in the hands of a Walpole could be moulded into a pervasive form of political censorship, even though general censorship of the press under law by the Stationers' Company ceased in 1694.[32]

The Executive and Parliament – The Die is Cast

From 1670 onwards, the Commons 'became immensely sensitive to the tactics used by the Court to circumscribe their activities or reduce their capacity for independent criticism. Naturally, they feared secret influence and they called time and time again for a statement about expenditure from the Secret Service Fund.'[33] Sir Robert Walpole was, by the 1720s, the controller of the Secret Service money and, in that capacity, was rightly regarded as the head of the Government's patronage system and thus the 'chief figure in the Ministry'.[34] He dedicated his efforts to an obsessive anti-Jacobite campaign, building up a 'vast web of counter-espionage with his own spies in all capitals and ports in Europe'.[35] He preferred to use ad hoc meetings of an inner Cabinet, meeting in the houses of the Chief Secretaries, instead of the full Cabinet which was large and unwieldy, or to have secret discussions with 'his tried and loyal supporters' or private individual interviews. 'He preferred the closet to the Cabinet', or at best a small efficient Cabinet in which he could secure a majority.[36] All the while his 'love of administration, his desire to see it based efficiently on knowledge [and information] was very much in tune with the more advanced opinion of his age'.[37] It is hardly surprising that it was Walpole's use of Secret Service money for covert purposes which activated some of the most heated exchanges between Parliament and Government on Parliament's right to be informed.

By the second half of the eighteenth century, the Commons could exercise its right to information in a variety of ways. A Member could move that 'a return should be made to the House providing statistical or other information about a specific subject',[38] such as the collection and management of the tax revenue, public expenditure and general statistics. 'But information about the exercise of the prerogative, e.g. treaties with foreign powers, dispatches to and from Governors of colonies, and returns connected with the administration of justice or the activities of one of the Secretaries of State could be obtained only by an address to the Crown.'[39] The House could not demand this information; it had to ask politely.

The Government also provided information by way of reports and papers circulated by command of the Crown. This was the usual arrangement for the reports and evidence of Royal Commissions. An increasing number of reports were ordered to be printed by the Commons, not the least of which were the reports of the factory inspectors to the Home Secretary, a point seized on by Karl Marx in *Das Kapital*. These were published every six months, and 'They therefore provide regular and official statistics of the voracious appetite of the capitalists for surplus labour'.[40] However, 'let us note that England figures in the foreground here because it is the classic representative of capitalist production, and it is the only country to possess a continuous set of official statistics relating to the matters we are considering', viz. capitalist economic exploitation.

Sir Norman Chester remarked how a requirement to provide returns and annual reports became a regular feature of Acts of Parliament. 'As early as 1787 an Act[41] placed an obligation on the Treasury to lay before Parliament annually an account of the produce of the duties of Customs, Excise, Stamps and the Expenses.' From 1803, the Treasury had to submit each year an account of the total revenues of Great Britain, together with an account of the Consolidated Fund and other financial details. Information was required on a regular basis on the activities of the Executive in areas of current concern.[42] The requests produced an increasing workload for departments, necessitating the creation of specialised officers. In 1832, a statistical branch in the Board of Trade was agreed to by the Treasury.

Special agencies, boards or even local councils created by Parliament inevitably had to report back to Parliament, sometimes directly, more usually via a Minister. Inspectors of Prisons appointed under an

Act of 1835 are an example of the latter, and the Registrar of Joint Stock Companies reported back via the Board of Trade. Even where a statute remained silent on the duty of publication, practice often dictated that reports would be submitted to Parliament via the Minister, e.g. reports of schools and factories inspectors.

Committees of MPs could take evidence and report with recommendations, providing 'a mass of information not only to Parliament but also for the Press and general public'.[43] However, these committees existed only for one session, and often could not complete their inquiries. They were not peripatetic, so witnesses had to be summoned to London. Nor was there a guarantee that a government would do anything about their recommendations. Between 1832 and 1862, 'Some 190 Royal Commissions were appointed to deal with subjects such as: Poor Relief; Municipal Corporations; Education; Military Promotions and County Courts'. They were appointed and had their terms of reference drawn up by government. Departmental committees, though not popular before 1870, were used. They comprised two or three officials, but were under no obligation to publish their reports. The Northcote–Trevelyan Report of 1854 on the civil service is a famous example of such a report which was in fact published.

Nor were changes in government administration the only development. In 1803 the House recognised the right of the press by reserving special seats in the public gallery for the use of reporters. Hansard Reports of debates commenced in the same year. Published debates became far more detailed; official division lists were published in 1836, thereby making it clear how particular MPs had voted. 'This made Members more consciously answerable to their constituents or to the outside groups interested in the outcome of their vote.'[44] More frequent publication of Parliamentary materials and greater availability of information became increasingly common. Parliamentary Questions became more ordered and routinised, as did MPs' questioning of Ministers on the floor of the House.

However, Government still had ultimate control over what became public. Certain areas, while not arousing a great deal of public interest, were sensitive; these included police special branch, aliens, subversives and foreign policy. In foreign policy, dispatches and 'blue books'[45] were doctored before publication, or correspondence was simply not acknowledged. The Reform Acts of 1832 and 1867 helped to dismember the old consensus which had developed throughout the previous century between Government and Parliamentary elites. The growth of the press, the emergence of strong political parties and organised party political conflict, the development of interest group politics[46] all contributed to a wider group beyond the two above which wished to be informed of public business. Until the 1830s, the battle for information had largely been fought out in a constitutional struggle between Crown and Commons, and between court and country. The reforms of the nineteenth century acted as a midwife to a prolonged labour for a fuller democracy. It was time for power holders not only to set the agenda for Parliament but to take active steps to prevent an unwished-for dissemination of information from departments of state.

Make no mistake, we have witnessed an enormous growth in the information business until the 1870s; government could not resist that. But information was provided on terms. The moment that compact was threatened by forces beyond the control of Government and Parliament, Government felt the necessity for legislation to maintain the culture of secrecy. 'As newspapers ... became almost as much a part of the political arena as the chamber of the House of Commons so most permanent officials learned to keep away from them.'[47] But not all officials or citizens wanted this isolation. Even in the eighteenth century, societies aimed at the spread of public opinion were legion[48] and included the Society for Constitutional Information. Trade and work associations emerged alongside older corporatist groups such as the Church, aristocracy, country gentry, the Inns of Court and the Universities.[49] Throughout the nineteenth century, however, a problem was developing within government departments. What if servants of the Crown broke their trust of confidentiality?

Officials and Secrecy in Central Government

The Northcote–Trevelyan Report of 1854 recommended competitive entry to the civil service based upon examination. Sir George Cornewall Lewis wrote:

One of the first qualities required in the clerks of a public office is trustworthiness. .... The honourable secrecy which has distinguished the clerks of our superior offices ... cannot be too highly commended. But this discreet reserve depends on qualities which cannot be made the subject of examination.[50]

Much had changed in the previous seventy years. In 1780, the typical 'Cabinet Minister had the assistance of only a few clerks. The Home Office contained only four rooms and sometimes handled less than twenty letters a day.'[51] The Treasury and Admiralty Boards with 'satellite and subordinate departments' were much larger. Most of the departments had a small staff who were largely engaged in copying documents and letters and other routine tasks.

By 1870, developments in administrative practice had altered departments beyond recognition. In the Treasury, the number of registered papers averaged between 2,500 and 3,000 a year in the period 1783–93; by 1800 it was 4,812. By 1820, the figure had risen to 22,288 and by 1849 it was 29,914. The Home Office was handling over 13,500 letters per annum.[52] The increasing number and routinisation of Parliamentary Questions and the increasing work-load of departments meant that a Minister could no longer answer all questions about his department impromptu. Notice of questions was required and permanent staff prepared the answers. The Home Secretary was particularly busy.[53]

As departments grew in size, the problem of confidentiality became more acute. Older clerks steeped in the traditions of Crown service were invariably able to maintain a discreet silence about their work. The increasing number of 'outsiders' appointed to senior posts were less tractable. It was not unknown for such senior officials to espouse a cause openly, e.g. free trade, or to liaise with MPs, to encourage the establishment of Select Committees and feed them with evidence. They advised in private and advocated in public. Reform, says Chester, was what they advocated.[54]

It was difficult for Ministers to perceive how such behaviour was compatible with individual ministerial responsibility. It could reveal antagonisms; it could pressurise a Minister into a course of conduct which he did not favour. Peel as Prime Minister referred to Trevelyan as a 'consummate fool' for publishing departmental information in a letter to the *Morning Chronicle*. What *was* expected is caught in the following lines of Sir James Stephen:[55]

Be assured that . . . my office is, and ought to be, that of a mere Subordinate . . . [an] effective and submissive Servant to its Head . . . he sustains the undivided responsibility for every decision taken here and that I am responsible only for supplying him . . . with all the necessary materials for forming such decisions.

Reports to departments by their inspectors and agencies often hit a controversial tone which governments found embarrassing and which was 'inconsistent with the character such reports ought to bear'. The Home Office instructed inspectors not to publish correspondence with the department or information outside the strict terms of their duties. The Education Minister censored and threatened to refuse to publish reports critical of government policy: 'It would be a mischievous principle, to lay down that the heads of each Department . . . should be compelled to print indiscriminately at the public cost everything sent into them by their subordinate agents.'[56] This problem would increase as departments syphoned off executive or regulatory functions to an ever-widening range of bodies.

Parliament had expressed its desire to be informed of the contents of reports from inspectors and agencies to departmental heads. The thrust of the argument was that Parliament had a right to be kept fully informed about the administration which it was responsible for financing, and this included the ungarbled comments of those who had direct oversight over aspects of that administration. The President (Secretary of State) of the Education Department expressed a point of general principle in 1863 when he stated that it was an issue of general importance 'whether in the Education Department there shall or shall not be that discipline which exists, and is found necessary, in every Department of the State'.[57] Administration was impossible without the loyalty of 'these gentlemen'.[58]

If the House chooses to say that the Inspectors are to report directly to it of course we shall instruct them to obey the order; but if the reports are to pass through our hands, I hold it to be the first principle of official duty to enforce that sort of reticence and reserve which all official men are bound to practise . . . no public Department . . . can be expected to carry on its operations with success, if it is obliged to print controversies maintained against itself by the very persons whom it employs to carry out the objects entrusted to its charge.[59]

Inspectors were thus neutered in the fashion of other officials. A Select Committee investigated the question of ministerial censorship and reported that Ministers had exercised their powers fairly and that no objection was made by Ministers to *statements of facts*. This loophole was finally to be sealed in 1911.

Legal Control of Information
Franz Kafka wrote that 'Official decisions are as shy as young girls'.

The Government did not find them as shy as it would have liked. Legislation, it asserted, was necessary and justified to protect official secrets.

A series of events from the 1830s onwards highlighted particular problems for Ministers and senior civil servants over unauthorised disclosure of official information. One concerned the sale and publication of diaries and memoirs kept by officials and diplomats and the Government's attempts to prevent publication by court injunction.[60] The legal question concerned the right of property in the memoirs – usually concerning foreign affairs – and the Foreign Office was pressing for right of ownership and delivery to it of the papers. According to the records, the first case of this kind occurred in 1833, and judgment was entered for the Foreign Office. The Government was successful in other cases. Establishing a right of property in the information that was in question in these cases was bound to cause legal complexity. Absent larceny or treason, and departments could find the position heavy going. Such was the case in 1847 when *The Times* published correspondence relating to the Congress of Vienna. The Foreign Office was advised that property rights were difficult to establish and publication was not prevented, in spite of the FO's rule that materials after 1760 were not available for public inspection. In other cases larceny was charged but an essential ingredient of the offence – permanent deprivation of the article in question in the case of temporary removal and copying – was missing.[61] There was no legal concept of 'official information' which was protected by the law against unauthorised dissemination thereby rendering it an 'official secret'.

By the 1870s, the large anonymous government department had been established; ministerial reponsibility was faithfully accepted and party loyalty and pressure would prevent Parliamentary majorities pressing for information which could make them a nuisance. But could the Ministers' servants be trusted?

In 1873 a Treasury minute on *The Premature Disclosure of Official Documents* was issued.[62] It expressed concern at what today we would refer to as civil service 'leaks' to the press. Dismissal was threatened by the Lords Commissioners of the Treasury in cases where officials were guilty of these offences which were of 'the gravest character'. The minute appealed to the civil servants' sense of honour, fidelity and trustworthiness – in short their bureaucratic professionalism. A further minute of 1875 warned civil servants of the serious consequences of close links with the press, and a Treasury minute of 1884 prohibited the publication of 'official information' without authority.[63] But neither the circulars nor minutes, nor an amendment to the law of larceny in 1861, plugged the holes. Home Office circulars of 1884 and 1896 to its factory inspectorates warned them not to disclose information to Parliamentary Committees nor to courts where privilege could be claimed. Robertson has shown how by 1914 Treasury minutes, memoranda and rules covered diverse matters. These included the production of information before Select Committees of Parliament, the political activities of civil servants, restriction of publication by officials of works from official sources, and standardisation of the rules governing publication by departments of their documents. Exceptions were made for 'internal documents, foreign relations, privacy of the individual, secret service and "scalping" and other such atrocities in war'.[64] These remained completely secret.

The Treasury assumed responsibility from the Admiralty for drafting a Bill making it an offence 'improperly [to] divulge official information'. This would cover the whole public service. After one abortive attempt, it passed into law as the Official Secrets Act 1889. Details of this legislation are provided elsewhere.[65] By 1903, however, it was clear to the War Office that the legislation had incurable defects as it placed on the State the burden of proving both *mens rea* and that it was not in the interest of the State that such communication take place. Newspapers which published leaked information were not punished, and convictions could only be secured where the Government testified to the truth of the information published. An official report of 1909[66] recommended greater powers of arrest and search and seizure. The most persuasive evidence to the committee had related to German spies, about whom there were numerous cases. Not one case had been reported by the police, although information had been provided by 'private individuals', fuelling speculation as to their identity and motives and whether they in fact existed.[67]

The committee's recommendations were aimed at espionage, and so it recommended that the Bill should be introduced by the Secretary for War and not the Home Secretary. This must rank as one of the most notable postures of disingenuousness by any government committee recommending legislation this century.

The Act of 1911

The Official Secrets Act (OSA) which finally emerged in 1911 did not simply strengthen the anti-espionage provisions to assist national security in section 1. Section 2 imposes the widest prohibition, on pain of criminal prosecution, on unauthorised dissemination of official information. And yet section 2 was not mentioned once in the Parliamentary debates, nor did the Government give a full explanation of the Bill. Parliament was anxious to pass the Bill to protect the security of the nation. 'There was no doubt, however,' believed Franks in his 1972 departmental report on section 2, 'that the Bill had, and was intended by the Government to have, a wider scope'.[68] Franks's own account of the circumstances is succinct, but eloquent testimony:

It was in these circumstances that the 1911 legislation passed through Parliament with little debate. The country was in crisis and it was late summer. The debates on the Bill in the House of Lords were brief and the House of Commons passed it in one afternoon with no detailed scrutiny and virtually without debate. The debates give a clear impression of crisis legislation, aimed mainly at espionage. Closer study, and reference to official sources, reveal a different story. This legislation had been long desired by governments. It had been carefully prepared over a period of years. One of its objects was to give greater protection against leakages of any kind of official information whether or not connected with defence or national security. This was clear enough from the text of the Bill alone. Although section 2 of the 1911 Act was much wider in a number of respects than section 2 of the 1889 Act, the files suggest that the Government in 1911 honestly believed that it introduced no new principle, but merely put into practice more effectually the principle of using criminal sanctions to protect official information. At all events, the Government elected not to volunteer complete explanations of their Bill in Parliament. And Parliament, in the special circumstances of that summer, did not look behind the explanations offered.[69]

The provisions of the Act require some explanation. Franks pointed out that misapprehension was common; that many 'leaks' were not leaks at all, but authorised; that the signing of a declaration of notice by all civil servants and government contractors, research workers and others does not mean that express prior authorisation for dissemination is *always* required, and the declaration does not mean that it covers *all* official information. The drafting was, however, ambiguous and misleading – one must suspect deliberately so. Franks also indicated that section 2 did not stand alone; it supported the culture of secrecy and confidentiality that was inherent in the working of our constitution which we have examined along with vetting for sensitive posts, security classifications[70] and privacy markings. Security classifications are: *Top Secret* – publication or disclosure would cause exceptionally great damage to the nation; *Secret* – publication, etc., would cause serious injury to the interests of the nation; *Confidential* – publication, etc., would be prejudicial to the interests of the nation; *Restricted* – publication, etc., would be undesirable in the interests of the nation. Privacy markings cover *Commercial – in Confidence*; *Management – in Confidence* and *Staff – in Confidence*. 'Confidential means secret.' The 'D Notice' system covering the press and media will be examined in the next chapter, together with other devices.

In 1972, Franks found the case for change 'overwhelming'. But section 2 lives on. It has had a remarkable durability. In December 1987, the Home Secretary, however, announced he was preparing a White Paper on 'reform' (H.C. Debs., 15 December 1987). Only once before, in 1939, has Parliament 'back-pedalled' on OSA legislation when it legislated that section 6 of the 1920 OSA, which concerned powers to obtain information in connection with offences under the OSAs, would only cover section 1 offences and not section 2 offences.[71] Section 1 is headed by the legend 'Penalties for Spying'. In *Chandler* v. *DPP*,[72] the House of Lords held that section 1 was not restricted to spying, as was commonly thought, but also covered conspiracy to commit sabotage or enter a prohibited place intentionally, regardless of motive. The OSA has mistakes in its drafting, its various Bill stages in Parliament have been characterised by incomplete information and erroneous explanation. It has been used to threaten an MP.[73] The legislation is among the most widely discussed of all laws in Britain.[74] Section 2 must be understood before we can appreciate how the legislation operates to create a climate of apprehension and caution among civil servants. Such an ethos is likely to survive all but a genuine and complete relaxation of unnecessary secrecy laws.

What is Section 2 About?
Under section 2(1), five types of information are subject to the section's protection. The first type repeats the kind of information protected by section 1, viz. information prejudicial to the safety or interests of the State.[75] It specifically refers to information relating to

a prohibited place such as a defence establishment (or a 'secret official code word').

The second category is information made or detained in contravention of the Act.

The third concerns information entrusted in confidence to any person by an individual holding office under Her Majesty – e.g. government advisers.

The fourth category covers information obtained in the course of his job by a person who holds, or has held, office under Her Majesty.[76]

The last type is information obtained by a person who holds, or has held, a government contract.

If *any person* possessing or controlling the above kind of official information communicates it in any of the five following ways[77] he or she is guilty of an offence under section 2(1).

1. If he or she unlawfully communicates it, viz. without authority or to a person to whom it is *not* in the interest of the State his duty to communicate it (s.2(1)(a)).
2. If he or she uses it for the benefit of a foreign power or 'in any other *manner* prejudicial to the safety or interests of the State' (s.2(1)(aa)).
3. If he or she unlawfully retains it or fails to comply with lawful directions regarding its return or disposal (s.2(1)(b)).
4. If he or she fails to take reasonable care of it or endangers its safety (s.2(1)(c)).
5. If he or she possesses or controls information which concerns munitions of war and communicates it to a foreign power 'or in any other *manner* prejudicial to the safety or interests of the State' (s.2(1A)).

Three kinds of person, as well as Crown servants, can be involved in the above offences: a private individual; an adviser to central government; a government contractor.

Section 2(2) concerns the unauthorised receipt of any of the five kinds of information within section 2(1). The offence is committed if, at the time of receiving information, the recipient does so 'knowing, or having reasonable ground to believe' that it was communicated in contravention of the Act. The quoted words would indicate that *mens rea*, or subjective guilty knowledge, is required under section 2(2)),[78] and a defence exists where receipt 'was contrary to his desire'.

The Ponting Trial

The law has been thrown into more than its usual state of uncertainty by the acquittal of the former Assistant-Secretary at the Ministry of Defence (MoD), Clive Ponting. Ponting's trial was a sensational event. He was a civil service 'high flier' who had responsibility for 'the policy and political aspects of the operational activities of the Royal Navy'. Ponting was concerned with drafting replies and answers on the sinking of the Argentinian warship *Belgrano* by the Royal Navy during the Falklands campaign.[79] He disagreed with his colleagues on what, and how, information on the sinking should be published. His belief that the Government was positively and deliberately misleading the Commons and a Select Committee[80] and the public, caused him to send two documents to Tam Dalyell MP. They were duly handed to the Chairman of the Select Committee on Foreign Affairs, who, in turn, handed them back to the Secretary of State at the MoD. Ponting was subsequently prosecuted for breach of section 2(1)(a). This section makes it a criminal offence for a person holding office under Her Majesty to communicate official information to any person other than a person to whom he is authorised to communicate it, or a person to whom it is his duty *in the interest of the State* to communicate it. In the course of the trial 'interest' and 'interests' were used interchangeably.[81]

Both prosecution and defence accepted that Dalyell was not a person authorised to receive official information under the terms of the Act.[82] Was an MP a person to whom it was Ponting's duty in the interest of the State to pass such information? This issue was central to Ponting's defence. In the trial,[83] McCowan J. consulted *Chandler* v. *DPP* where Lord Reid observed that the term 'State' did not mean the Government or the Executive but 'the realm' or the 'organised community'. Lord Reid also believed that a Minister or a Government did not *always* have the final say on what was in the public interest, although *in cases concerning the defence of the realm* a different approach would be necessary. *Chandler* was such a case.[84] McCowan J. directed the jury that '*interests* of the State' (sic) were synonymous with the interests of the Government of the day, adopting Lord Reid's narrower interpretation regarding defence. The offence indicted in *Chandler* was a conspiracy to commit an act of sabotage within a prohibited place 'for a purpose prejudicial to the interests of the State' under section 1. In the context of national defence the State was the 'organised community', 'the organs of Government of a national community' and responsibility for armed forces and defence fell to the Crown, viz. the Government of the day advising the Crown. This, as Lord Devlin suggested, was not a blue-print to suggest that the interests of the State were *always* the same as those of the Government of the day. The 'duty' referred to in section 2(1)(a), McCowan J. ruled, is an official duty under the terms of his office and authorised chain of command. It did not refer to a moral or 'public' duty. But surely this begs the question.

A fuller ruling is necessary on these words in the context of section 2(1)(a) as there is ample scope to argue that whereas 'interests of the State' in section 1 refers to national security, the words in section 2(1)(a) qualify the 'persons lawfully permitted to receive information, so excluding the communicator from committing an offence'.[85] The Crown accepted in the Ponting trial that the leak had nothing to do with national security.

It remains a severe criticism of our system of government that there is no equivalent of the US Civil Service Reform Act 1978, which protects civil servants who 'blow the whistle' in the public interest from punishment by administrative disciplining.[86] The Act protects those servants who leak information which they reasonably believe reveals violation of the law or regulations or 'mismanagement, a gross waste of funds, an abuse of authority, or a substantial and specific danger to public health or safety'. Where the disclosure concerns foreign intelligence and counter intelligence, it must be made to designated officials who have to inform the appropriate Congressional Committee. Similar protection covers FBI agents and other officials. Reports of investigations are submitted to Congress, the President and the Complainant.

A further complicating factor arising from the Ponting trial concerned the issue of *mens rea* – the subjective criminal intent on the part of an accused which it is necessary to establish to secure conviction. Ponting's lawyers sought to show that he did not have a guilty mind when he contacted the MP. It is accepted that convictions under section 1 require proof of intent[87] – although section 1(2) and section 2 of the 1920 Act allow the jury to infer intent from objective factors, e.g. 'his conduct' or 'known character'.[88]

The offences under section 2, excluding section 2(2), do not require *mens rea*; although there has been judicial difference of opinion on the matter apropos of section 2(1).[89] In Ponting's trial the judge ruled that a conviction under section 2(1)(a) did not require proof of intent.

Section 2(1)(*aa*) makes it an offence when the accused 'uses the information in his possession . . . in any . . . *manner* [as opposed to purpose in section 1] prejudicial to the safety or interests of the State'. Only section 2(2) expressly introduces a subjective mental element: the prosecution must prove that the accused *knew* or *had* reasonable ground to believe that receipt of information was in contravention of the Act.[90]

Stated in fairly dispassionate academic terms the position might seem relatively straightforward. But when the Act is put into practice and prosecution is attempted before a jury, then unless a confession is forthcoming, as in the case of Sarah Tisdall, or concerns straightforward allegations of fact, it can prove to be impossible to secure a conviction. In the case of *Ponting*, failure to convict no doubt related to a jury refusing to be browbeaten by a judge, prosecution handling the case less adroitly than it should, a feeling that the Government was actively involved in manipulating an outcome, and the Attorney-General appearing to prejudge guilt in a radio broadcast.[91] And Ponting's lawyers mounted a very successful campaign outside the courtroom.[92] Yet *all* the vital rulings in law went against Ponting. In law, the Crown (Government?) could not have asked for more, and no judge could have provided such, since juries were last imprisoned before *Bushel's* case[93] in 1670 for returning verdicts against the judge's direction.

Links in the Chain

Where there is a chain of individuals communicating and receiving information, the problems involved in securing convictions are legion, as the trial involving Jonathan Aitken showed in 1971.[94] Does *mens rea* have to run through the chain? The balance of opinion would suggest 'no' if offences under section 2(1) are charged. But if receipt is involved, section 2(2) requires *mens rea*. Can receipt be brought under a charge in section 2(1)? This would depend upon whether 'obtaining information *in contravention of this Act*' refers to section 1 of the Act, or the Act as a whole. Section 1 is restricted to purposes that are prejudicial to the safety or interests of the State. Section 2 is not so restricted.[95] Franks believed it referred to contravention of the Act as a whole, and though this seems the likelier interpretation, judicial opinions have differed.

Despite the fact that the Act and its two thousand or so offences have been described as unworkable and fit for 'pensioning off', a view supported by Ponting's acquittal, the Government reminded civil servants in the DHSS of its parameters shortly after the acquittal. Nonetheless the Government have a new weapon at hand to protect official secrets – the law of confidentiality – where no embarrassing or inconvenient jury decisions can be returned. We shall return to this theme later.[96]

But further problems attend the Act. The role of the Attorney-General – whose *fiat* is required for a prosecution under the Act – has been described as invidious inasmuch as the decision to prosecute is his. Franks found no evidence of political interference with Attorneys-General in the past. Events since Franks cast doubts on the continuing accuracy of that view,[97] and in the Peter Wright episode an embarrassed Cabinet Secretary was forced to admit in open court in Australia, by the Attorney-General himself, that decisions on prosecuting, or not prosecuting, had not been the responsibility of the Attorney-General.[98] The proximity of the Attorney-General to the Government makes it very difficult for the office-holder to argue persuasively that he is an 'honest broker', regardless of his identity.

Franks found that section 2 was saved from absurdity by the 'sparing exercise of the Attorney-General's discretion to prosecute', although the matter still gave rise to 'considerable unease'. The case for reform was overwhelming, he believed, but he still envisaged a central place for the Attorney-General, who would retain control of prosecutions in the major areas where Franks recommended the law should operate. Not one government department had supported the *need* to protect all forms of information within the scope of section 2 by the criminal law. Rather, section 2's 'catch-all' quality was useful in instilling the fear of God and maintaining a culture of secrecy. An 'appropriate alternative' was difficult to conceive, the Government argued, and Franks accepted that over-reliance on voluntary forms of internal restraint by the press and media would be undesirable. They may have a 'responsibility' to publish what is in the public interest, but Government has a constitutional responsibility to protect the nation, which cannot be 'abdicated on the basis that a failure to exercise them will be made good by the responsible behaviour of others'. And, as we all know, the press in particular do not always act with the requisite degree of responsibility.[99]

Franks's specific recommendations for reform included the recommendation that the criminal law should be used for un-authorised disclosure of information relating to the defence or security of the realm,[100] of information relating to matters concerning or affecting foreign relations or the conduct of such relations, and of information relating to proposals, negotiations or decisions connected with alterations in the value of sterling or those relating to bank reserves. Only information classified 'Secret' or 'Defence Confidential' would be subject to prosecution, i.e. where unauthorised disclosure would 'cause at least serious injury to the interests of the nation'. Classification and declassification procedures would be laid down, and proper classification would be ensured by the Minister before embarking on a prosecution. His certificate of classification would be conclusive evidence of proper classification, and the court would not inquire into the effect of disclosure on the interests of the nation.[101] The prosecution would have to prove that it was information communicated in contravention of the Act and so classified. Cabinet documents,[102] criminal investigation and law enforcement information and confidential information would be protected by the criminal law.[103]

Franks recommended a general advisory body, which would be non-statutory, to advise on a wide range of classification issues. Its members would be representative of affected interests, e.g. press and media, and members of the Government, and would be appointed by the Prime Minister.

But Franks has never been acted upon. Use of the Acts has not abated. Before Franks reported, there had been 30 prosecutions with 26 convictions under section 2 of the Act.[104] Since 1946 there had been 20 prosecutions under section 1 of the Act for spying.[105] There were 19 convictions. By 1 August 1978, a further five prosecutions had been brought under section 2.[106] These involved three cases, one of which was concluded. In the same period there were six prosecutions under section 1, with four convictions, and a fifth under section 7.[107] Between 1 August 1978 and 9 February 1983, there were 11 prosecutions leading to 10 convictions under section 2.[108] There were five completed cases under section 1, three of which led to prosecution. One further case led to a conviction under section 2 alone, and another to a conviction under section 7 of the Act alone. In an additional case to the five, the police charged under section 1, but the Attorney-General did not consent to prosecution. From 10 February 1983 until 24 April 1986, there were nine cases under section 2, leading to five convictions, though one of these was subject to a successful appeal. In one further case, the Solicitor-General had authorised a prosecution. There were three prosecutions under section 1, and one authorised prosecution under section 7.[109] These figures do not, of course, cover cases where confessions have been given *and* resignations tendered *in return for immunity*, as in the case of Ian Willmore.[110]

The OSA are designed to operate *in terrorem*. If the Government miscalculated the public sentiment badly in the case of Ponting, it is doubtful whether the acquittal in that case would influence more than a handful of individuals to act as he did where they had a sincere, well-motivated and morally felt duty, not simply to their political overlords but to Parliament and the nation. The OSA should be seen for what they are: the legal framework of a tradition of government which is steeped in secrecy and confidentiality which have been used 'viciously and capriciously by an embarrassed executive'.[111] The Attorney-General and the Government have both reiterated subsequent to Ponting's trial that they would deal with the OSA as before.[112] As we shall see in chapter 6, the Government has resorted more and more to the law of confidentiality.

The Shepherd Bill

In November 1987, a Private Member's Bill sought to repeal section 2. It bore the same title as the Government's discredited Protection of Official Information Bill of 1979, although it differed in important respects.

Under the Bill, six classes of information or 'articles' would have been protected by the criminal law insofar as unauthorised dissemination might lead to criminal prosecution with the consent of the Attorney-General or, in some cases, the consent of the DPP. The areas covered were: defence, international relations, security or intelligence 'the unauthorised disclosure of which would be likely to cause serious injury to the interests of the nation or endanger the safety of a British citizen' (clause 1(1) (*a*) and 1(2) (*a*) information). Further classes covered information likely to be useful in commission of offences, or in facilitating an escape from legal custody or likely to impede the prevention or detection of offences or the apprehension of suspected offenders; and information supplied by an individual in accordance with any statutory requirement to do so or in connection with an application for a statutory grant or benefit or permission and where there is an express or implied duty to hold it in confidence. Other information was to be protected by administrative action, i.e. disciplinary proceedings.

A Crown servant was only to be guilty where he had *mens rea* in disclosing in breach of his official duties. Likewise, a Government contractor would have to possess *mens rea* for an unauthorised disclosure. The burden of proof was on the prosecution. Other parties would be guilty, if with *mens rea* they made an unauthorised disclosure of information as classified above. Other offences covered wrongful detention and failure to comply with instructions as to its return or disposal. *Mens rea* had to be proved.

A defence that the information had been publicly available in the UK *or* elsewhere (cf. the FOIA of the USA) was provided. A public interest defence to a criminal charge was also available if the defence could prove 'that the disclosure or retention of the information or article was in the public interest insofar as [the defendant] had reasonable cause to believe – [not conclusive proof] – that it indicated the existence of crime, fraud, abuse of authority, neglect in the performance of an official duty or other misconduct and that he had taken reasonable steps to comply with any established procedures for drawing such misconduct to the attention of the appropriate authorities without effect'.

Information under clause 1(1) (*a*) and 1(2) (*a*) must be properly classified by a Minister at the appropriate time. Classification may be challenged by the defence, and the Judicial Committee of the Privy Council would be asked to make a 'conclusive determination' of the propriety of the classification on a mandatory reference from the Attorney-General where it was challenged. The classification procedure would be laid out in regulations approved *affirmatively* by Parliament. An annual report was to be made to the House on the operation of the regulations and their review procedure. The Bill was to cover those departments and agencies listed in the Parliamentary Commissioner Act 1967, as extended in 1987. The Bill applied to Northern Ireland.

The Bill was welcomed as a relaxation of the ambit of section 2, but it was widely criticised for not going far enough in making public provision of official information. We can pick up on this point in Chapter 7 below. It should be noted that the Bill provided for the publication of manuals used by scheduled authorities in making decisions affecting the rights, privileges and benefits or obligations etc of 'persons'. These would include interpretations, rules, guidelines, practices and precedents and the provision was inspired by Australian legislation (see Chapter 2). Authorities would have to publish an annual statement of the documents so available and where they may be inspected and copied. Annual reports to Parliament would indicate the steps taken by departments to facilitate access to its information.

The Bill brought a statement from Mrs Thatcher that she intended to reform section 2 – although there were misgivings that such a Bill would not be a liberalising measure (HC Debs. 12 November 1987). In fact the imposition of a life-long statutory duty of confidentiality for *all* officials, enforceable by the criminal law, was widely suggested. A three-line whip on Tory MPs helped to kill the Bill in January 1988.

It is now time, however, to examine a tier of government which has more immediate impact upon more people on a daily basis than central government. Local government has responsibility for administering a substantial body of programmes ranging from education, planning, public health, the environment, to social services and child care, housing, trading standards, highways and numerous licensing and regulatory responsibilities. Its gathering and use of information rivals that of central government in bulk, if not quite in subject matter. It does not have the protection of OSA; that only covers information acquired by a Crown servant or officer or government contractor while in the course of his job or an individual in receipt of it, although information in the possession of local authorities may be such. Yet in too many cases local authorities have been as closed as Whitehall. What gives the subject added interest is that our first approach to a freedom of information act affecting a tier of government has involved local government.

Local Government

The most important development in our constitutional history has been the supremacy of Parliament as an institution over other governmental institutions, and the supremacy of the Crown in Parliament as a legislature. The law of Parliament is supreme, and local authorities are the creature of Parliamentary statute,[113] and statute affords them wide powers to administer.

A persistent theme of relations between central and local government in this century has been the growth of centripetal tendencies as central government has removed function after function from local government responsibility, or has sought more effective control over local government spending. Today, local government accounts for 28 per cent of public expenditure and employs in the region of 3 million people. How the money is spent, and what local authorities are getting up to, have always been high on the agenda of central government.

When central government pursues tight monetary and expenditure policies to restrict public spending, its demands for information from local government will correspondingly increase. The statute-book has seen a plethora of statutes requiring local authorities to provide information to central government and its departments, the Commission for Local Administration (the local Ombudsman), the Auditor and Audit Commission, members and the public.[114] With the Local Government Act 1986 the Government obtained powers to prohibit and restrict the publicity exercises of local authorities. Section 2 prohibits the publication of material which 'in whole or in part appears to be designed to affect support for a political party'. Section 3 restricts the use of sections 137 and 142 of the Local Government Act 1972.[115] The former authorises expenditure by authorities of a rate of 2p in the pound in a financial year, which in their opinion is in the interests of the area or any part of it, or some or all of its inhabitants, providing it is not the subject of other statutory provision. Section 142 concerns the provision of information by local authorities affecting local government. It has been held by the High Court that use of section 142 to persuade an electorate of the authority's view of the effects of rate-capping and the retention of an advertising agency to help in persuasion was invalid.[116] The section permitted explanation and factual information, not political persuasion, Glidewell J. believed.[117]

The 1986 Act was prompted by the highly successful campaigns of local authorities against central government. The Act provides the belt and braces from the Government's perspective and allows codes of recommended practice to guide authorities on the content, style, distribution and cost of local authority publicity. The House of Lords, in the passage of the Bill, rejected a provision that the codes, which have to be approved by Parliament, should be mandatory. The Government has indicated that the matter is not closed and wishes to introduce further legislation. The strength of feeling on the Government side was expressed by a former Secretary of State for the Environment[118] when he informed a Select Committee that he had been at the 'wrong end of by far the most expensive publicly financed propaganda campaign . . . finding that my hands were almost totally tied as to what I was entitled to do at public expense as part of my departmental duties in reply'.[119]

Local Government, the Public and Information

Since the Poor Law Reform Act 1834, a system of compulsory local authority audit has existed in England and Wales. The Municipal Corporations Act 1835 opened up the books of the corporations to inspection in the legislature's attempts to ferret out corruption which had been rampant in the commercial oligarchies administering the cities. Duties to provide information to Ministers and auditors increased as the century developed and as central government became more and more jealous of its powers of supervision over local administration. Public knowledge of local authority affairs did not appear to become an issue until later in the nineteenth century when local government administration became more widespread and more coherent. Following a judicial decision that reporters were not allowed as of right to attend and report council meetings, an Act of 1908 was passed allowing press access to council meetings, but it could be avoided by delegating business to a committee. Nor were agendas circulated in advance under the Act. Analogies with Parliament, which had been reported freely for well over a century, were not regarded as pertinent, as Parliament is a legislative body, whereas councils and committees are executive. It was not 'practical politics' to administer in a 'gold-fish' bowl.[120]

In 1960, Margaret Thatcher MP secured the passage through Parliament of the Public Bodies (Admission to Meetings) Act, which opened up council meetings to the press and public. Minutes of councils and committees[121] had to be published. Even after the 1972 Local Government Act, which opened up committees to the press and public, problems remained. The legislation did not cover sub-committees, though local authorities were urged to be open in their administration. Research conducted in 1984 showed that while many authorities opened up their sub-committees, with exceptions, to the public, a substantial number of those who replied did not.[122] Other studies found authorities adamantly refusing to provide information which they were under a legal duty to provide.[123]

There were pronounced elements of secrecy in too many authorities which did not assist their cause at a time of highly publicised scandals relating to corruption of standards and rule by high-handed political caucus across the political spectrum. Nor was there much evidence to show that local authorities had geared themselves to inform the public better of their rights to receive information and assistance or to make complaint or to participate in decision-making in planning,[124] urban renewal,[125] development[126] and housing,[127] to name but a few. In 1972, the Bains Report[128] urged authorities to introduce, where they had not already done so, a corporate approach to management with overall co-ordination of policy-making, which often ended up in the hands of ruling political heavyweights and the Chief Executive and a cadre of senior officers. The period throughout the 1970s and 1980s witnessed an increasing politicisation of local government politics,[129] at least in intensity if not pervasively,[130] with issues being fought out locally on the lines of party political allegiance reflecting, very often, national political conflict. Ruling parties, backbenchers and opposition emerged as terms of political currency.

Politics, Members and Information

The ante-chamber confidential discussion became more and more closed in a growing number of authorities, and one-party groups emerged which were often advised by, and sought the advice of, officials. Ad hoc groups, advisory bodies, working parties and the like emerged to attempt to maintain confidential discussion within political groupings. Constitutionally, this produced difficulties.

First of all, the local authority in law only knows of the existence of the council, committees, joint committees, sub-committees and officers as executive bodies. The law does not adequately reflect the political reality of administration and its organisation. Secondly, the emergence of political groupings has helped to increase the alienation of those who are not privy to a ruling group's policies and politics while, in urban areas at least, there has been an increasing co-option of non-elected members into council bodies, most notably from bodies who are under-represented in terms of elected representatives, e.g. ethnic minorities, minority groupings, council tenants, under-35-year-olds.[131] Thirdly, officers are frequently placed in a difficult situation as their duty is to advise members as a whole – not as political groups of ruling members who can shield officers by conventions such as ministerial responsibility and advisers' anonymity. Fourthly, in law members are members of the council as a whole, not members of political parties. It is around this latter point that recent legal controversy has centred.

Members of the council have a common law right to inspect the books and papers of the council. Conflicts over the scope of the right have produced an explosion of litigation.[132] Two opposing positions are present in the case law: the corporate responsibilities and duties of members of the corporation to the corporation, and the duty and responsibilities of members as representatives of a wider range of community interests which they are elected to represent.

Members do not have a 'roving commission' to examine the documents of a council.[133] They must establish a 'need to know' in order to perform their duties as councillors, and any irrelevant motivation or any ulterior, indirect or improper motive may be raised as a bar to their inspection.[134] Where a member is also a member of a specific committee, he or she has the right to inspect the committee's documentation, barring improper motive, etc., on the part of the member, though this ought not in principle to be easy to establish on the part of the committee or council because of the strong *prima facie* right of the member to inspect.[135] Where a member is not a member of a committee, he or she has to establish a 'need to know' a committee or sub-committee's documents. The claim of such a member is not as strong as that of a member of the actual committee, although the courts will be reluctant to second-guess a council's decision to allow inspection to a non-committee member.[136] A member of a parent committee will, even though not a member of the sub-committee, usually have a right to see documents of its sub-committee, and even a right to attend the sub-committee.[137]

Some recent case law has developed these principles. At common law it has been established that a ruling party can, *pace* the standing orders of the authority, which must be followed if they cover the subject area unless *ultra vires*, appoint *only its members* to the committees of the authority.[138] In *R. v. Sheffield City Council ex p. Chadwick*,[139] it was held that it was *ultra vires* for a policy committee to delegate functions to a sub-committee of ruling party members alone *simply to avoid* informing opposition members of decisions in the formulation of the budget. It was unlawful to use a sub-committee for purely party political purposes. The case involved alternatives to the actual budget recommendation that was made and could support a suggestion that a 'need to know' will cover alternative policy options. The councillor was entitled to attend the meeting and see the documents, although strictly speaking it was only operating in a recommendatory capacity in settling the budget.[140] Where the leaders of a party group met informally with officers and made what in effect were decisions *on behalf of* the council, they were acting in an executive capacity and were covered by the common law 'need to know' principle. The metings were within the formal framework of the council structure, and not outside it, and the councillor could establish a need to know and a right to attend.[141] There seems no reason in principle why a 'need to know' might not exist in relation to a 'working group's', etc., papers and documents if they are council papers. It would depend upon the facts.

Local Government (Access to Information) Act 1985 (ATIA)

The law relating to members' rights and the public's rights to information in particular was reformed by the ATIA. A circular accompanies the Act.[142] This Act constitutes an FOIA for local government, and there is an immediate irony in the fact that it was passed with the approval of the Government, which had steadfastly refused such legislation for itself. The Act provides for greater public access to the meetings and documents of principal councils, i.e. essentially county, district and London borough authorities, and regional and district authorities in Scotland.[143] It opens up council, committee and sub-committee meetings to the public, and provides for access to local authority information. 'Information' in the Act includes an expression of opinion, any recommendations, and any decision taken. Meetings must be closed to the public, and information will not be available where 'confidential' items, as specifically defined, are dealt with.[144] This is where a government department provides information upon terms which forbid public disclosure. It is thereby also under the OSA. It includes cases where publication is prohibited by court order or statute.[145] Under the terms of the Act, an item is not confidential simply because a party gives the information in confidence.

Information can be exempt under the Act if it falls under one of 15 categories. If exempt information is involved, the authority *may* exclude the public from its meetings and refuse access to information containing such items. The list of exempt categories covers information relating to employees and office holders of the authority; tenants of the authority; applicants and recipients of any service provided by the authority, or of financial assistance in their capacity as applicants; it also covers information relating to the adoption, care, fostering or education of any child, or to the financial or business affairs of any person other than the authority unless already required to be registered under various statutes. Further exemptions protect the contractual and prospective contractual interests of the authority for as long as exemption is necessary to protect the interests of the authority and the identity of those tendering for contracts for goods or services. Labour relations are covered in certain situations. Instructions to and opinions of counsel are given a total exemption, as is 'any advice received, information obtained or action to be taken in connection with any legal proceedings by or against the authority', or 'the determination of any matter affecting the authority', or where such is contemplated. 'Determination' refers to a formal administrative ruling, for example after an inquiry. The legal opinions of officers and other information is protected when given in connection with such determinations and legal proceedings or where they are contemplated, and this would require more than a 'vague anticipation'. Exempt information covers those situations where the authority seeks to impose statutory orders or notices, especially important in the planning area and where disclosure would defeat the purpose of the order, e.g. a building preservation notice. Information relating to the prevention, investigation or prosecution of crime is exempt, as is that relating to 'protected informants'.[146]

Unless the 'Proper Officer' believes it to contain confidential or exempt information, the public will have access to officers' reports for items on the agenda of meetings and advance notice of agenda, meetings, their place and time. A reasonable number of copies of reports and agenda must be available at the meetings. The provisions requiring public notice may be waived where the chairperson is of the opinion that the item should be considered at the meeting as a matter of urgency 'by reason of special circumstances' which *must be specified* in the minutes.[147]

An important dimension to the Act concerns 'Background Papers', namely those documents relating to the subject matter of the report which 'disclose any facts or matters on which, *in the opinion of the proper officer*, the report or an important part of the report is based and have, *in his opinion*, been relied on to a material extent in preparing the report'. The information is available for specified periods before and after the meeting.[148] Minutes are open for inspection. Additional information has to be published.[149] Interference with rights under the Act is a criminal offence.

The Act covers a wide range of principal councils and has been extended to cover joint consultative committees of health and local authorities.[150] The Act also extends members of authorities' rights of access to information in the possession or under the control of local authorities and relates to any business to be transacted at a meeting of the council, its committees or sub-committees. A member does not need to establish a 'need to know' as under the common law where he or she is not a member of a specific committee, but some of the exemptions will apply to requests, especially those relating to employees, recipients of housing or services, children, contracts, the legal immunities apropos of advice and the prosecution, prevention or investigation of crime. These exemptions would *not* apply to a request at common law. However, the rights of a council member under the Act are more extensive than those of the public, as the right to go through background papers is not restricted to those papers which the 'Proper Officer' believes formed the basis of the officer's report to a material extent.

The legislation leaves important matters of judgment in the hands of the 'Proper Officer'[151] and the chairman of a meeting. This includes selection of items or reports which are exempt, materials in background papers which were relied upon to a material extent, and in the case of the latter those items which as a matter of urgency require incorporation without the statutory notice of three clear days. No specific procedure for challenging such decisions is contained in the statute, so it will be a matter of pressurising councillors or seeking relief via the Ombudsman or the courts. The Widdicombe Report[152] of 1986 suggested that the Proper Officer should be the chief executive for these decisions. A proposal that a special complaint/appellate procedure should be contained in the Act to resolve the matter inside the uthority was rejected in the passage of the Bill. The absence of such a procedure gives support to the proposal of Widdicombe that a new statutory power of assistance for individuals wishing to challenge a decision by their local authority in the court should be available –

1. Where there are important implications for an authority's services at large or, on procedural issues, for its conduct of business generally.
2. Where there are important issues of principle where clarification of the law is desirable.
3. Where there is evidence of persistent breaches of the law.[153]

One further point concerns the fact that the Act preserves the right to exercise a power of exclusion to suppress or prevent disorderly conduct at a meeting.[154] It has been decided that a chairperson can exercise this right in advance of a meeting; this would prevent the public seeing how members voted when it came to a subsequent ratification of the chairperson's decision.

Some Food for Thought

The Access to Information Act only addresses the formal mechanisms of local authority decision-making, a point we shall develop in the next chapter. There are numerous other statutory provisions which seek to render local government more open in its decision-making by providing information and allowing participation in decision-making. A point of crucial significance is the fact that part of central government's restriction on the activities of local government has taken place by transferring some of the latter's existing functions to public corporations and commissions, a point to which we shall return. Various circulars enjoin authorities to provide information to the clients of their services such as social services.[155] Parliament has passed an enabling Act which will open up personal files to the subjects on whom information has been collected. The Act is effectively restricted to local government.[156] Other codes such as the *National Code of Local Government Conduct* for councillors are in addition to standing orders of an authority and seek to prevent abuse of information and breaches of confidentiality by declarations of interest – apart, that is, from financial ones, which are covered by the law. Officers have a duty not to disclose information which would amount to a breach of confidence, unless presumably there was a greater public interest in disclosure than in maintaining a confidence.[157]

The practice of closed or secretive local government is considered in the next chapter, where an examination is undertaken of the guiding principles that inform or must be taken to be presupposed in our system of government. What promises are there, so to speak, which legitimate power, and what differences exist between central and local government? Both are operating in the public interest and have monopolies of power in important respects which are exercised on the public behalf. Is government in either respect too powerful for the devices of accountability which exist? It was the Widdicombe Report's belief that, for abuses in local government, the problems would be largely resolved if members and officials were made to operate within the law. Two questions are pertinent. Firstly, is the law itself an adequate safeguard? In relation to central government it would appear that it is hopelessly inadequate. For local government there is fuller legal provision which is easier for citizens to utilise, but its formal properties have little relevance to strengthening democratic principles, and it is these which legitimate public power. But, secondly, what principles are we talking about, and what does their application entail? It is time to return to the centre.

4
Claims and Counterclaims

The development of the secret state in Britain goes back centuries. The British have not been forced into addressing fundamentals in the face of revolution for three hundred years. Nor has the nation been compelled to reassess basic principles of governmental right. We are a conservative and placid race. But we do have basic principles which governments purport to abide by in their process of rule – the Rule of Law being the most obvious. This chapter will seek to describe the actual operation of government today, the claims for responsible government and the continuation of the practices of a secret state. In the opening chapter, a theory of communicative competence as developed by Habermas was described. What do the following pages tell us about the desirability, necessity or feasibility of that theory? Is there a systematic distortion of communication and information by Government? If so, why is there not the political will or pressure to do something to change practices? Would freedom of information legislation of a kind which he saw in operation elsewhere effect such changes, or do existing practices run too deeply to be altered significantly?

Principled Government

The stormy episode of Michael Heseltine's resignation as Defence Secretary from Mrs Thatcher's Government in January 1986 throws into dramatic relief some of the relevant issues. The factual details of the event need not concern us now, but Mr Heseltine alleged that the Prime Minister had engineered the breakdown of constitutional government.[1] She had cancelled an agreed Cabinet meeting specifically to thwart his efforts to show that it was in the national interest that a British-owned helicopter-manufacturing company – Westland plc – was taken over by a consortium with a British component and not an American company. He claimed that the Prime Minister's conduct was in breach of collective ministerial responsibility and that his own individual ministerial responsibility necessitated that he went public on the issue. Within two weeks, the Defence Secretary's major protagonist in the Cabinet resigned because of his role in authorising[2] a leak through the Press Association of a confidential[3] letter from the Solicitor-General to Mr Heseltine. This was a major breach of confidence. The Defence Select Committee pressed for the attendance before it of the civil servants who were involved,[4] but eventually settled, albeit reluctantly, for the attendance of the head of the Home Civil Service and Secretary to the Cabinet, Sir Robert Armstrong.[5] He had conducted an internal inquiry into the leak, knowing beforehand what its conclusion would be. The whole episode was wonderful political drama. But important themes run through the episode concerning the principles of constitutional government. Mr Heseltine declared pointedly 'that the case against him was being put by "unidentified sources" '. 'We have no documents, no statements, no piece of paper that we can examine, we have just whispers on the telephone. Now, that is the way British Government is to be conducted. . . .'[5a]

Michael Heseltine revealed the machinations of contemporary Cabinet government, and his allegations of Prime Ministerial presidency set off a process that led to the release of more information about Whitehall's inner workings than we could normally have hoped for, although not all that the Select Committee wanted. Even now, certain crucial points have not been fully clarified.[6] A court of law might have uncovered more information and have left a record of events that was more readily acceptable.[7] But this is high politics. Political survival depends upon political support, and this the Prime Minister had in abundance.

From this imbroglio[8] how much light can be shed on the basic principles upon which constitutional government is supposedly conducted in the British State? How much information has to be given about matters of government for claims of governmental power to be legitimated? What are the leading principles of constitutional government? Are they realisable – or only idealistic or rough guides which imperfect men and women are urged to strive towards by tradition, the system or public expectation, knowing that in the world of practical politics their realisation is impossible? Are they mere

shams which conceal the actual operation of power in the contemporary State and from which, like Milton's flames in *Paradise Lost*,
nothing but 'darkness visible' emerged? The truth is probably a
mixture of all of these.

Constitutional Principles and Central Government

In an important recent work, Norman Lewis and Ian Harden have
argued for an immanent critique of the actual operation of public
power and government in the British tradition when set beside the
nature of the constitutional principles which act as a talisman within
our system: 'If these are your claims, your ruling principles, are you
being true to them?'[9] The method of the immanent critique, very
simply, is to identify the basic rules or principles which are taken as
fundamental to a set of particular relationships. The question is then
asked: 'To what extent are they actually observed in practice?'

The two principles on which they fasten are openness and
accountability: '*With due respect to the need for confidentiality in sensitive
areas of public activity*, the constitutional response must surely be to
bring public business into the sunlight.'[10] Lewis and Harden's
argument is part of a wider critique of an absence of suitable concepts
of law, public and constitutional, for analytical and practical
purposes. I wish to use as a springboard their belief in openness and
accountability as centrepieces of our immanent or inherent, as
opposed to 'real' or living, constitution. However desirable these
principles are, how far do they or can they go? What counter-
arguments can Government posit in its own defence? Lewis and
Harden in the passage cited qualify the degree of openness by giving
due consideration to 'confidentiality' in sensitive areas. Even if we
accept such principles, who defines 'sensitive'? Is it the *ipse dixit* of the
Prime Minister or Minister? Is it Parliament? How 'sensitive' and for
whom? The Government too has its own arguments. Is it open to the
Government to argue that openness is not one of the legitimating
principles? A government strives to fulfil its manifesto pledges after a
successful election. It makes public and Parliamentary statements. It
acts after inquiries – whether public, as in the planning and
environmental fields, or internal, as in the Westland episode itself.[11]
It is as open as it ought to be. Any more openness would interfere with
what *are* its major objectives, the realisation of which ensures

legitimacy: namely, efficiency and responsiveness. Efficiency in the meeting of objectives, and responsiveness to the claims and needs of its citizens. Bentham may have asked for publicity in everything. He also asked for frugality in everything, Government might assert. Too much openness would be too costly for efficiency and responsive action. Without openness, it must be asked, how do we know what objectives are and how efficiently they have been met? Without effective accountability, how can we gauge the degree of responsiveness of Government?

Ministerial Accountability

By the eighteenth century, ministerial responsibility to Parliament had become one of the focal points of constitutional attention, although the concept lacked precision. George I stopped attending Cabinet meetings regularly in 1717, reasoning that his Ministers now had to answer to Parliament for their advice to him. He could no longer protect them. The difficulties in establishing *individual* culpability led to the convention of collective responsibility of a government for its actions. If they were responsible collectively, then the Government should respond and initiate, i.e. govern, collectively. That means unanimously. Disagreement in public could not, would not, be tolerated. It took until 1975, in the litigation concerning the diaries of the former Secretary of State, Richard Crossman,[12] for the courts to insist that, in law, proceedings within the Cabinet are protected by confidentiality, at least for as long as confidentiality requires.[13] As recently as the late nineteenth century no minutes were taken of meetings, and Asquith stated in 1916 that only the Prime Minister took notes or a record for the purpose of the letter to the Monarch[14] to advise on the collective decisions of the Cabinet.

Once a Minister heads a Ministry, and it becomes a matter of public record that an area of administration falls within the responsibility of that Ministry, the Minister at its head assumes responsibility to Parliament for the administration of the Ministry, and his servants, traditionally, remain anonymous. He has to answer the questions about the Ministry's business, though he may not always accept the blame for what goes wrong. It depends upon the seriousness of the shortcoming and whether the Minister knew or ought to have known of it. On many crucial items, the Minister does not have immediate access to the research resources of his advisers, so he cannot ignore their advice.[15] If the Minister is to be individually responsible, then he must be accountable to Parliament by providing information in debates and at Question Time[16] and by responding to investigations from Select Committees: 'A Minister does not discharge his accountability to Parliament merely by acknowledging a general responsibility and, if the circumstances warrant it, by resigning. Accountability involves *accounting* in detail for actions as a Minister.'[17]

The Defence Committee did not believe a full account had been given by the Government on the Westland affair, which I referred to earlier, so that doubt was cast on the conduct of civil servants whom they were not allowed to question. The Government had not been as 'forthcoming . . . as the House . . . might have expected'.[18]

We need to examine the contemporary practice of Government and to compare these practices with the constitutional principles we accept. It will be necessary to look at the position of civil servants and their relationship with Ministers. In the Westland affair, the public witnessed a Minister giving information through his civil servants, as it would, he claimed, have appeared improper for him to have supplied it; a Minister praying in aid the support of named civil servants; and an invitation by the Select Committee to the civil servants to come to the Committee to tell the story as it really was.[19] The discussion will examine the methods whereby information is provided to the press and media by officials, Ministers and MPs – how, in other words, the Press Officer, the lobby system, the Press Association and 'D Notices' operate. Their collective objective is unattributable disclosure which seeks 'to influence without accepting responsibility'.[20] We will examine the relationship between Government and broadcasting. Our study will look at the practice of quasi-government and the deliberate creation and perpetuation of obscurity in administration. We will examine the practice of local government and its resort to secrecy or openness. Throughout the chapter we will assess the practice with reference to the principles.

Collective Responsibility

How collective is governmental decision-making? It depends upon the Prime Minister. Ministers are given a secret rule-book, *Questions of Procedure for Ministers*, and Cabinet secretarial staff are issued with *Talking About the Office*.[21] We are fortunate in having a recent monograph by Peter Hennessey[22] which, within the confines of the information he was able to gather, is an authoritative account of contemporary Cabinet government. If the account reveals that decision-making is anything but collective, then how can there be a shared responsibility in any meaningful sense beyond responding to a vote of no confidence from the Commons by resignation *en masse*?

Hennessey draws on the 1952 *Questions*, which he claims is similar in most vital respects to the one in current use.[23] The Cabinet is described as the final court of appeal on interdepartmental disputes. The restrictions on reproducing Cabinet memoranda are laid out, and the record of proceedings is limited to the decision taken and 'such summary of the decisions as may be necessary for the guidance of those who have to take action on them'. The Secretary should avoid recording the opinions of Ministers. An additional Annex may be used for matters of exceptional secrecy.

Rule 18 stipulates that Cabinet documents are the property of the Crown and must be returned to a successor or the Cabinet Office on relinquishing office.[24] A former Minister may at any time have access in the Cabinet Office to copies of Cabinet or Cabinet Committee papers issued to him while in office. Conventions govern the use of information from one government to a succeeding one. Each Minister will announce and defend his own area of interest once arrived at collectively.[25] Rule 21 leaves the method adopted by Ministers for discussion among themselves of questions of policy as a domestic matter. It is no concern of Parliament or the public. 'The doctrine of collective responsibility of Ministers depends . . . upon the existence of opportunities for free and frank discussions between them, and such discussion is hampered if the processes by which it is carried on are laid bare.' The composition, terms of reference and chairmen of Cabinet Committees should not be disclosed.

Rules 22–26 cover *Protection against Unauthorised Disclosure of Information* and emphasise the importance of maintaining confidentiality within the 'narrow circle of knowledge' of those responsible for the formulation or execution of a particular policy. A Minister's *own* views on a policy should not be publicised. This is honoured almost as much in the breach as in the observance.[26] Rule 25(vi) allows 'confidential' leakage to responsible editors, lobby correspondents, etc., for 'reasons of state'.

The remaining rules cover junior Ministers, Parliamentary Private Secretaries, statements in Parliament, White Papers, setting up committees of inquiry, and public behaviour and private business while in office.

Cabinet Committees

The Cabinet is not the centre for decision-making. For this, or these centres, we must look *inter alia*, to Cabinet Committees. Six Cabinet Secretariats reported to the Secretary to the Cabinet in 1986. The position of the Cabinet Secretary is pivotal. It was a Cabinet Secretary who urged the Government to be fuller in their explanations for actions while stating in court that Ministers and officials are necessarily 'economical with the truth'.[27]

In 1983, Mrs Thatcher disclosed the four main standing committees of Cabinet: the Home and Social Affairs Committee chaired by the Lord President of the Council; a Legislation Committee chaired by the Leader of the House of Commons; the Overseas and Defence Policy Committee and the Economic Strategy Committee, both chaired by herself. To these might be added a committee for security, intelligence and their budgets. However, Hennessey has commented that by the winter of 1985–6 there were at least 160 groups within the Cabinet Committee network. He identified five types of committee:[28] *Standing*, i.e. permanent (for the duration of the Prime Minister); *ad hoc* or 'single issue';[29] *Ministerial*, where civil servants do not participate; *Official* for civil servants alone, and *Mixed* for both Ministers and civil servants.

The actual creation, administration and utilisation of such committees will doubtless vary according to the particular style of the Prime Minister. Since 1979 the tendency has been to avoid committees, circulation of Cabinet papers and Cabinet debate wherever possible. Informal ad hoc groups might be stacked against an erring Minister,[30] or a colleague might be asked to prepare a paper just for the Prime Minister with his back-up team of civil servants or outsider specialists. A typical follow-up is a meeting at No. 10 with the Prime Minister and 'her team': 'a mixture of people from the Downing St. Private Office, the Policy Unit and Cabinet Office, with one or two personal advisers and sometimes a Treasury Minister'.[31] The style is not quite presidential, Hennessey argues, but much of the 'collective spirit' of the Cabinet system has been syphoned off to committees and informal groups.[32] This may be simply a more emphatic tendency in what has been happening since the end of the Second World War. Only one decision on nuclear weapons in 40 years, for instance, was approved by the whole Cabinet – the decision to proceed with the 'H' Bomb.

The former Central Policy Review Staff (CPRS) was an attempt better to inform and co-ordinate governmental decision-making.[33] It comprised 'outside' experts and academics. The Head of CPRS had 'a seat at the table of Ministers and Ministerial Committees'. To be effective in influencing policy at this level one needs 'to have vast access to information at least as good as all the departments who are putting forward their voices as well as time and staff'. Often CPRS did not have such facilities. Their papers had a 'shallow' feel to them, the last-minute effort of a 'bright spark' which was set beside a paper on a subject prepared by senior officials and advisers who had worked on a paper for months.[34] By the mid-1980s, the Prime Minister had her own policy research unit in place of a Cabinet one.

Our system of Cabinet government is not collective in any real sense, as the information and details of policy-making are not presented to the whole Cabinet, but are invariably kept within the narrowest possible range of Ministers. So much is no doubt a consequence of more government and more specialisation. It is not the framework for full, free and frank discussion of government policy within the confidence of the Cabinet. But it might be argued that this does not really matter. If the Government loses the confidence of the House it must go to the country. That is what is central, along with mute agreement, in collective responsibility. No Minister can claim a right to know what another is doing unless the matter touches upon his *own* sphere of responsibility. Then he must provide the information for Parliament to account for his *own* area of responsibility. Timing of release of information is, of course, vital, but while a Minister in the Cabinet, with the Prime Minister's approval, believes it best that Cabinet colleagues are not informed, it is unlikely that Parliament should be. How, and when, does Parliament get informed?

Parliament and Information

As the 'Grand Inquest of the Nation' Parliament can ask Questions. It can demand debates. It can summon witnesses and call for evidence before its Select Committees, especially the Public Accounts Committee (PAC) and the Select Committees which are departmentally related. By these processes it holds Ministers responsible for their departmental administration. Parliamentary proceedings, like those in courts, are protected by absolute privilege.[35] The mechanisms of Parliamentary Questions and debates are geared towards the provision of routine information: how many prisoners on remand; how many deportations; how many school closures? – the stuff of Parliamentary life. The more probing investigation exercises are conducted by the Select Committees of MPs who can have outside specialists advising them.

There is a prevailing mood of disappointment in the work of the Select Committees which were created in 1979, especially apropos of their oversight over finance and expenditure.[36] They are established to oversee and scrutinise the policies, administration and expenditure of related departments, their various agencies and fringe bodies. Members are appointed by the House of Commons, and the party balance usually reflects the balance of the House as a whole, as does the division of chairmen.

John Biffen has described how by February 1982 'about 750 departmental memoranda had been submitted to the committees. In the first three years there had been about 150 Ministerial appearances . . . and over 700 official witnesses.'[37] Select Committees have power to subpoena the attendance of witnesses and to order presentation of documents. Failure to comply is a contempt of Parliament. Nevertheless a *Memorandum of Guidance for Officials Appearing Before Select Committees* exists.[38] This may not always be applicable to the Public Accounts Committee because of its unique authority. The *Memorandum* supported the Procedure Committee, which reported:

It would not, however, be appropriate for the House to seek directly or through its committees to enforce its right to secure information from the Executive at a level below that of the Ministerial head of the department concerned (normally a Cabinet Minister) since such a practice would tend to undermine rather than strengthen the accountability of Ministers to the House.

Presence of witnesses is requested rather than demanded. Ministers decide which officials are to appear, and they remain 'subject to Ministerial instructions as to how [to] answer questions'.

Information should, the *Memorandum* explains, be provided, subject only to the terms of the *Memorandum* and 'the requirements of good government and national security'. Requests may also have to be refused where they would 'appear to involve excessive costs'. The following items should also be excluded: advice to Ministers; interdepartmental exchanges on policy issues; the level at which decisions were taken or the manner in which a Minister has consulted his colleagues; Cabinet Committees and discussions thereon; advice given by a Law Officer; information supplied in confidence; questions in the field of political controversy; sensitive information of a commercial or economic nature, which although understandable is drafted in a very vague and potentially broad manner; matters which are or may become the subject of sensitive negotiations with governments *or other bodies*, quasi-judicial functions or cases before the courts or Parliamentary Commissioner.

Where a 'closed session' is held, there are guidelines on 'sidelining' or expunging classified or confidential information from the testimony. Departmental responses should be made within two months. A refusal to appear or to allow officials to appear occasioned the Leader of the House to guarantee that time will be given to debate the matter on the floor of the House. The Director of General Communications Headquarters[39] was not allowed to testify in 1984. Nor were the civil servants in the Westland case.[40] An outright refusal to appear might constitute a contempt of Parliament; in reality a vote of censure would have to get a majority, and no doubt Ministers could rely upon MPs of their party at least being very careful not to encroach upon ill-defined executive privileges. The Government is adamant that the confidentiality of relationship between a Minister and civil servant shall not be threatened by 'cross-examination' before a Select Committee of MPs, however much Select Committees might claim that they are upholding Parliamentary supremacy in contra-distinction to Government's claim that committees only exist by virtue of Ministerial responsibility to Parliament. It is not right, the Government maintains, to allow officials to be questioned with a view to establishing the appropriate *locus* of fault in conduct, or the conduct itself, of individual officials.[41] It is claimed that committees have received more useful information from officials than Ministers on occasion.[42] Pressure has been put on the Leader of the House by chairmen to obtain more information on nationalised industries and to inveigle more information out of government departments, and committees have a long-standing practice of showing papers and drafts to them for comment and further information.[43]

Select Committees, like governments, suffer leaks. The Committee of Privileges has investigated the breach of the rule which prohibits the publication of evidence taken *in camera* or publication before report to the House, or the publication of deliberations of a committee. Members of committees are 'prime misfeasants' and the code contained in the *Notes on the Practice of Lobby Journalism* is not enforced.[44] The press show scant regard for the rules, and the House is reluctant to punish the press, as evidenced in the case of the journalist from *The Times* in 1986 who published details of a Select Committee's confidential report.[45] The House has power to punish a breach of privilege with imprisonment[46] or withdrawal of a Press Lobby or Press Gallery pass. The Committee recommended that a pass be withdrawn for certain serious breaches.

Before leaving Select Committees, we should note a point which is relevant for a later discussion. There is no Select Committee for the Lord Chancellor's Department, so that not only the judiciary but the administration of the courts and prosecution policy and legal aid are not subject to Parliamentary scrutiny via Select Committees. Nor indeed is the administration of Public Records for which the Lord Chancellor is responsible.[47]

In December 1987, it was announced that a Science and Technology Service was to be introduced to advise the all-party scientific committee, independently of Government.[47a]

MPs themselves are under a duty, by resolution of the House, to disclose private interests in debates or proceedings of the House or its committees or in their official transactions. A compulsory register has existed since 1975.

Ministers and Civil Servants

The Duties and Responsibilities of Civil Servants and Ministers has been the subject of a report from the Treasury and Civil Service Committee[48] as well as featuring in a variety of committee reports and government memoranda. The background to the TCSC Report was the low morale in the civil service, the banning of trade unions at GCHQ, the *Ponting* trial, and the *Note of Guidance on the Duties and Responsibilities of Civil Servants in Relation to Ministers* issued by Sir Robert Armstrong.[49] The guidance, which 'was not intended to break new ground', reasserted the tradition of civil service confidentiality and allegiance to the Minister, and the responsibility of Ministers to Parliament:

Any civil servant whose loyalty is put under strain is advised to refer his complaint to his superiors, even up to his Permanent Secretary . . . but in no circumstances to seek by his own actions to frustrate Ministers' policies or decisions.[50]

The Committee was surprised that principles of the 1930s were still considered adequate for the late 1980s. It was also uneasy about Sir Robert Armstrong's equation of the Crown with the Government of the day. The Crown may be symbolic of the nation, the Committee ruminated, to which 'civil servants and others may owe a loyalty higher and more lasting than that which they owe to the government of the day'. The official view stated by the Cabinet Secretary was of an undivided loyalty owed by the servant to the Minister. In return the Minister should, Sir Robert believed, 'read, mark, learn and digest the information and advice which the Civil Service has to offer . . . and to take that seriously'.[51] Too much, the Committee believed, was left to happenstance. What was needed was a set of guidelines promulgated by the Prime Minister after consultation with other political leaders in the Commons and spelling out the duties and responsibilities of Ministers to Parliament and the civil service.

The wider concerns of the report are obviously activated by the 'low morale' which exists when senior civil servants, especially, feel their career prospects are jeopardised if they do not give *politically* acceptable advice to Ministers. More immediate was the concern over the accountability of an anonymous civil servant who acted without the authority or knowledge of a Minister and for whose actions the Minister will not accept responsibility, and the situation where a civil servant feels obliged to reveal what his Minister is doing because the latter's behaviour is not in the 'public interest', or so the civil servant believes. On the former situation, the Committee, in agreement with the Defence Committee, believed that an internal departmental inquiry which is not fully reported to Parliament cannot qualify as accountability. The latter situation poses several problems.

In the case of a moral dilemma, Sir Robert believed a civil servant could take the matter up as a last resort with the Permanent Secretary of his Department. The Cabinet Secretary, and through him the Prime Minister, may be consulted. The Government has endorsed and acted upon this view.[52] In the case of Ponting and Colette Bowe,[53] these procedures were found defective. The First Division Association (the trade union for leading civil servants) has argued for a Code of Guidance to reinforce the position of the civil servant with possible redress from the Ombudsman or resort to the chairman of the appropriate Select Committee in the Commons. Sir Douglas Wass has called for an 'Inspector-General for the Civil Service' who would be independent of Ministers and who could hear civil servants.[54] Requests for guidelines have fallen on deaf ears.[55]

The Government also rejected the proposal for Ministerial *Cabinets* or private offices staffed by special advisers as well as career civil servants and the Minister's Parliamentary Private Secretary. It rejected splitting up the two offices of the head of the Home Civil Service and the Secretary to the Cabinet, both currently held by one official. A conflict of interests was not seen to exist.

The Committee could not regard as justified any leak by a civil servant which is designed to frustrate the policies or actions of a Minister. Indeed, it went further: 'Civil servants who leak information should face the sack or internal discipline', not punishment through the courts.

These conclusions, and a good deal of the Report, are superficial. The Report offers no scope for debate on what might be a 'justified leak' by a civil servant such as is recognised in other countries.[56] The Committee appears to endorse the view that such leaks are never *totally* defensible, even presumably when informing of evil or criminal acts. The concluding comment in the previous paragraph reinforces what is probably the current legal position on the subject of discipline and punishment. Even if the OSA could not be successfully invoked, a civil servant who communicated, in whatever form, information which would embarrass his Minister, whom he believed to be acting against the public interest, would have no right to claim wrongful dismissal if sacked. For civil servants are not under a contract of employment, although such a status may be ripe for legal reassessment.[56a] The Government in fact introduced a clause conferring contractual status, for limited purposes, on Crown servants in its 1987–8 Employment Bill. Even if they were under such contracts, as are other employees in the public sector, it seems on the balance of authorities that it may be an implied term of a contract of employment that an employee cannot be sued for revealing the confidences of his employer if it is in the public interest to reveal such confidences and this outweighs the maintenance of confidentiality. However, such a 'defence' may not be available for wrongful dismissal. Public interest may not be invoked to render a dismissal wrongful where the reason for dismissal was a breach of confidence. The defence of public interest is a defence to an action for breach of confidence whether or not contractual.[57] It will not necessarily make a dismissal wrongful which would, without that public interest, be lawful.

The law protects civil servants against unfair dismissal, but the tribunal is concerned with the 'fairness' and 'reasonableness' of the *process* of and reason for dismissal, and breach of confidentiality may well be a reasonable ground. Similar problems attend demotion or transfer to a far less satisfactory job, in so far as such action by an employer is unlikely to constitute constructive dismissal in response to a breach of confidence by a civil servant. If a Minister is abusing his position by deliberately misinforming Parliament, the only safe course for the civil servant is to ask for a transfer. If he or she does inform an MP of an abuse, it could well mean the Minister's resignation. It is regrettable that a civil servant who has taken the necessary internal steps by appealing to higher officials without success, and who has not been transferred, should be left with damaged career prospects by following his or her conscience and going public where such a course is justified.

Outright lying to Parliament may indeed be rare, but Sir Douglas Wass described the more usual practice where 'by judicious presentation and omission [the Minister] gives an impression to Parliament which is not the impression which would be formed if someone had all the evidence'.[58] Presentation and timing are everything, and these are matters of ministerial prerogative.

Sir Robert Armstrong's *Memorandum* and government responses promote a duty of confidence into an absolute and inflexible rule admitting of no exceptions. The civil service in the late twentieth century has changed irreversibly from the anonymous monolith of the early twentieth century. It has greater pressure of work because of increased and varied duties; it operates under the constant attention of the news media and the press; it is more vociferously unionised and organised around staff associations at all levels; it campaigns far more on behalf of its own causes.[59] On the government side, there is more intervention in senior appointments; there are certainly demands for more 'activist management and devolved responsibility to more junior line officials' bringing them occasionally into the limelight.[60] Their identity and level of responsibility will become easier to assess, although the Cabinet Office has argued that this development around the Financial Management Initiative will merely strengthen ministerial responsibility.[61] The public wants more publicity about administration, and the civil service are asked increasingly to advise not only on policy, but on presentation of policies for public acceptance.

Government and Media[61a]

The Treasury and the Civil Service Committee believed that Ministers who require their press officers to do more than present and describe their policies should make political appointments. How do governments use the media?

In 1984, a century after 'one gentleman of the press was given official permission to enter and remain in the Members' Lobby', the Lobby[62] celebrated its centenary. No formal resolution of the House authorised the event of 1884 and informal practice predated that year. The 'famous secret' of the Lobby takes place twice daily, and Lobby journalists see the Leader of the House and Leader of the Opposition on Thursday afternoons. Ministerial briefings of the Lobby developed, some suggest, from 1926 and a visit to Downing Street during the General Strike. Regular daily briefings emerged only after 1945.

The basis of the Lobby is a 'cosy collusion' whereby snippets of information will be given on the basis that the source is not identified. Even the politically uninitiated will appreciate that there are elements of a 'corporatist embrace' in the relationship inasmuch as the press cannot be controlled but they can be compromised if given anonymous 'confidences' by those in the know.[63] The Lobby is a voluntary group which regulates itself and operates according to a convention which the Government would not wish to cease.[64] The enforced hypocrisy has been too much for a growing number of national newspapers. However, securing reform has proved difficult,[65] even though it would only establish a more open 'on the record' form of journalism. In March 1987, the Lobby voted to continue the practice of unattributable quotations.

Outside the Lobby, leaks unless authorised are subject to the usual process of law. In such cases journalists have been imprisoned for refusing to name their sources in disclosing incompetence in Whitehall.[66] In 1972, the offices of the *Sunday Times* and the *Railway Gazette* were raided because of disclosure of a DoE document advising the closure of 4,600 miles of railways. In 1973, *Newsweek* was informed that photographing an employment office was a breach of section 2.

Successful prosecution followed the publication of military intelligence information by Duncan Campbell *et al.* in 1978 in the *ABC trial* – even though the information was otherwise published. In 1987, the offices of the BBC in Glasgow were raided following publication of an article on the 'Zircon' satellite intelligence system.[67] And so on.

The Cabinet Manual *Questions for Ministers* says the only safe recipients of neutered information are the Lobby correspondents: 'But Ministers should not at any time refer to such meetings; to do so would endanger the very special relationships with the Lobby which have been developed over many years'. In Harold Wilson's premiership, the Prime Minister had to authorise any broadcast by a Minister 'in a private and non-Ministerial capacity', had to be given all details of public-speaking engagements, and had to give approval before a Minister could write a letter to a newspaper.[68]

Formal rules govern the Lobby and are issued by the Parliamentary Lobby journalists.[69] Breach is most unlikely to lead to exclusion.[70] The Lobby has often been used to discredit and to disinform, but it is a practice that will outlive any FOIA reform, as witness General Alexander Haig's description of his character assassination by 'Reagan's henchmen' in his book *Caveat*. To achieve this, the President's men opened that 'great smithy of information' – the Government – to the press. They 'escorted reporters inside in a way hitherto unknown in Washington'. The press had 'never had sources like this' – it told them everything. 'And of course, it would not risk losing these sources by offending them, so it wrote what it was given.' In the USA the press still has the matter better organised, as each large newspaper has a bureau at Congress.

The Prime Minister has employed a private press spokesman since 1917. From 'around 1936', government departments 'first felt the need to possess a press officer'. 1939 saw the establishment of the Central Office of Information headed by a Minister of Information.[71] The office, but not the Minister, survived the Second World War. Departments have their own information officers and press officers to brief the press and media and present the departmental public image. Their importance in presenting ministerial policies in a favourable light has been acknowledged,[72] as has their role in press manipulation during the Falklands campaign, for example.[73] Weekly meetings of departmental press officers take place. The position of the Prime Minister's Information and Press Officer is crucial, and there has been increasing criticism that they are used for party political and anti-Opposition purposes, and not purely governmental ones.[74]

D Notices

Yet another corporatist embrace is illustrated by the D Notice system. Originally established in 1912 and entitled Admiralty, War Office and Press Committee, the relevant body is now known as the Defence, Press and Broadcasting Committee. Established on a voluntary basis and deriving no legal basis from OSA or other Acts of Parliament, its membership comprises senior civil servants from the relevant departments,[75] representatives of certain press and publishers' agencies, societies and associations, and latterly the BBC and Independent Television News. The Secretariat and expenses are borne by the Government. The Secretary must be fully informed of the facts behind a D Notice, which is issued to limit or prevent publication of information which would be against the public interest. The Secretary applies and interprets the scope of D Notices, i.e. what is detrimental to the national security of the country. According to the Memorandum of the Committee submitted to the Franks Committee in 1972[76] it is not otherwise concerned with the national interest, although the Secretary 'is instructed to bring to the notice of the Chairman of the Committee (or his deputy) any cases which lie at or beyond the border-line of the D Notice system for consideration as to whether Ministers should be informed of what other action should be taken'. The system is 'designed to protect national security while at the same time safeguarding the freedom and independence of the press and is based on mutual trust and confidence'.[77] Since 1982, D Notices cover eight topics:[78] names of the heads of MI5 and MI6; British agents and addresses used by the security services; defence plans; defence equipment; nuclear weapons; radio and radar transmissions; cyphers (codes) and communications; civil defence and photographs of defence establishments.[79] They were issued personally to editors of the national and provincial press, various news agencies and relevant publishers as well as the BBC and ITV.

The corporatist element is emphasised in that these notices are not creatures of law but are voluntary, represent an exclusive relationship between the State and private or quasi-governmental organised interests, and are self-regulatory, although they cover some similar areas as the OSA and breach could involve a prosecution. Indeed compliance itself is not a *legal* guarantee of immunity. This was evident in December 1987 when the Government invoked the civil law of confidentiality to prevent the broadcasting of a Radio 4 programme on the security services, although it had been cleared by the Secretary to the Committee. Failure to agree to D Notices will mean exclusion from the circle of trusted recipients of information. The close interrelationship between the press and Government made any significant alteration of the D Notice system by a reform of section 2 less than likely, though we shall have to see how it operates alongside the law of confidentiality. In fact, throughout 1987 the system was under strain because the Government had effectively by-passed it on two occasions.

This takes us to another facet of the contemporary State – the public/private interface and the corporatist tendencies in the distribution and exercise of power. What do we know of the networks through which contemporary government chooses to influence, and what ought we, or our representatives, to know? What are the consequences of Government seeking to achieve public ends via private or quasi-public institutions? Broadcasting offers an interesting illustration.

Broadcasting, Information and Political Censorship

Government influence and control over broadcasting is not a novel issue of concern, although it has spawned notorious episodes including the banning by the BBC of Duncan Campbell's *Secret Society* programme on the 'Zircon' information satellite system in 1987 and the prohibition by injunction of a programme on Radio 4 on the security services: *My Country Right or Wrong*. Regulation of broadcasting in the round and its future are important issues, but they take us beyond our brief.[80] What is of present concern is the ability of Government to censor, influence or regulate the nature of political information which is broadcast. Governmental influence may not be directly exerted but may operate through the mediation of public corporations which are, ostensibly, independent.

The BBC consists in a formal, legal sense of twelve governors, appointed effectively on the 'say so' of the Prime Minister, though formally by the Queen in Council. A Chairman and Vice-Chairman are appointed likewise. Members of the IBA and the Cable Authority, which regulate commercial TV and Cable TV, respectively are appointed by the Secretary of State. The BBC's formal powers and responsibilities are contained in its Charter of Incorporation; the IBA's and the Cable Authority's are contained in the statutes establishing the bodies. In a formal sense, both the BBC and the IBA[81] are given a wide range of discretion in their activities,[82] and are provided with minimal legal standards on quality, balance and impartiality. Both have internal codes and guidelines on taste and decency, violence and other matters. Both must refrain from editorial comment on current affairs. In the case of advertising the IBA has a Code of Guidance and works in close relationship with the TV companies' representative body, the Independent Television Companies Association. The Home Secretary has formal powers of veto, though in the case of both bodies they can announce that a veto has been effected and he can request the broadcasting of certain items.[83] Only five veto directions of a general kind have been given, and none on a particular broadcast. The IBA has the power to issue formal directions to a broadcasting company; but it invariably achieves its ends informally and by influence rather than by resort to its statutory powers, or it refers to its guidelines and decisions implemented by regional officers.[84] There is a tendency for controls on programme content to be greater in the independent sector than in the BBC as boards and executives are closer to programme makers and more knowledgeable about current operations.[85] The Minister has power to revoke the licence to the BBC, and the IBA may suspend or revoke contracts with programme contractors. Since 1980, a Broadcasting Complaints Commission has existed to cover both the BBC and the IBA. It is appointed by the Home Secretary.

The early history of the BBC reveals a marked element of subservience to Government. In 1926 the Chairman, Sir John Reith, at the Prime Minister's prompting refused to allow the Leader of the Opposition to broadcast. By the 1960s, a degree of independence had been firmly established, assisted without doubt by the advent of commercial TV. In 1972, for instance, the BBC resisted ministerial pressure not to broadcast *The Question of Ulster* because of the general political sensitivity of the subject.[86] However, Stuart Hood has suggested:

The BBC's relationship to the centres of political power in this country is government less by conspiracy than complicity; in this connection Reith's diary entry from the General Strike – 'they know they can trust us not to be really impartial' – still accurately defines that relationship.[87]

It might appear curious that such a degree of influence existed, for it was not until after 1955 that news bulletins made any reference to election campaigns. A semi-formal Party Political Broadcast Committee (PPBC) has existed 'in which sharing out of time takes place between delegates of all the parties with representatives in Parliament, the BBC, and IBA and party organisations'. It is chaired by the Lord President of the Council. The SDP-Liberal Alliance has contested the sharing of time to achieve balance and impartiality in news and current affairs coverage on the BBC. After an inconclusive court hearing,[88] the BBC promised to produce a pamphlet explaining its rules and procedures for achieving such balance and to give *limited* publicity to results of monitoring of its practices. Political broadcasts covering elections are formulated through the PPBC.[89]

Since 1937, BBC staff, on appointment or promotion, have been politically vetted by MI5. This was a negative form of vetting; the subject is not informed and cannot therefore correct false or inaccurate information. In April 1986,[90] the BBC undertook to restrict the extent of vetting to security-sensitive posts.

Controls on good taste, sex and violence are pervasive, making TV, it has been alleged, 'the most censored form of communication in our society'.[91] Between 1959 and 1985, the BBC and the IBA[92] banned, censored, delayed or doctored 48 TV programmes. Other forms of censorship are contained specifically in the law, and include a novel extension of the law of confidentiality.

For Northern Ireland, internal and external censorship by the Government is vigorous, if not always respected by the respective broadcasting authorities.[92a] In an attempt to maintain 'impartiality', i.e. the status quo, they must not show scenes which might encourage Republican sentiment, and must not criticise the armed forces. On this and on all subjects in the UK, political impartiality must be maintained, so that if one suggested a school was falling down this would not be impartial unless a government spokesman could say it was not.[93]

The Northern Ireland (Emergency Provisions) Act 1978 prohibits collecting, recording, publishing or attempting to elicit any information concerning the police, army, judges, court officials or prison officers, which is likely to be of use to terrorists. It is an offence to collect or record any information which is likely to be useful to terrorists in carrying out an act of violence, or to possess any record or document containing any of these types of information. The Act, as drafted, would cover ordinary journalistic practices, although the consent of the Northern Ireland DPP is required to bring a prosecution. A defence of lawful authority or 'reasonable excuse' may be made out.

The Prevention of Terrorism (Temporary Provisions) Act 1984 applies to the whole of the UK. Section 11 provides that persons are under a duty to disclose to the police any information which might be of material assistance in preventing an act of terrorism or in apprehending, prosecuting or convicting someone suspected of terrorism. The Attorney-General has previously threatened to adopt a hard line under this section after reporting by BBC crews in Northern Ireland. It was invoked in March 1988 after the death of two British soldiers at a funeral.

These legislative provisions, understandably, help to maintain an ethos of caution, but authorities would not wish to be seen to be using them oppressively. There are more subtle forms of political persuasion. The Foreign and Commonwealth Office has close and informal contacts with the BBC World Service, and every day delivers a 'selection' of cables it has received. The World Service is bound to 'plan and prepare its programmes in the national interest' according to the BBC licence, and its hours and languages of broadcast are prescribed by the FCO. Under clause 13(5) of the licence, the World Service has to obtain and accept from the FCO 'such information regarding conditions in, and the policies of Her Majesty's Government towards countries' in planning and preparing its programmes. Any complaints from foreign governments about broadcasts are invariably made to the FCO, which duly presents them to the BBC while maintaining to complainants that the BBC is independent. Many complaints come from right-wing countries with whom our Government has important diplomatic or commercial arrangements.[94] Closer to the home front have been studies indicating pro-Government bias in the news programmes covering the miners' strike of 1984–5[95] and overt pressure on the IBA and TVS not to rebroadcast in their existing form a series of programmes on the Greek civil war of the 1940s, or to sell them overseas.[96] The interpretation offered of the war was not favourable to the 'establishment' version, it was claimed. The inquiry into the complaints was not made by the Broadcasting Complaints Commission but by Channel 4 itself internally, 'because of the seriousness of the allegations'. The issue centred on the alternative versions of the truth emerging from historical events.

In 1972, the Irish Government banned the appearance of members of illegal organisations on the media. The Annan Committee Report rejected such a move in the UK, arguing that 'these organisations are a political force in Northern Ireland; and it would be unrealistic for the broadcasters not to recognise them'. In 1985, however, the BBC governors postponed the screening of *Real Lives*, a programme concerning members of Northern Irish para-military organisations after the board of management had passed the programme for screening. The governors had reacted, it seemed, to overt pressure from the Home Secretary and senior officials, and for the first time vetted a programme before it was broadcast. The decision was taken shortly after the Prime Minister had spoken publicly of the need to starve terrorists of publicity. Only one BBC governor dissented. The Home Secretary believed that, while censorship under the criminal law would be wrong, he should be allowed to convey the Government's view of the public interest to the BBC. The Chairman of the Governors was approached directly by the Home Secretary after the Board of Management, largely comprising directors of the BBC, decided not to show the documentary to the governors, fearing that the Board's 'editorial independence' might be undermined. The Home Secretary was adamant that it was *not* a question of not maintaining balance, but of the undesirability of broadcasting the committed and extreme views of terrorists from both sides of the division in Northern Ireland. Under the Charter, the governors carry legal responsibility, are the ultimate management authority and are the 'independent' judges of programmes on the public behalf. It will be recalled that they are appointed by the Crown on the recommendation of the Prime Minister.[97]

General De Gaulle once said, 'They have the newspapers, I have the television.' A former director[98] of the BBC asked why the Prime Minister should have both. Whether the governors acted from good motives or bad, the episode has left a damaging taint on the BBC's image. The functional confusion of the roles of governors and managers, and the BBC's dependence on the acceptance of an appropriate licence fee, i.e. their income, by the Home Secretary, leaves a situation ripe for political exploitation. By law the Home Secretary had a power of veto; was this not the appropriate route rather than via the back door, which compromised the governors?[99] Other episodes suggesting covert pressure have followed.[100]

Annan found the IBA position more clear-cut. It contracts out and then supervises. The BBC has a confusion of roles. What is required is a clear division between governors and management. The board of management should manage; the governors should vet standards in the public interest, and the licence seeks to ensure that appropriately experienced individuals are appointed. Here lies the snag. How representative of the community are the governors? How far afield does the Prime Minister's search go? What safeguards are there to prevent the packing of allies and like-minded souls on the Board? If the example of the Public Appointments Unit is anything to go by, precious little. This is maintained in the Cabinet Office and keeps a central list of the 'Great and the Good'. The criteria for admission to the list, and the fact that it is open to self-proposal, are not made public.[101] Information about the operation of the unit has been denied on the ground that it was 'purely a matter of internal efficiency'.

The IBA has not escaped criticism for refusing to exercise independent judgment.[102] In early 1985, it prevented Channel 4 from showing a film about a former employee of MI5 who claimed that MI5 had acted illegally when tapping people's telephones, including those of CND and NUM leaders. The IBA gave no reasons for the ban initially, but subsequently claimed that the film might have contravened section 2 of the Official Secrets Act had it been broadcast. A subsequent application in the courts for a declaration of the illegality of the Home Secretary's action failed, though not because of any weakness in the evidence contained in the programme itself.

The Peacock Committee Report on the Financing of the BBC[103] recommended a greater reliance upon the ordinary law of obscenity, defamation and sedition, etc., rather than upon regulation. Such a trend is already in existence[104] and has come close to Parliamentary endorsement.[105] In the autumn of 1987, the Home Secretary announced his intention to establish an independent watchdog to reflect public interest in the development and maintenance of standards. The Committee further recommended a greater reliance on pay-as-you-watch TV and on the auctioning of commercial sector broadcasting contracts. The dangers in choosing wealth as the only significant factor in public broadcasting are all too obvious as regards the overwhelming support that such a criterion is likely to create for one political party and political creed. When Fox's Libel Act of 1792 placed power in the hands of juries and not judges to decide not only the facts, but whether the facts amounted to libel in charges of seditious libel brought by the Crown, the Crown managed quite well without the assistance of the offence. Newspaper owners had become the friends of government and less likely to publish seditious libel.

TV represents the most immediate and effective mass persuader and conveyor of information in our culture. As we enter an era of direct satellite broadcasting of transmissions from overseas and the encouragement of an integrated European TV system, the need for vigilance to ensure political balance is as great as ever, possibly greater. It is as great as the need to maintain standards of taste and decency. Government and money must not have the only word on settling those issues.

Government, Non-Departmental Bodies and Private Organisations

Openness and accountability are two of the legitimating principles of our governmental system, though they have to be weighed against other principles such as efficiency, responsiveness and security. Collective and individual ministerial responsibility are predicated upon the former. If we set these claims upon which legitimacy is dependent against actual practice, the constitutional principles are invariably suborned. Democracy is based upon voting and representation for all those whose personal attributes do not disqualify them. In order to vote meaningfully, I must know what I am voting for. My representative must convey what the Parliamentary elites have done in their stewardship of the 'gubernatorial power' and what, in return, he or she has done, or the legislative assembly has done, to investigate that stewardship. It comes to this: we cannot guarantee that we will know all that is relevant, and the system of government has not been devised in which we could. But we can ensure that vigilance and suitable pressure have been applied to ask the right questions, and get the best answers.

Openness and accountability cannot be taken as absolutes, because we do yield to countervailing pressures which are present in appeals to efficiency, responsiveness and security and which are duties of government. Sir Humphrey's advice to young Bernard concerning open government, 'My dear boy, it's a contradiction in terms. You can be open, or you can have government,'[106] is far too strong, but there is a scintilla of uncomfortable truth for the advocate of open government. The lines between openness and accountability, and efficiency, responsiveness and security, represent clashes between degrees of participatory and representative forms of democracy. But make no mistake, they are clashes over forms of *democracy*. The lines are always shifting as encroachments are made on the nature of the government prerogative and its assertion of the prevalence of politics and policy in government and administration. The encroachments demand justification for the exercise of collective power through reasons, rational explanation, debate and institutional structure. That area of pure politics will never disappear entirely; our present task is to confine it to its legitimate realm and not to allow it to rule arrogantly and rudely where it does not belong.

The chapter so far has concentrated on Whitehall. What about government beyond Whitehall which is not subject to the democratic pressure of our high politics? We all know who can vote; less easy to assess is on what issues we can vote.

The points which follow are complex,[107] but they involve the following themes. Outside the formal and constitutional structure of government emerge bodies which are Government/Parliament created by a variety of devices. We saw in Chapter 3 how governments sought to control and censor such agencies. These bodies are responsible for particular areas of administration which fall outside a department's specific responsibility to administer directly, but which might be under the direction or guidance of a Ministry which can be achieved by a variety of devices.[108] If public expenditure is involved, either by way of grant in aid from the sponsoring department or by direct vote from Parliament, then the Comptroller and Auditor-General (CAG) would have the duty of scrutiny and inspection of accounts.[109] What concerns us is that these bodies themselves become repositories of vast amounts of information, and secondly they establish relationships with sponsoring departments which are not on the record of any public document. The subject of nationalised industries and the public corporations which manage them, and indeed the boards of privatised industries, and the relationships of these bodies with Ministers, is a case in point. The relationship between these bodies and Ministers is of a confidential nature, and it is impossible to fathom whether nationalised industries are under a greater degree of political control than the arm's-length statutes establishing them would suggest. These points are dealt with elsewhere,[110] as are the frequent complaints of industry consumer councils that they are deprived of sufficient information to play a meaningful role in protecting the consumer interest on service and prices. In 1980, it was estimated that the electricity industry had fourteen classifications of secret information.[111] When a monopoly industry is privatised, as in the case of British Telecommunications (BT), the Government establishes a regulatory body which, as with BT, supervises the licence which the Government has issued to BT to provide telecommunication services to the consumer. In 1984, the National Consumer Council wrote:

Without a clear statutory definition of whose interests the Office of Telecommunications is supposed to be looking after there is a danger that OFTEL will take whichever side can make life easier for OFTEL; this is unlikely ever to be the consumer.[112]

The procedures for enforcing licensing conditions are cumbersome. OFTEL will have to rely upon BT for much of the information which it requires for effective regulation – 'it is not in BT's interests to be open and frank'. In his annual report for 1985,[113] the Director-General of OFTEL stated his discontent over BT's licence terms, which provide only for the corporation to supply information on specific request. He would like to be supplied with information on a regular basis. Prior to the sale of British Gas, its employees were warned by an internal circular not to talk about the sale to 'outsiders'.[114]

If, for example, a government hives off to an independent agency executive powers to regulate, license or control an aspect of commerce or finance in the public interest, how do we or our representatives know that the public interest is being maintained? Indeed, does the Government know that the public interest is being maintained? In deciding whether to assume a responsibility for regulation or supervision of a sector or activity, the Government has to make a political decision. These decisions are made through the traditional channels of government decisions, followed by legislation, Royal Charter or whatever.

Government then has to decide how to carry out its programme. Is management best achieved – in the case of an industry – by a Minister or a manager or a Board? Is privatisation best achieved by complete sale, by retention of shares, or by a partnership with the private sector? Is regulation best achieved by a government department or by an independent body – if so, how independent[115] – or by an organised interest already in existence with which the State can enter into bartering relationships and which can speak on behalf of a client group? In this latter range of questions, it has been suggested, the Government is acting more as a legal agent.[116] It has to choose the instruments through which its objectives can best be achieved. Very often this will be through law. The legislation is invariably facilitative: authorising various things to happen, allowing others to happen. It is usually widely drafted. It lacks specificity. It does not provide answers, nor does it help to pinpoint responsibility. It does not insist on publication of details and it rarely gives public interests, e.g. the consumer, an opportunity to be fully informed or to make a meaningful contribution.

Inevitably, in the case of formal institutions established by Government, there is a duty to inform the Minister on whatever he directs; to present accounts to him or to the Comptroller and Auditor-General; and to make reports, in the case of statutory bodies inevitably to Parliament. But Parliament has itself found it difficult to break through hollow ministerial answers, or in the case of nationalised industries to obtain corporate plans.[117] Where the Government or its agencies collect information in the course of inspections, refusal to publicise information is far from rare. The Ministry of Agriculture, Fisheries and Food is refusing to allow public examination of the detailed information on the 400 pesticides already approved for use in Britain, and no timetable has been set for safety review. The Health and Safety Executive for years refused to establish a public register of companies licensed to handle hazardous chemicals and to release details of firms convicted of breaking regulations[118] – the result of a misinterpretation of provisions under the Health and Safety at Work Act. In the NHS 'accountability is generally limited to inspection and reports, which for the most part remain firmly within the system' and which are not regularly reported in the reports of health authorities.[119] Even the Health and Safety reports fail to give details of the criteria of standards adopted by inspectors in investigations.[120] One final point concerns the power under the Competition Act 1980 for the Monopolies and Mergers Commission to investigate the efficiency of a nationalised industry or water authority. Investigations can take from six to nine months, and the MMC will decide whether the industries' practices are operating against the public interest. The follow-up procedure to its reports which are presented to Parliament is unsatisfactory, and usually follows an informal procedure with agreements in private and written Parliamentary answers which draw little comment from MPs. Responses from industries are placed in the House of Commons library, which is not open to the public. One has to apply to the sponsoring department or the industry. The MMC has failed to define the 'public interest' and what is contrary to it. It investigates in private[121] and does not hold press conferences.

For the more 'apparent' of public outposts, the Cabinet Office and Treasury published in 1985 a guide for departments.[122] This is a detailed document setting out three main criteria: systematic review of existing bodies; good value for money for the taxpayer; rigorous examination of proposals to establish non-departmental public bodies (NDPB) and whether the private or the voluntary sector could perform the tasks under consideration. While establishing an NDPB implies a degree of independence from ministerial control,

the responsible Minister is answerable to Parliament for the degree of independence which an NDPB enjoys, for its usefulness as an instrument of government policy, and so ultimately for the overall effectiveness and efficiency with which it carries out its functions.

The Guide is voluminous in its *internal* controls, e.g. the necessary information-flow between public bodies and Ministers for meeting objectives and realisation of roles, keeping statements of accounts, and providing information which is consistent with the Treasury's Financial Information System.[123] Its public dimension is meagre. The chapter concerned with 'Public Disclosure of Information' is the shortest in the Guide, concentrating on Annual Reports, remuneration and expenses, and the information that should be provided to Select Committees. The report only deals with public bodies in a formal sense; it does not cover bodies or interests with which the Government enters into private concordats and which in legal terms are private enterprises.[124] Nor does it have much relevance to the subterranean world of advisory committees. These are often advisory in name only, possessing *de facto* executive powers. They report in confidence to the Minister, and their meetings and minutes are not public.

When the State enters into close working relationships with private concerns, the problems posed for the constitutional 'Watcher' include establishing what has been devolved on to the private body by way of public responsibility. A classic case of this kind was the administ-

ration of the civil legal aid scheme by the Law Society.[125] A further
example is the State's reliance upon the accountancy profession to
formulate appropriate standards of good practice in the keeping of
accounts and the supervision of audits. A recent process of bartering
involved the Government's desire to extract undertakings from the
Institute of Chartered Accountants that the latter would take a much
more active role in providing information to the Bank of England on
the financial affairs of banks and financial institutions whose books its
members audited. The profession managed to avoid the incorporation of these duties in legislation on the undertaking that satisfactory
internal criteria were met.[125a] Who makes decisions? How? Where?
Under what controls? With what publicity? If we do not know what is
going on, we cannot hope for answers. It must be conceded that this is
not so much a right for individuals, unless their lives are directly
affected by such decision-making, as for Parliament. Parliament
knows little of what goes on in this twilight world – indeed, one of the
benefits of privatisation from the Government's perspective is that
Parliament's interest ought thereby to be reduced.

It is quite clear that in dealing with mighty client groups, not even
the Government is always fully informed. The CAG has commented
adversely upon the failure of the companies within the armaments
industry to supply adequate information of profit levels and pricing to
the Treasury. Many of the important contracts are not open to
competitive tender.[126] The Review Board for Government Contracts
– a joint non-statutory CBI/Treasury-nominated body – reviews the
appropriate profit formula for non-competitive contracts every three
years. Its recommendations are used as a basis for discussion between
the CBI and the Government. It also reviews individual contracts
referred to it. The CAG has criticised the industries for failing to
reveal the details behind the information which they provide to the
Board: 'I question whether this denial of information is consistent
with the Government's responsibility to Parliament to account for the
basis on which they have accepted the recommendation.' The
Treasury did not know how to get this information while still
retaining the 'co-operation' of the industry.[127] It is a big money-
earner and a big employer. It cannot be told, it has to be persuaded, to
adopt suitable approaches after *quid pro quo* bartering. It is impossible
to know whether this is in the public interest.[128]

A similar theme concerns the DHSS and the Pharmaceutical Price
Regulation Scheme which is regulated by the DHSS and is non-

statutory. Companies which are not exempt from
submit accounts and production and sales figu
Companies may be asked to reduce *overall* pr
considered too high. There is no enforcement
PPRS does not apply to individual drugs but to
profitability, which allows a variety of accounting sleights o.
drug companies to distort the real profit level. The DHSS lac..
adequate information and inside knowledge on costs and did not
know 'whether they had played a good hand or had been the victim of
a bluff'.[129] The chairman of the Public Accounts Committee has
asked officials whether 'the Department . . . [is] really serious about
wanting to get a good deal for the tax-payer'.[130] The PPRS was
revised in 1986, but it has not properly addressed the problem of
obtaining adequate information from the drug companies.

This is an enormous theme, and is too complex to pursue in depth
here.[131] At issue are the methods by which Government governs.
Anyone with an interest in freedom of information and open
government must understand that the topic is not exhausted by
allowing individuals to have access to public documents. It is
centrally concerned with knowing how these dense networks operate.
Only when we know this can we hope to know what questions to ask
and who to put them to.

Local Government

Openness and accountability apply equally to local government as to
central government. The arguments apropos of the ascendancy of
those principles over efficiency, effectiveness and responsiveness have
already been detailed and need not be repeated here. The latter group
implies the former. It must be borne in mind that local government
does not embrace problems which affect national security unless civil
defence and emergency planning[132] and police affairs outside the
Metropolitan area are included. 'Policing' is a sensitive topic in those
localities where police committees of local authorities and police
authorities wish to be informed about policing policy and operational
items relating to the police. Traditionally Chief Officers of police
refuse to cover such matters in any detail in their reports to such
authorities or to be drawn into answering detailed questions.[133]
Information addressed to the Chief Constable from the Home Office

confidence is not addressed to the authority, nor is it in the authority's possession, and his position as an officer of the Crown probably means that members of the authority have no right to demand and receive it.[134]

In the previous chapter, the legal requirements for the openness of local government were noted. The Local Government (Access to Information) Act 1985 will open up to council members and the public the opinions and advice of officers at all levels. The Government has used the ideologies of openness and accountability for its own purposes: to claim that it has assisted in open government – at the local level alone. This was particularly pointed when it restricted the Access to Personal Files Bill to local authorities, excluding its own administration which impinged directly on individuals. Government might claim that it has rectified an abuse of democratic government by making local government more fully answerable to its electorate and ratepayers, especially business ratepayers.[135] Many remain convinced that the real problem lies within central and quasi-government.

Nevertheless bureaucratic conflicts, as well as ideological political conflicts, are a pervasive feature of local government administration. How can these features foster a secrecy or lack of information which militates against openness in the public interest? What follows looks at some of the more closed pratices of authorities in response to legislative duties to open up administration. It must be said that the 'fault' is sometimes that of the legislature or the Government – its legislation does not cover the real problem or it missed its target. Secondly, authorities might see in legislation which affects their procedures and powers the heavy hand of 'some bright spark in Marsham Street'.[136] Resistance is geared more towards a perceived unwarranted interference by central government in local government's affairs. Be that as it may, local authorities are there to govern and administer, and as such their responsibilities are built upon openness and accountability. But to what extent?

Three basic kinds of information can justifiably claim the protection of confidentiality in local government. The first relates to a political group formulating policies outside the structure of official channels and *before* it constitutes council business. Such a protection must be carefully circumscribed. A second concerns information on individuals, the disclosure of which to others would amount to an unwarranted interference in their privacy. A third category covers information where the local authority is acting in a business or regulatory capacity, or is taking legal advice and where disclosure would harm or prejudice its legitimate management or destroy legal immunity. The 1985 Act deals with the latter two categories directly, and indirectly with the first.

The formulation of party policies will become more of a vexed question. The courts have contributed to the party political contest which dominates in some local authorities where old political understandings have been upset by the arrival of third parties and politicians prepared to use local political fora in a contest with central government or to repeat national conflict at a local level. In *R.* v. *Sheffield City Council ex p. Chadwick*[137] the High Court held that a member of the city's Policy Committee was entitled to see the reports of alternative budget proposals which were before its sub-committee. The sub-committee had been appointed purely on leading party political lines. The exclusion of the applicant, a member of the opposition party, was unlawful because party political reasons for drawing up sub-committees were invalid[138] and the member had a right to know by virtue of his membership of the parent committee. It was accepted by the judge that there could be information which was so sensitive that a member of the parent committee would not be entitled to see it. This would be very rare, however.[139] It seems that, at common law, if ruling parties wish to propose alternative strategies and discuss political points confidentially, they must organise *outside* the formal structure of council, committees and sub-committees.[140] The Widdicombe Report deplored this, arguing that it should be possible to have recommendatory non-executive committees to which the public and council members who are not members of the committees in question would have no access and no right to information. His point is that it will have to be referred back to appropriate committees or the council for resolution, at which stage the provisions of the 1985 Act come into play. Widdicombe's solution to exclusion was to suggest that the standing orders of a local authority should stipulate that the constitution of decision-taking (not deliberative) committees should reflect *as far as practicable* the balance of political power in the authority. The Chief Executive would be responsible for the detailed application of the rule and for deciding which information councillors could see.[141]

Widdicombe also proposed that outside 'advisers' should not vote on executive committees, that their names should be publicised, and that party groups should publicise the identity of those attending their meetings and that their activities in relation to council business is restricted. These proposals would cause endless controversy about what is a deliberative/recommendatory committee and what is an executive one, *de facto* if not *de lege*, and how far into the background papers of a deliberative committee a member of the local authority or a committee to which its recommendation is referred is allowed to delve. At present, if the political party in power or in opposition wishes to discuss matters informally, it must do so *outside* the formal structure of the council. Establishing a need to know at common law is going to be difficult where it is a non-executive, informal[142] group. The ideal must cede to the practical reality of party politics. If the group is advised by officers, a member's right to know will be similarly established; is it information in the possession or control of the council or is it an informal, off-the-record opinion to individuals constituting a political group, but not a formal committee or sub-committee? Widdicombe's suggestion that if this facility is provided to one party, it should apply to all, has merit.[143] Among the other recommendations, the provision of a Question Time for the general public at the end of council meetings and the opposition right to place items on the agenda are found in more advanced authorities.

Where powers are delegated to an officer, Woolf J. has stated 'that in respect of decisions taken by officers the rights of councillors to be informed' (at common law) also depended upon the need to know. Under the terms of the 1985 Act, an officer's decision will come back to the record of a committee, etc., and come within that Act. Decisions cannot be delegated to one member alone.[144] An increasing number of authorities are delegating to an officer who must consult with the leader or a committee chair before deciding. The need-to-know provision applies, as does the statute. Where the officer reports 'what he is told to write' and this is all that is presented to a committee before a decision, or where a report is written that is tendentious and omits facts and alternative possibilities, what then?[145] Files often contain contrary evidence from sources that are not presented in report. *Chadwick* would suggest that members can ask for and receive alternative proposals; under the AIA they ought to form part of the background papers which the public can see if not exempt. Some authorities have adopted the following standing order:

Officers preparing reports for members have a duty to take into account all relevant information. This must include any arguments that are counter to those expressed in the report. Any background documents that do not support the arguments expressed in the report must be mentioned along with those that do.[146]

A preserve on information is, in local government as in other forms of government, a means of securing influence, allowing the 'right' conditions for the exercise of decision-making to prevail, courting political favour with the electorate by knowing where to go for results, and diminishing the efficiency of the opposition by exclusion. Local government has been subjected to legally imposed processes of open decision-making which have invited judicial intervention in a way that other areas of our public administration have not. This is not to say that such intervention has been pervasive or necessarily influential. It is in stark contrast to the position in central government and its agencies and client groups.

However, stories about evasion of the 1985 Act are legion. These do not simply involve members as described above. Below is an extract from a memorandum to all members of a council which is not untypical of the devices used to circumvent the Act:

To All Members of the Council: as you will be aware the above Act places onerous new responsibilities on Local Authorities with regard to the availability of information to the press and public. Consequent upon this issue it is encumbent on a Local Authority to provide, in connection with any report considered, a background list of information which has been relied upon to a material extent in compiling the report. For practical purposes this list of information will, in most instances, need to be supported by a copy of the document concerned and kept available with the papers for the statutory period of four years.

This requirement, however, only applies to reports which are considered by the Authority through the Committee process and whilst matters are dealt with in this manner there is no alternative other than to abide by the requirements of the Act.

In considering the Health and Housing Committee Agenda a number of items on which reports arise are likely to present considerable problems to officers in compiling the information. I refer particularly to the following:

(a) Housing Progress Report.
(b) Progress Report – Council House Sales.
(c) Housing Rent Arrears Statistics.[147]

Whilst they do not relate to written reports, it is also relevant to consider in this context the under mentioned items:

(d) Home Improvement Grant and outstanding commitments.
(e) Housing Waiting List.
(f) Housing Stock Figures.

As these items are of course purely informative in nature and prior to the Council Meeting . . . the Chairman and Vice-Chairman of the Committee have exercised their delegated powers to authorise that in future they are no longer dealt with through the Committee system. Instead updated situation reports will be sent direct to Members for their information and they will then be able to take up any queries privately with the Officers concerned.

Further devices include: calling bodies a working party or group and not a committee or sub-committee; charging excessive fees; and taking no steps whatsoever to publicise the existence of rights to access.

One potential weakness concerned the recipients of a service provided by an authority in so far as such information could be exempt, even as against the recipient himself where he had provided it. The Access to Personal Files Act, which we examine elsewhere,[148] may help to overcome this problem in housing and social services. Education files, it is promised, will be made available under other legislation and may formalise in law the pressure of teachers' unions, education authorities, and government circulars[149] enjoining access to personal files by the subject of the files. It is worthwhile examining the Education Acts of 1980 and 1981,[150] which will be looked at in the following chapter, and the Housing Act 1985,[151] which involved legal duties to provide information, open up practice, allow for participation in decision-making and provide for rights of appeal or challenge.[152]

Under the Housing Act 1985, section 104, a housing authority is required to publish information 'about its secure tenancies in such form as it considers best suited to explain in simple terms and so far as it considers appropriate the effect of' terms of the tenancies and other statutory duties.

Under section 105 a duty is imposed on an authority to make and maintain 'such arrangements as it considers appropriate to enable those of its secure tenants who are likely to be substantially affected by a matter of housing management' to be informed of its proposals and to make their views known to the authority within a 'specified period'. The authority has a duty 'to consider representations so made and to publish their arrangements which are to be available for inspection, free of charge, at all reasonable hours at the authority's principal office', or which can be provided to a member of the public for a reasonable fee. 'Housing management' relates to the management, maintenance, improvement or demolition of dwelling houses let or to related services or amenities; or to a new programme of maintenance, etc., or a change in the practice or policy of the authority which is likely substantially to affect its secure tenants as a whole or a group of them. Housing management does not include rent payable under secure tenancies or charges for services.

Last of all, section 106 imposes an obligation on a landlord authority to publish a summary of its rules on determining priority in allocation, exchanges and transfers, and to maintain and furnish such rules to the public upon request at reasonable charge. The authority has also to provide an applicant with certain information on himself and his family which *he* has supplied to the authority, but under the section it does not have to provide information which it has obtained from other means. This position is now covered by the Access to Personal Files Act, which may remedy a substantial potential for abuse in misusing information, e.g. for racist purposes,[153] or for using inaccurate information.[154]

Research questionnaires to Directors of Housing indicated that the means used to publish the details of tenancies under section 104 varied, although 76.4 per cent said it was by a 'package'. Many provided examples of what were impressive documents, although only eight of these out of a total of 185 had any details of a complaints procedure for housing complaints; one additional return said in the event of a complaint 'see a solicitor'. Eighty-seven per cent of the respondents felt that section 104 was a desirable measure, but only 50.8 per cent felt that the section had made any difference to their actual practices. The methods employed to involve tenants in discussion varied enormously, but consultation via tenants' associations was a widespread practice, as was co-option of tenants' representatives on to housing sub-committees. In spite of the wide variety, evidence of active assistance by the authorites in helping to establish tenants' groups, to help them understand the process of decision-making and the best way to influence decision-makers, was virtually non-existent. The real crunch came when Directors of Housing were asked whether the tenants had questioned or challenged the 'appropriateness' of the procedures. Only four said 'yes'. More to the point, tenants had only challenged an authority's decision that they were *not* substantially affected by a matter of housing management on four occasions. A total of 40.9 per cent of the responses said that consultation had changed the authorities' decision, usually on minor points; while 74.7 per cent of authorities believed that they should not be under a specific legal duty to take seriously, rather than simply consider, the views of tenants: 'it was not an appropriate matter for law'. As one response expressed it: 'Endless discussions will rarely affect a party political vote, frequently predetermined at group meetings and such an obligation would be of no practical value.'

Generally in relation to sections 105 and 106 there was a profound sense of legalistic overkill: 'Procedures stagnate decisions – previously matters were settled much better by doorstep negotiations.' 'Legalism is not an appropriate response to the involvement of the client, and this code is something of an empty shell. It imposes a heavy administrative burden on authorities with large stocks, but the results of consultation are negligible.'

The duties to publicise and to consult would appear to have been largely an exercise in apathy and going through the motions. The above duties were introduced in the same statute that introduced the 'right to buy' council properties for tenants. The Government in recent legislation has given authorities wide powers to privatise council estates and their management and to take away tenants' security of tenure under the 1980 Housing Act.[155] In *Short* v. *L.B. of Tower Hamlets*,[156] the Court of Appeal ruled that tenants had very limited rights under the Housing Act in relation to discussions of a *proposed sale* of their tenancies to a private concern, and in other respects gave a very narrow ruling on the impact of the Act on tenants' rights to be consulted.[157]

It would be easy to say that rights to be informed and to make contribution to the actual decisions affecting people's lives must give way to executive will, especially in the pursuit of economic objectives. But deeper lessons lie in the history of the housing legislation. To be informed, to be consulted and to participate is meaningless unless we actively develop the skills required to assess and analyse information; to use information to press a case or a point of view; to use information through processes which are not closed or foreshortened, in which alternatives will be seriously considered, and which do not constitute a distortion of communication in Habermas's sense. Unless we give pressing thought to these points, public decision-making will remain the private concern of elite politicians and their trusted confidants. In some circumstances, this is inevitable; as a pervasive practice it sets the framework for a 'fraud on the majority'. The biggest threat to democratic standards comes when privatisation is proffered as a form of accountability in itself.[158] Its proponents argue that we can vote with our feet. A monopolised or oligopolised market offers little alternative direction in which to aim our feet. The arguments that the vote is the quintessential feature of democracy, and that to vote between alternatives one must be informed on what the alternatives have done and propose to do, are weakened by the simple expedient of reducing those issues on which we can vote by declaring them private. Regulation will then replace democratisation.

Central government's invitation to private enterprises to provide initiatives, or combine in joint efforts with the centre, to combat urban decline has been one of the major features of urban politics since 1980. Use of the private sector has been seen as a way of reducing the role of local government in planning, housing and development, education and commercial initiatives. The various assortment of task forces, action teams, Financial Institutions Group, Inner City Enterprises Limited and the Urban Development Corporations witness a movement away from the role of local government and the spearheading of private initiatives with central government pump-priming or financial support. Needless to say, this takes us into the public/private interface where democratic forms of accountability or rights to information as in the 1985 AIA are absent. The 'commercial confidential' escape route will be invoked to ensure that all but a minimum of information about the real nature of decision- making is reported to the public and Parliament.[159] Indeed, an annual report of the London Dockland Development Corporation spoke well of its consultation processes while deprecating the duty to attend public inquiries because of the cost in terms of directors' time.[160]

The Government has argued that the local authority is incapable of adaptation for effective operation in a business environment. Speed and confidentiality are required, along with flexibility of recruitment. Widdicombe noted how criticism of local public/commercial enterprise centres around an absence of openness and accountability.[161] Where local authorities had established such private sector companies, on their initiative or at government insistence,[162] Widdicombe proposed more specific legislation and articles of association, better reporting provisions and audit provisions, and a majority of councillors on such companies. What *degree* of openness will be generated, however?

5

Openness as a Practice or Non-practice

Our discussion so far has centred on the creation and maintenance of secrecy in Government and public administration. A major governmental prerogative concerns its power to control the flow and timing of information. How does Government provide information? The previous two chapters have discussed the emergence and contemporary practice of a secret state. Now we must look at the converse side and examine how much information is provided, and on what terms. My first aim is to inquire into the circumstances in which Government has to declare its position and provide information through political pressure to legitimate its exercise of power. Government intervention and regulation have spawned a wide range of *fora* through which decisions and proposals can be challenged or objected to, in addition to the traditional legal and political structures. This chapter will examine the practices and procedures of open and closed government and to what extent they are advanced or negated by informal networks of relationships within a complex institutional framework. The 'corridors of power', it has been confidently asserted, 'are studded with doors' through which the public, Parliament, the Ombudsman, academia, the press, etc., 'pour in'.[1] What do governments give, and what are they made to give?

It is appropriate under this heading to examine the Data Protection Act 1984. This is an access Act for individuals and it covers both the public and private sectors. On the surface, it appears to be the most comprehensive access legislation we possess. Deeper inquiry reveals problems.

Central Government

Public Records Act
The first point to make is that government papers are available, after

selection, 30 years after they came into existence.[2] Government inquiries frequently produce information in advance of this date which would otherwise remain undisclosed in any detail – the Franks Inquiry into the causes of the Falklands War is an example.[3]

The subject of public records was examined by the Wilson Report of 1981.[4] This found that many documents were not available when administrators or researchers needed them. It was impossible to know whether this was by accident, bad judgment or design. About 99 per cent of public records are destroyed because they are regarded as unimportant.[5] Sir John Donaldson MR has criticised government apathy.[6] Wilson found 'maximum destruction' at the first review of documents after five years, and only at the second review after twenty-five years were historical factors considered. In 1962 the Public Records Office stated that departmental records produced each year amounted to 100 miles of shelving – it received about one mile. Because only one department, Defence, had established a body of academic experts to assist its selection, the Public Records Act established an Advisory Council on Public Records consisting of lawyers, MPs, senior civil servants and historians. It does not advise on selection; departments do: 'Therefore its members have no means of knowing which records have been withheld, and why.' Security papers are not usually transferred. Sensitive information on national security is scrutinised by a Cabinet Office Committee.

Papers which are recommended for extended closure[7] include: 'exceptionally sensitive papers' whose disclosure would be against the public interest; documents containing information supplied in confidence, the disclosure of which would, *or might*, constitute a breach of good faith; personal documents whose disclosure would cause distress or embarrassment to living persons or to their descendants. In 1971, papers of 'political or commercial sensitivity' were added.

The Lord Chancellor has responsibility for public records, and he is not answerable to a departmentally related Select Committee, thereby avoiding effective Parliamentary scrutiny. Where a Lord Chancellor has been a member of a government whose papers are eligible for release, a conflict of interest can arise.[8]

The Cabinet

There are conventions restricting the disclosure by the government of the day of the papers of a previous government without the consent of the previous Prime Minister concerned and the consent of the Queen.[9] A practice also exists whereby Government in office denies itself access to a previous Government's papers if of a different political party. The conventions on release to third parties cover ministerial minutes, and other documents written by a former Minister in the course of his duties are not publicly available. It covers advice to Ministers from their officials. Information in the public domain, such as letters to trade associations, trade unions and MPs, is not included in the Government's self-denial, nor is information known to a foreign government nor the written opinions of law officers. Lord Hunt believed that common sense would bridge the gap between this convention and the need to keep present Ministers informed where 'continuity of knowledge is important', although clearly the fact that civil servants must possess such continuity of knowledge affords them a certain degree of superiority.[10]

If it were felt that a previous Minister's Cabinet papers should be disclosed to his successor, the permission of the former would be sought. A strong plea has been made for an incoming administration to be supplied with sufficient 'information on potential immediate problems and on the difficulties of implementing specific proposals to ward against initial errors during its first year in office'.[11] Difficulties have been caused over specific projects, e.g. Concorde, or constraints of forward commitments on public expenditure and economic policy.[12] It was felt that greater contact should be encouraged between officials and opposition parties than is practised at present, which is usually restricted to discussion of the machinery of government. Any wider practice is regarded as 'taboo'.

The Departments

Tradition in Whitehall dictates that a Minister and not an official must answer inquiries from MPs – although the status of the MP may well be commensurate with the ministerial status of the reply.

A recent report of the Comptroller and Auditor-General[13] indicated that the departments listed in the Table on pages 137–41 published annual reports.

Most of these bodies are not ministerial departments,[14] but non-ministerial and non-departmental bodies.[15] The Department of the Environment (DoE) published an annual report in 1983, but none since. The DoE also introduced MINIS – the Minister's Information

	Number printed (where known)	When published	Reporting period (calendar year except where stated)	Delay before publication (months)	Output and performance measures (output only except where stated)	Information about departmental management (none unless stated)	Audience
ACAS Annual Report	8000	Apr 1986		4	Some	Yes	SoS[4], Parliament, Industrial Relations Practitioners
Annual Review of Agriculture*	3250	Feb 1985		2	Some		Parliament, Farmers
Office of Arts and Libraries*	1100	Jan 1985		1	None		Parliament, Libraries
Certification Officers' Annual Report (ACAS)	3500	Apr 1986		4	Some	Yes	ACAS Chairman, SoS, Industrial Relations Practitioners
Report of the Charity Commission*	1100	June 1985		6	Some		Parliament, Charities
Civil Service College Principals' Annual Report	2000	Aug 1985	Financial Year	5	Comp[4]	Yes	College Advisory Council, Departments
Civil Service Commission*	2500	May 1985		5			The Queen, Public, Staff
The Crown Estate*	904	June 1985	Financial Year	3			The Queen, Public, Landowners
Report of Comm for Customs & Excise*	1350	Nov 1985	Financial Year	8	Comp	Yes	Parliament, Trade interests

Report							
Statement on the Defence Estimates	4410	May 1985	Financial Year	2	Some	Yes	Parliament, Public
Dept of Education & Science Annual Report*	1700	July 1985		7		Yes	Parliament, Libraries, Public
Dept of Environment Annual Report	3000	July 1983	Financial Year	3	Some	Yes	Public
ECGD Trading Results	3000	Oct 1984	Financial Year	6	Some		Parliament, Exporters, Banks
Annual Report of DG[4] of Fair Trading*	1500	May 1985		5			Parliament, Public
Government Actuaries Dept Annual report	400	Mar 1984		3			Actuaries, Public
Health & Safety Commission Annual Report*	2900	Nov 1984	Financial Year	7	Some	Yes	SoS, Employers, Public
The Health Service in England	3800	Nov 1985		11	Comp	Yes	Public, Health Service
Report on the work of Prison Dept*	2500	Dec 1985	[1]	9	Some	Yes	Prison Dept, Public
Report of Comm. of Police for Metropolis*	3000	June 1985		6	Comp		Home Secretary, Public
Report of HM Chief Insp. of Constabulary*	1400	July 1985		7	Some		Home Secretary, Police
Report of HM Chief Insp. for Fire Services*	1200	July 1985		7			Home Secretary, Fire Services

Annual Report under the Industrial Development Act 1982*	1600	Sept 1985	Financial Year	5			Parliament, Public
Report of the Board of Inland Revenue*	3300	July 1985		7	Some	Yes	Parliament, Public, Staff
IBAP Annual Report*	1300	June 1984		6			Parliament, Farmers, Public
Report of the Land Registry*	400	Sept 1984	Financial Year	5	Comp	Yes	Lord Chancellor
Annual Report of the Law Commission*	300	Feb 1986	Nov-Oct	4	Some		Parliament, Public, Legal Profession
Manpower Services Comm Annual Report*	10000	July 1984	Financial Year	3		Yes	SoS, Staff
Dept for National Savings Annual Report	4000	May 1985	Financial Year	1		Yes	Press, Public, Staff
Northern Ireland Agriculture	500	Sept 1983	Financial Year	5	Some		Parliament, Farmers
Ordnance Survey Annual Report	1500	Sept 1984	Financial Year	5		Yes	Dept, Contacts, Special
Property Services Agency Annual Report	15000	Nov 1984	Financial Year	6		Yes	Clients, Contractors, Staff, Public
British Overseas Aid	5000	July 1985		7			Embassies, MPs, British Council
Public Records Office Annual Report*	950	July 1984		7			Lord Chancellor

Public Trustee Annual Report	750	Nov 1984	Financial Year	7	Some		Lord Chancellor, Trust Managers
Registry of Friendly Societies Report*	2000	Sept 1984	Financial Year	5			Parliament, Building Societies
Agriculture in Scotland	1400	June 1982		6	Some		Parliament, Farmers
Prisons in Scotland*	1400	Nov 1984		11			Parliament, Prisons, Public
Report of Ch Insp of Constab for Scotland*	1500	July 1984		7		Yes	SoS, Police, Public
Health in Scotland	750	Sept 1985		9	Some		SoS, Health Service, Public
Report of Ch Insp of Prisons for Scotland	1300	Nov 1984		11			Parliament, Prisons
Rep of Ch Insp of Fire Services for Scotland*	1200	Sept 1984		9	Some	Yes	Parliament, Fire Services
A commentary on the Scotland Programme	500	Feb 1986	Financial Year		Comp	Yes	Parliament, Press, Public
HMSO Annual Report	3500	Oct 1984	Financial Year	6	Some	Yes	Staff, Contractors
Science & Technology Report	6000	Oct 1985	Financial Year	6			Small companies, Graduates

| Annual Report of Council on Tribunals* | 200 | Dec 1985 | August-July | 4 | Public, Clients, Contacts |

Notes

* — Statutory requirement

[1] — Covers the period 1 January 1984 to 31 March 1985. Future reports will be for the relevant financial year.

[2] — Most of the information for this table was gathered in the Autumn of 1985

[3] — In addition to the reports covered here, a number of departments issue management documents. These include:

Cabinet Office/MPO — Management Documents
Customs & Excise — Management Plan
DOE — MINIS documents
Health & Safety Commission — Annual Plan of Work
Inland Revenue — Senior Management System

MAFF — MINIM (Ministerial Information in MAFF)
MSC — Corporate Plan (also separate corporate plan for MSC Scotland and Wales)
OPCS — Financial Management Objectives, Targets and Budgets
DHSS — Divisional Management Accounts
DTp — Departmental Plan

[4] Abbreviations: Comp — Comprehensive
DG — Director General
SoS — Secretary of State

System – to inform the Minister of his departmental administration, but it only gave information on about 1 per cent of annual expenditure in the DoE. MINIS concentrated upon:

systematic annual reviews of objectives, tasks, costs and performance measures; much greater precision in the definition of tasks; much more precise performance measures; more specific attribution of costs and staff numbers to tasks and management functions; presentation of the results to Ministers . . . and publication of the results. The system or its equivalent should be used in departments and made available for public inspection and sent to the public for small cost.

MINIS has been resisted by Government departments; a form of it was, however, extended to the Ministry of Defence. Financial Management Initiatives (FMI) for departments concentrate upon informing managers within departments on the meeting of perform-ance objectives and costs to help ensure their responsibility for the performance of programmes. They have little public dimension apart from being within the purview of departmentally related Select Committees. The Treasury and Civil Service Committee has argued the case vehemently for departmental annual reports to explain policies and provide sensible performance indicators and information on FMIs as a back-up for the general annual reviews.[15a]

Although the Government has published more and more details of its policies and priorities in the form of White Papers[16] and more speculative Green Papers before drafting and publishing Bills where necessary to implement programmes, its efforts are, naturally enough, geared primarily to informing Parliament. In 1977, the then head of the Home Civil Service, Sir Douglas Allen, issued what is known as the Croham Directive urging the publication of more background information behind departments' decisions. The direct-ive had some success,[17] although it was restricted in its objectives as it excluded policy matters, and it was regarded as a dead letter by the incoming Thatcher administration.

Parliament has to assist it the Parliamentary Commissioner for Administration (PCA), who investigates cases referred to him by MPs alleging maladministration in the conduct of a department's affairs where the complainant concerned has been affected, and as a consequence hardship or injustice has been caused. He conducts the investigation in private and has access to all the relevant files and documents; he can interview witnesses and demand information, even from a Minister, and he can take evidence on oath. Where a

Minister believes, and issues a notice, that disclosure of information either in content, or as a class of information or documents, would be prejudicial to the safety of the State or otherwise contrary to the public interest, the PCA must not disseminate the information beyond himself and his officers.[18] He is not allowed access to documents of Cabinet proceedings or of Cabinet Committees. A certificate from the Cabinet Secretary approved by the Prime Minister is conclusive. We shall see that case law has given judges more scope than the PCA, although his powers were to be equal to those of judges *vis-à-vis* investigation and examination.

The PCA is unlikely to require access to Cabinet papers in any event, since his office is shaped to cater for the more routine grievances. On one occasion the Government has found it necessary to issue a certificate on Cabinet documents. This arose out of the PCA's investigation into the *Court Line* episode, which concerned misleading statements made by the Secretary of State in the Commons. The certificate was limited under section 8(4) of the Parliamentary Commissioner Act to the actual transactions of a Cabinet Committee and did not include drafts of its papers. He was informed of the outcome of the Cabinet Committee's discussions and the Minister was interviewed.[19]

Successive Commissioners must be criticised for their limited use of the media and press and the scant publicity which their reports have received. These are presented to the MP who sponsored the complaint, the departmental head, and the person alleged to have taken the action complained of.[20] The PCA presents an Annual Report before both Houses of Parliament and 'such other reports with respect to those functions as he thinks fit'. He compiles quarterly volumes of reports of select cases which are published, and he has power to lay before Parliament a special report where an injustice caused to an individual by maladministration has not been, or will not be, remedied. These reports contain a large amount of information on the day-to-day workings of the Departments of State under his jurisdiction, a service which will doubtless be replicated when the proposals to extend his jurisdiction over certain non-departmental bodies are operational.[21] For most individuals, this information will be of little interest, although it could be of use. It is vital for MPs on the Select Committee on the PCA. The reports of this body and the Select Committees which we examined in the previous chapter and the Public Accounts Committee provide information that would not be published but for their existence. 'For centuries, Parliament has been at the centre of the nation's information network', even if it is not the only centre.[22] How adequately is Parliament informed in order effectively to perform its responsibilities?

Parliament and Information

We have looked at Select Committees before. Parliament as an 'information centre' requires further treatment. There are up to 40,000 Parliamentary Questions (PQs) put to Ministers in a session in Parliament: 'the House debates 7–8 hours a day, five days a week for some 36 weeks a year. The magnitude of information in Hansard is apparent.'[23] MPs are informed by constituents, by civil servants via PQs and Select Committee appearances, by lobbies and interest groups and by their own political parties, by employers and trade unions, by all-party subject groups to which they are members, and so on. MPs have limited resources for back-up staff and so the assistance of the House of Commons library could be invaluable:[24]

There are too many questions and too few staff to guarantee that more than a small number of answers are checked by others before they go to a member. This is in stark contrast to most large organisations, such as the Civil Service or nationalised industries where information sent to Parliament will have been vetted several times.[25]

The library contains official documents which are not published outside Parliament, e.g. the *Instruction Book for the Guidance of the Metropolitan Police* and the *Governors' Handbook* for prison governors. Certain facilities of the library are available for Members of the European Parliament. Peers have their own library. Broadcasting of Commons and Lords proceedings has taken place, in one form or another, since 1968.

Englefield[26] has more recently described Parliamentary proceedings to assess their role in extracting information from Government spokesman on, for instance, the stages of a Government Bill through both Houses and the relevant standing committees, Government and Opposition motions, adjournment debates, the variety of PQs[27] and ministerial statements. During the Committee stage of Bills, it has become usual for MPs to be supplied with more information than previously in the form of Notes on Clauses. These will not include

arguments drafted by civil servants, but they will contain explanations of clauses. Ministers are likely to face oral Questions about
once every four weeks, although every week the Prime Minister has
two sessions of Parliamentary Questions, each lasting about 15
minutes.

In 1970 Parliament, in response to growing demands from MPs
and outside organisations for information, discussed the introduction
of a computer-based information-retrieval system in the Commons
Library. A scheme was introduced in 1980. The data base draws
together most of the existing visible strip indexes on to the Parliamentary on-line computer-based indexing system (POLIS) which is
in the Library. About 60,000 entries a year are added, covering PQs,
private notice questions, debates, bills, statements, reports, evidence,
Treaty series papers, deposited papers from Ministers, departmental
publications (both HMSO and non-HMSO) and unprinted papers.
By the end of April 1985, POLIS had over 190 external organisations
subscribing to its services.[28] The House of Commons Public Information Office receives about 70,000 inquiries per annum and uses
PRESTEL.[29]

The Speaker is the final authority on the admissibility of
questions.[30] It might be claimed that the 'obligation of the Minister
answering to the High Court of Parliament is exactly that of a witness
before the High Court of Justice: to tell the truth, the whole truth and
nothing but the truth',[31] but the analogy is not exact. Parliament is
essentially a talking shop not a court of law, and while Ministers who
mislead or deceive can be treated severely, a Minister who answered
in total candour would be regarded as politically naive. Among the
devices used to curtail the whole truth are: refusing to answer; bland,
inconsequential or partial answers; declaring that the information is
not available in its requested form or that statistics as required are not
kept; timing the answer to avoid embarrassment in the media and
press, e.g. on Christmas Eve; or 'I shall write to the Hon. Member' or
'I shall place the document in the Library'. One example cited by
Christopher Price was a question to the Environment Secretary on (a)
Current and (b) total expenditure of every local authority in England
in 1981/82 showing its estimated final block grant entitlement and
any penalties to be imposed.[32] The Minister replied that he would
write, and sent the raw print-outs from the DoE computer.[33] Price has
argued that a system of rapid assembly of information in questions
(PQs) in a form in which it can be extracted and used has not been

maintained. Neither MPs, the Library nor specialist lobbies have yet assembled the resources to utilise effectively the more informative answers to PQs. This point has been repeated by the director of a public relations company, who wrote that 'there had been no systematic review of how citizens can obtain information from either their Legislature or Executive'.[34] A growing number of lobbyists from commercial and voluntary organisations have obtained passes to gain access to the Votes Office and Sales Office of the House of Commons and Lords for documents not published by HMSO, and this has led to fears of favouritism and abuse. The following were suggested:

1. A list of types of documents whose publication and general availability would be beneficial should be agreed.
2. A sales point, outside the Palace of Westminster, should be established, where all these documents would be available to personal callers, or for telephone or mail order.
3. The sales point should publish a list of all daily documents available which would itself be available on a subscription basis – a significant expansion of HMSO daily lists.

While these would not solve every problem, these suggestions would, it is submitted, be a useful addition.

In February 1988, the House of Commons voted to allow an experimental period of TV broadcasting of its proceedings. Its impact on the conduct of the House will be a fascinating study.

Parliament and Expenditure – A Case Study

The role of departmental Select Committees in examining the expenditure programmes of related departments has been viewed as disappointing. The accusation has been made that the examination of finance requires painstaking discussion of detail and analysis, and that most MPs do not care about and/or are not very good in this role.[35]

Government requires money – lots of it. The most effective way to oversee Government is to know how much it is spending and on what. Constitutional fundamentals,[36] such as they are, have dictated that Parliament should authorise and oversee expenditure and the raising of revenue. The Comptroller and Auditor-General has agreed that the lay person who wishes to be informed of expenditure in central or local government should be assisted by way of reports and explanations. However, the prime recipient should be Parliament or elected members of local government.[37] For MPs, there is a 'mountain of estimates, accounts, reports and other material produced in ever-increasing volume on all aspects of public business'.[38] However, 'the quantity of information made available is frequently not matched by its quality', nor is it made available at the right time, and there is 'a significant lack of analysis and statement of objectives, and those to whom information is directed often have neither the will nor the organisation to make the best use of it'.

Accountability, either by way of *ex ante* control or *ex post facto* scrutiny, depends upon information.

The fundamental requirement is the provision of the right information, at the right time, to the right people, as a basis for timely and effective action. In this context there is little benefit in information for its own sake. It has value only where it is provided for a clear and defined purpose. Clear objectives are needed both by those supplying the information and by those receiving it.[39]

From this the Comptroller, Sir Gordon Downey, believed two questions flowed: Does Parliament get the information it needs? Does Parliament make effective use of the information it gets – or could get? There are three basic documents covering the first question:

1. The Public Expenditure White Paper – a Government forward-planning document.
2. The Supply Estimates presented to Parliament by Ministers for the former to approve, which they always do.
3. The Appropriation Accounts, showing how actual spending has compared with the Estimates approved.

All these documents, Sir Gordon has said, are 'seriously flawed'.[40] The first is not priced in real terms, and there is no 'ready means of directly linking the expenditure plans with the Supply Estimates on which Parliament exercises its function of control'. The Estimates ignore 'incalculable capital assets and other resources acquired and paid for in recent years'. The Accounts will reveal a purely technical overspending of voted expenditure – however small. They will leave Parliament ignorant on the effects on health care of hospital spending of almost £10 billion per annum.[41] The answer may not lie in more and more information in the Estimates and Accounts but in 'publishing more annual reports on Departments and their operations, as a vehicle for a more analysed and selective account of their activities and achievements against plans and objectives'. This would better inform not only Parliament, but the public who wished to know.

On Parliament's ability to handle the information, the CAG was equally pessimistic. Supply debates were rarely used for supply itself, and even 'the relatively recent change to link debates with certain nominated Estimates does little to provide any coherent coverage of the aims, purpose and objectives of the major funds involved. . . . A Parliament which *de facto* gives up its control of Supply gives up much of its constitutional control of government and accountability.'[42] Parliament as a whole lacks the resources and expertise to use the information it can extract. But this is to overlook the Committee of Public Accounts (PAC). This draws on the work of the National Audit Office and its 800 or so staff. Under the National Audit Act 1983:

The NAO has direct and independent access to documents, records and information in all Government Departments, and produces a series of analysed reports dealing with the efficiency, economy and effectiveness with which Departments have used their resources.

The PAC is the most developed form of *ex post facto* accountability of departmental administration that we possess, the Comptroller and Auditor-General believed. It will be examined shortly. One pertinent point concerned the role of Financial Management Initiatives, which we examined elsewhere, and which are used internally by departments to set clearer objectives, better management arrangements, effective incentives and improved output measures and performance indicators: 'a natural development would be to see it coupled with external reporting arrangements to Parliament which would provide additional assurance and information for selective Parliamentary follow up as necessary.'[43]

Local government is not covered by the 1983 Act, but by the Local Government (Finance) Act 1982 which established the Audit Commission. Nor are nationalised industries under the 1983 Act. Satisfactory accountability is still a matter 'on the table' and was likely to be achieved by an 'agreed partnership' between industry chairmen, Ministers and Parliment. The omens from the past are not good if nationalised industry reports are anything to go by.[44] Nor should we regard privatisation as a process which will rid essential industries of secretive governmental influence and direction in the expectation that private business is not public business and therefore has no constitutional dimension to it.[45] In relation to nationalised industries four points were essential:

1. The need to improve the quality of information, particularly on output related to pre-set aims, performance and results.
2. The need for Parliament to define its own needs and to develop its own organisation and resources to deal effectively with the information it receives.
3. The need to review the extent of accountability to Parliament for public expenditure.
4. The need for a changed culture away from governmental secrecy, over-caution, fear of unfavourable facts or potentially unwelcome conclusions about plans, objectives and results.

Sir Gordon's article was succeeded by a National Audit Office Report to Parliament on Financial Reporting to Parliament.[46] This report amplified many of the points already made, e.g. only 34 of 184 introductory notes to the 1986–87 Estimates commented on the level of service provided, and the report noted the Treasury's argument that a volume basis giving an indication of service levels would undermine the cash basis of planning.[47] The report also noted the antiquated nature of supply procedure and documents informing Parliament of expenditure proposals and accounts, and which are:

1. *Financial Statement and Budget Report* (FSBR), which sets out the Budget, short-term economic forecast and Medium Term Financial Strategy which provides the framework for economic policy for up to five years ahead.
2. *Annual Statement*, usually published each November, which sets out the Treasury's latest economic forecast and the planning totals for the next three years, and provides the broad departmental allocations of expenditure which has been agreed during the Public Expenditure Survey (PES).[48]
3. *Public Expenditure White Paper* (PEWP), which covers the whole of the public sector and is published in January. It provides a more detailed expenditure plan for each public expenditure department, looking three years ahead with estimated and actual outturn of the latest six years.

4. *Supply Estimates* (above), derived from the Public Expenditure Survey and the White Paper. The Main Estimates are presented in March.[49]

5. *Appropriation Accounts* – the end of the cycle, published in the autumn after the end of the financial year. Audited by the Comptroller and Auditor-General (CAG), they can include the CAG reports.

The National Audit Office is critical of the Public Expenditure White Paper on the following grounds. There is no distinction between aims (high-level) and objectives (specific planned achievements), and these terms are used interchangeably. Objectives tend not to be qualified, although some are targeted, e.g. the Department of Transport's target that 90 per cent of driver vehicle licensing applications should be processed within ten days. Targets concentrate on manpower rather than target *achievement*. Aims and objectives are not complete, e.g. not all functional lines within departments are covered and only 46 per cent of functional lines have sections of text which contain aims and objectives. Lastly, even where aims and objectives are well defined, it can still be difficult to relate these to the programme structure.

In general, Introductory Notes to Votes in the Estimates are bland or vapid. An absence of figures in volume terms, *how much* service is provided, meant that assessment of levels of service was impossible. Yet Parliament based its supply on assumptions of levels of service, and 'it is arguable that it should also receive systematic outturn information on the levels actually received'. The rules on departmental audit are set out, but what is missing is an express formulation of the principles to rationalise the rules. Neither Accounts nor Estimates set out clearly enough whether objectives were realised and what the aims of expenditure in substance are.

Research commissioned by the National Audit Office[50] to investigate Parliamentary use of the Estimates and Appropriation Accounts found that Select Committees did not find it generally worthwhile or productive to perform systematic scrutinies of the Main Estimates and only the PAC seemed to use Accounts positively in consideration of CAG reports. Methods used to select Estimates for scrutiny varied from consultation between clerks and specialist advisers, to direct lobbying after a reduction in service.

From the reports there emerges a general agreement that not only is more information required for Parliament, but it is not using that which it receives as efficiently as it ought if it takes accountability seriously. The NAO recommended:

1. The Public Expenditure White Paper retains its status as a document for public expenditure, planning and overall control, setting out the Government's spending plans within the framework of the medium-term financial strategy.
2. Estimates should include better information on objectives and targets for all major sub-heads, and should be supplemented by information elsewhere to enable Parliament to examine and approve Supply Expenditure.
3. Departmental annual reports should round off the cycle. Comment upon these has been made above, although the Government is not persuaded that a uniform system is required for reporting.

Behind this information and its shortcomings lies the Public Expenditure Survey Committee. This is too detailed and complex a programme to describe here,[51] but it concerns the wrangling and horse-trading within and between departments and the Treasury over prospective items and levels of expenditure. The process ends up with the 'Star Chamber' of senior Cabinet Ministers who arbitrate on contested bids. The completed results will contribute to the Autumn Budget Statement.

The Comptroller and Auditor-General (CAG) and the Public Accounts Committee (PAC)

The primary responsibility of the CAG is to examine the accounts of designated bodies and to issue reports for the PAC of the House of Commons. As we have noted, the reports of the CAG have been accused of being 'unambitious', 'constrained' and 'coded', and of failing to explain causes and effects. The CAG cannot examine 'policy' itself, only the impact and expenditure implications and value-for-money aspects of departmental programmes. Instead of reporting boldly, giving substantial reasons, 'The CAG has preferred to work discreetly, through informal pressure within Departments, and to give time and opportunity for people to remedy the weaknesses themselves'. The CAG responded[52] that his reports were checked by departments and had to avoid political controversy in their tone.

They were prepared for the PAC, which is a formal and businesslike body with more extensive powers than any other Select Committee. The Accounting Officer, usually a Permanent Secretary, has to appear before it, and it has access to all necessary information – providing the department possesses it.[53] In defence procurement and pharmaceutical production, the departments do not have all the information that the PAC would like, as we have seen elsewhere.[54] The flow of information often relates to the symbiotic relationship between the department and the trade association or manufacturing company. Elsewhere the PAC has criticised the Ministry of Defence in particular for failing to give information on the accounts of bodies in advance of a proposed privatisation.[55] This takes us to a further problem.

Alice in Quangoland

Governments do not exist in splendid isolation. They stand at the apex of the administrative structure of the State. They have to rely upon others in the public and private sector to help promote, administer and deliver governmental programmes. In the case of resort to public corporations to administer or regulate an area of activity, the statute usually does not reveal the real relationship between a Minister and the chairman of a management board of a nationalised industry, a relationship which operates behind the scenes. The same is true of a corporation established by Royal Charter, although the charter is invariably supposed to recognise and preserve a body's independence from Government. The charter will describe and define the body's objects, constitution and powers to govern its own affairs, although as we saw in the previous chapter with the BBC, the formal terms of the charter may not reflect the reality of its operations.

Advisory bodies are usually set up by administrative/ministerial *fiat*, and although the 'Minister concerned should inform Parliament of his action in establishing an advisory body; a Written Answer to a P.Q. is usually sufficient'.[56] Legislation will be necessary where advisory bodies will require significant continuing government funding. They inevitably advise in confidence. Royal Commissions are advisory bodies of a formal and prestigious nature appointed by Royal Warrant of the Crown issued through the appropriate

Secretary of State. The reports are published as Command Papers laid before Parliament. The reasons for establishing such a body are diverse.[57] Functions can be hived off by creating a corporate body under the Companies Acts, although Parliamentary approval should usually be sought before departmental responsibilities are hived off in this way. 'Departments will need, in the absence of legislation, to devise suitable arrangements to ensure that Ministers have sufficient information about, and control over, the companies' activities.' This has been true in some privatisation programmes which have seen sponsoring Ministers retaining a significant degree of influence over companies via the Memoranda and Articles of Association and special holdings of 'golden shares' and the like.[58] The last category concerns bodies which are private but which enter into close and detailed working relationships with the State. Trade associations, the Confederation of British Industry, multinational and national companies, professional associations, trade unions and pressure groups come to mind. The means adopted by Government to achieve its policy objectives are of crucial significance.

If, however, a non-departmental advisory body is acting as a *de facto* executive body, details of the arrangements will rarely be forth-coming. The relationship is one of confidentiality between the Minister and his advisers. Important features of the operation of such bodies will not be within the formal terms of reference of ministerial responsibility. More secluded will be the operations of such bodies and their relationships with organised interests and the network of multi-layered pluralistic or corporatist relationships which sprout from their existence. Government needs advice, assistance and information from specialist professional, commercial or industrial concerns. In return, a trade-off may be bartered around degrees of self-regulation and administration and exclusive rights to enter into certain areas of exploitation, or utilisation of resources may be offered. Governors deem this to be in the public interest. The point is, if, for instance, wealth creation is the only or the pre-eminent criterion of public interest, do we know that wealth is actually being created where information is not forthcoming or adequate? If 'private' bodies operating in the public interest are not subject to the pressures of democratic accountability, because they do not have to account for what they are doing on the public behalf,[59] are forms of accountability based upon commercial practice and accountancy practice adequate? These might inform us of financial accountability. But what of social and political accountability?[59a] Who should know, and how much?

In the field of competition policy we have the Office of Fair Trading (OFT), the Monopolies and Mergers Commission (MMC), and the Secretary of State for Trade and Industry. The City Panel on Take-Overs and Mergers has recently been ruled to be susceptible to judicial review even though ostensibly a private body in form, but the impact of that decision is marginal to our present concern. The OFT would like to possess fuller powers to get at the books and obtain information from the business concerns it investigates and keeps under review.[60] The MMC carries out formal hearings in private,[61] and it has recently been the defendant in court proceedings when it proposed to give documentation to the take-over target of the bidding company's proposed merger, including that part of the latter's confidential submission dealing with future financing plans and tactics apropos of the take-over bid.[62] It was 'entirely unprecedented for a company to have to hand over such documentation to the bid for company for the latter to comment upon'. A sniff of this sensitivity was repeated when a report by the Stock Exchange into the share-dealings surrounding the take-over of Westland plc in early 1986 was not published, even though the report might be instrumental in formulating new Stock Exchange rules.[63] Much of the work of the OFT and MMC is geared towards putting the Government in a good bargaining position to extract undertakings from private and indeed public bodies to avoid open proceedings in court. The scene is set, in other words, for off-the-record deals to pursue the public interest. What Government wants is information, knowledge or favours; what regulated bodies or those on exclusive licences receive is akin to favouritism. Is the trade-off really in the public interest? How do we know? What quality of information have we got? What should we strive for? Where does political responsibility begin and market responsibility end? This is of lasting significance regardless of whether Government seeks to privatise public markets and assets as at present, or whether it seeks the co-operation of vested interests in the economy such as employers or trade associations or trade unions and the like, or whether it buys out essential industries in the private sector while still seeking to gain the benefits of commercial con-fidentiality and official secrecy in their undertakings. The problems relating to the trade-offs on information and power were identified with the Government and interest group interface in a classic passage from Beer's *Modern British Politics*:[64]

... The needs of the class or interest in question should be considered not simply because they are legitimized by the design of the good society, but also because this element (whether stratum or lesser community) carries out a function important to the social whole. This justifies giving it power to protect itself. ... it also means that the knowledge of those performing this function may well be necessary for the good governing of the wider community. They have special skills, experience, expertise which government must have at hand if it is to understand and control the complex and interdependent social whole. ... a special emphasis is given to this need by the conditions of government in modern industrial society. As control extends into the complex and technical affairs of the economy, government must win the cooperation of crucial sectors and show sensitivity to their values and purposes. Not least, it must elicit their expert advice. These sectors are the seats of technical, professional, and scientific knowledge indispensable to effective policy making. ... For the proponents of functional representation in modern times, this contribution is especially 'knowledge'.

A particularly significant example of this was apparent in the way the Government wishes to use the accountancy profession not simply as guarddogs but as bloodhounds and retrievers for the Bank of England when checking the books of banks and other financial institutions in their audit. The Government settled for a non-statutory scheme whereby the profession would inform the Bank of England of any irregularities. This would take the profession outside its usual 'confidential' relationship with its clients. It was notable that contemporaneously the profession sought legislative immunity from negligence suits in respect of its members' auditing of books.

The Government's action was prompted by the collapse of a merchant bank and the initiation of new financial markets after the relaxation of restrictive practices in the Stock Exchange and elsewhere.[65] The British Bankers' Association remonstrated with the Government, pointing out that it was wrong for the Bank of England to pass on information it received to government departments other than the Treasury. 'Customers are entitled to expect their affairs to be kept secret unless there are cogent reasons to the contrary.'[66] Similar protestations were uttered by the City's support for government proposals to limit the amount of information that has to be given on a shareholders' or members' register.[67] These are documents which are difficult to obtain and invariably obscure.[68] The registrar, usually a clearing bank, is inevitably reluctant to allow even cursory glances at the register without a reference to the secretary of the company in question. Certainly requests to take notes or subject the information to detailed scrutiny would have to be accompanied by detailed reasons in writing. The law merely requires a fee, which is discretionary, and 10 days' notice. One request about British Telecom revealed that 28 per cent of share capital was held by unnamed corporate bodies.[69] A Department of Trade and Industry paper has suggested the end of annual returns to Companies House, and only those shareholders with more than 1 per cent of share capital should have to register. The powers of the Securities Investment Board to provide and demand information in the regulation of the securities industry will doubtless be watched with interest[70] in the late 1980s to see how it oversees regulation in the newly 'liberated' financial markets.

Non-statutory bodies frequently distribute information on behalf of the Government. A typical example is the non-statutory training organisations which are established by industries and which disseminate information on training schemes and reports on various activities, often in close alliance with the Manpower Services Commission. Conversely, the Director-General of Telecommunications has a duty to encourage the preparation of codes by associations to help safeguard customers' information.

While some voluntary organisations have been active or vociferous in their support of FOI legislation,[71] the Press Council, surprisingly (or perhaps not),[72] has not been active on FOI, nor on reform of contempt, libel or obscenity laws. The Council is a self-regulatory body for the press industry and its reputation is not one to be envied.

Local Government

Local government is local, elected and increasingly under statutory obligations to be open to the public and the press.[73] Where central government gives information, it is invariably as an act of grace and favour or instrumental necessity. In the world of quasi-government, there is no elected representation, no public voting and no political accountability, and very rarely are there duties to inform the public in even the most exiguous of terms of what is being carried out on the public behalf. It is worthwhile noting these points when we consider the range of non-departmental bodies the Government has created, and the close links it has attempted to forge with organised interests, usually of a commercial, financial or engineering nature, to rejuvenate the economic infrastructure; to assure responsibility for education programmes; to exploit the removal of planning restrictions, and to administer housing schemes. Democratic involvement is not on the agenda, and indeed the democratic nature of local government is a reason for that tier of government being excluded from governmental responsibilities if it will not operate as a business manager. As one chief executive expressed it: 'We are being pressed to become like commercial organisations, yet what commercial organisations are being pressed to become as open as local authorities?'

Local government will not disappear. In our constitutional design it poses very particular problems of openness and information. Its record, as we saw, is mixed. We should not assume that all senior officers and leading members of local government are advocates of open government. A chief executive expressed the quintessential conflict between serious open political debate and public access to meetings as follows:

I have serious reservations about the current craze for so called Open Government. It is my considered opinion, and I believe it is the opinion of many of my colleagues, that the quality of debate and the quality of decision making in local authority committees has fallen very very considerably ever since, with the coming into operation of the Local Government Act 1972, the press and public have been admitted to committees. There is no doubt whatsoever that not only do members play to the gallery and spend far more time scoring cheap political points off each other than ever they did before, but perhaps even more importantly Officers are reluctant now to come out with ideas and to enter debate with the same freedom that they were prepared to do when the committee was closed, and there was no risk of seeing a headline in the local paper 'Chief Executive Clashes with Opposition Leader etc.' I also believe it is true to say that as a result of this so called open government, far more decisions are now in fact taken in private than ever was the case before.

This raises the question of the cost of freedom of information legislation, which was alluded to in Chapter 1. The quality of decision-making falls as rational input from professional officials declines and politicians engage increasingly in point-scoring and being seen to be effective by sectional interests whom they represent, rather than by the community as a whole. The chief executive quoted above described a climate which was not conducive to the giving of advice in public with commitment and candour. Decisions were becoming less influenced by professionals and were far more frequently the result of informal agreement between political heavyweights in group meetings. As a consequence, the quality of decisions had dropped enormously. This was the price of openness. There was less real or meaningful debate of the underlying issues, interests and implications in decisions. The views of the chief executive deserve respect, and we will encounter their analogues in central government in Chapter 7. In other words, efficiency was deleteriously affected. It is well to remember, however, that in the period before committees were opened to the public there were widespread examples of corruption in local government, and countless examples of arbitrary decisions riding rough-shod over local views where secrecy assisted unresponsive government.

There are numerous and important statutory duties imposed on authorities to provide information to central government, the Audit Commission, the Commissioner for Local Administration, members of authorities and the public. I have conducted research on these provisions, and this is published in detail elsewhere.[74] Authorities' duties to publicise information for comparative purposes on man-power, levels of service, accounts and rates under sections 2–4 of the Local Government, Planning and Land Act 1980 were examined in their operation. The style and format of reports varied enormously, 'reflecting the individual styles and commitment to open communication of the individuals who wrote the material, prepared it and presented it, as well as the local authority concerned'. Some were impressive documents, but virtually all respondents said that public reaction was apathetic. Only one of 32 reports studied contained information about what to do if one were dissatisfied with a service and wished to complain to the authority or subsequently to the Commissioner for Local Administration. The CLA has said that the annual report is an appropriate place in which such information should be conveyed, although this suggestion has met with no support from central government[75] or the local authority associations.

One chief executive put the point eloquently in expressing his frustration at the lack of public feedback:

I think we are all a bit cynical of the worth of the information in terms of public consumption. I would dearly love to receive searching questions from the public about information contained in our Annual Report . . . but in the three years we have been publishing a report I have received no feedback from the public whatsoever.

A few comments are in order. The provisions seem to owe more to political populism on the part of central government than to any rational design to make government more open and accountable. The Government envisages a ratepayer assiduously filing through dry details, comparing his authority's performance with that of other authorities so that he can register his objections. There has been no real effort to sort out what the public wants to know; no real attempt to break down unresponsive bureaucracy where it exists to local government. It is, in short, political buck-passing. If the intention to open up government had been serious, then more work should have been carried out to test the market, by the authorities concerned and by independent assessors. The comments on sections 2–4 from chief executives are pertinent for any subsequent FOIA involving central government:

There are scant minimum requirements for disclosure of information by encouragement or discouragement. For the most part the problem is about interpretation, practice, attitudes or defensiveness on the part of councillors as well as officials. Few local authorities have systematically set out to research the market to test the demand for more information, or its quality. [As] far as I know none has really taken a conscious decision to aim information at the broadest group of people, and to employ all available skills and resources to that end in the way that a newspaper does, or T.V. or radio do. In many areas where there are ethnic minorities, the problems of communication are particularly acute. Legislation is largely irrelevant. Will and attitude are far more important.

The following examples of open practices and provision of information irrespective of statutory duties (and before the 1985 Access to Information legislation) were provided in the responses. As well as free newspapers, reports mentioned local meetings, decentralised committees and co-option on to council committees, and a wider publication than necessary for planning applications (e.g. all were placed in the local press). Mention was also made of a quarterly town forum and an internal appeals/complaints structure for most licensing decisions; a rent arrears panel had been established to act in an advisory and counselling capacity towards tenants in arrears, and panels also existed in other social service fields. Frequent meetings were cited for General Improvement Areas (GIA)[76] on both an individual and a group basis. Some authorities said they had designated senior officers, or sometimes Chief Officers, to meet group deputations or to deal with more persistent complainants. It has to be said that previous research had found local authorities to be

somewhat deficient in providing opportunities for public participation in decision-making on, e.g. urban renewal, GIA or Housing
Action Areas'[77] programmes, school and education management or
structure plan exercises, or in the provision of obvious accessible
complaints procedures for disgruntled citizens, electors, etc.[78] One
reply to the question said, 'Yes – it is our practice and no details are
necessary.' One metropolitan county authority[79] allowed any
member of the Council to introduce and speak to a petition for two
minutes. It will then be referred to the appropriate committee and
placed on the agenda of the next meeting, and the member is able to
attend, obtain all necessary information and speak to the matter. In
one authority visited, the Chief Legal Officer described a comprehensive internal complaints procedure for complaints which a
member has been asked to refer to the Ombudsman. The officer,
however, had not heard of the Code of Practice on Complaints
Procedures issued by the Commission for Local Administration.[80] It
is of interest to note that a High Court judge recently ruled that the
holding of extra meetings beyond statutory requirements might be
desirable where the authority is obliged by law to be seen to be acting
fairly. In the case in question, the authority was granting planning
permission in circumstances where it had a direct interest.[81] At the
more formal level of procedures where something has gone badly
awry, or appears to have done, authorities have been advised on how
to proceed by ad hoc inquiries in preference to statutory ones.[82]

As a general point, the better authorities provide information and
are relatively open. But they are a minority, as is shown by recent
work detailing the number of authorities who publicise grievance
procedures.[83] When statute has been introduced it tends to leave too
much to goodwill, or it tends to over-formalise without giving
adequate training, which can lead to legalism, delay and woodenness.
Appeal provisions in the Education Act 1980, which allow parents the
opportunity to appeal against a school allocation decision by an
authority which affects their child, are pertinent. Appeal committees
must be established by Local Education Authorities, and the
chairman must not be a member of the authority's education
committee. The procedure is spelt out in Part II of Schedule II of the
Act and Codes of Practice, and provides for oral presentation of a case
– with representation if desired, private hearings and written
communication of decisions. Certain criteria have to be considered by
the panel. Section 8 of the Act concerns the provision of information

about schools and admission arrangements and imposes a range of duties on LEAs and governors, etc., to publish their arrangements and policies on admissions to schools, details of the number of places available at schools, as well as details of Appeal Panels. Regulations have provided for publication of school examination results, school rules and discipline and other information as required.

These provisions are heavily used and, it was felt by senior education officers,[84] by the more vociferous, articulate and pushy parents for reasons which are entirely selfish and which are often detrimental to the overall welfare of parents and children and the educational policies of the authority. A decision of the High Court will have exacerbated these apprehensions.[85] The philosophy of the Act is one of an open-market freedom of choice, though only a minority of the more articulate will benefit and no extra cost to the public purse will ensue. This should be compared with the 1981 Education Act, which concerned children whose parents or guardians wished them to be assessed for Special Education Needs (SEN), relating for example to a disability. The LEA must notify a parent if it proposes making an assessment of the SEN of a child, informing them of the procedure; of an officer from whom information may be obtained; and of the parents' right to make representations and submit written evidence. If an assessment is made, a decision with reasons must be given to the parent. If an SEN assessment leads to no provision of special facilities, appeal lies to the Secretary of State, who may direct the LEA to reconsider. If an authority decides that an SEN determination should be made, it makes a statement of the child's SEN. A dissatisfied parent may make further representation to the authority and can require meetings and further meetings with the LEA. Appeals from this stage are to the Appeals Panel established under the 1980 Act (above) against the statement of the SEN, and because their decision is not binding on the LEA as under the 1980 Act, further appeal lies to the Secretary of State.

Recent reports have suggested that the Act is very difficult to invoke,[86] unlike the 1980 Act. It should be noted that the 1981 Act will involve additional expenditure, unlike the marginal cost of the 1980 Act for central government, although local authorities will have to administer the Act. The reports indicate that too little information is given to parents, or it is provided piecemeal at each of the numerous stages outlined above, leaving parents at a disadvantage because they are unsure what happens next. Only a third of LEAs described in one document all the basic procedural steps for assessment.[87] Many authorities discouraged parents' utilising their rights under the Act. Studies promoted by the Department of Education and Science[88] reveal that the Act involved too much paperwork and too little available information and co-operation among the departments and professionals. The 1981 Act was promoted as an Act that would require little money to administer. This is patently not the case. Procedures require skill, training, understanding and instruction. Legislation does not work by itself, however much central government might wish that it did. Authorities, likewise, were not provided with additional funding for the 1985 Access to Information Act, because it was claimed that there were few financial implications. This either reveals a belief that the Act would not be utilised or simple disingenousness, since central government has persistently claimed that cost is one of the major reasons against establishing FOIA for itself. Not all the blame is central government's, for in the question-naire returns on the 1981 Act, only 10 LEAs sent detailed documents for parental consumption. A large majority had such documents, but only for internal consumption by the LEA.[89]

Beyond the Scope of Duty

We examined the effects of the Local Government (Access to Information) Act 1985 in the previous chapter. Some authorities had gone further than the provisions of the Act and are still more open than the Act enjoins. The Association of London Authorities has asserted that decisions based on inadequate reasoning or information must be open to scrutiny and challenge and has insisted that greater openness enhances equality of opportunity by paving the way for greater public participation, particularly for those who have historic-ally suffered discrimination.[90] Members of the public, it continues, should have internal rights of appeal where information is refused; the public should be allowed to ask questions at council meetings and make deputations to the Council, and the timing and location of meetings should take account of the needs of all sections of the community, particularly those disadvantaged because of special needs. Personal manual files should be available, as are computer files, although here events have been partly overtaken by the Access to Personal Files Act which we examine in the concluding chapter. Authorities should have a complaints procedure for any grievance raised by a member of the public which should include a right of appeal to a body with a preponderant councillor component. Information on the Commissioner for Local Administration, the Data Protection Registrar and Tribunal (see below) should be readily available and well publicised. As well as urging the use of plain language the Association enjoins all members and chief officers to complete a comprehensive declaration of interests from which authorities will compile a public register of interests. The Charter is already operational in some London boroughs and requires declarations of pecuniary and personal interests. In the case of committees, refusal to comply means members will not be appointed to sit on committees. This had led to litigation where the stipulation was held *intra vires*.[91] The Charter stipulates that training for these new duties is essential and that there should be annual performance review exercises by committees of their obligations under the Charter.[92] Elsewhere, authorities have established methods to review performance in service areas, to gauge satisfaction or otherwise and to improve performance, an exercise which is based on being fully informed of what is happening in a service area.[93]

Not all authorities, or their associations, have been as positive. One has called in the police to remove a council member who claimed he had a right to be at a meeting of the working group which he claimed was a committee.[94] The Government has condemned such practices as 'partisan', restricting 'the ability of individual councillors and minority groups to participate fully in policy formulation devices aimed at preventing free and effective access to information' and keeping information provision at a minimum. What is sauce for the goose surely . . .[95]

A National Code of Local Government Conduct is in existence and deals, *inter alia*, with the disclosure of pecuniary and other interests.[96] The law provides for the disclosure of pecuniary interests by members – the Code seeks to cover other interests which may interfere or conflict with a councillor's public duties. Rule 6 says: 'As a councillor you necessarily acquire much information that has not yet been made public and is still confidential. It is a grave betrayal of trust to use confidential information for the personal advantage of yourself or anyone you know.' Breach of the Code could constitute maladministration.[97] Widdicombe, in addition to the reforms which he advocated and which were examined in the previous chapter, recommended that councillors should not have a right to inspect documents in which they have a pecuniary interest if those documents are not open to public inspection. The Code, he suggested, should be amended to indicate that councillors hold office by virtue of the law, and sectional loyalties, as well as private gain, may create conflict with councillors' public duties, and that *all* councillors should be statutorily required to have regard to the Code as part of their statutory declaration on accepting office.[98] As we saw elsewhere, Widdicombe's proposals amount to a Bill of Rights for those affected by local government administration. But can anyone honestly argue that what is good for local government is not applicable *a fortiori* to central government? The buck has been well and truly passed. This was also the case with the Access to Personal Files Act which the Government restricted to local authority housing and social service departments and which I will examine in the concluding chapter.

The Data Protection Act was not so restricted, and applied to every holder of personal computerised data in the public or private sector. It is a major access statute and will be a significant development of openness as a practice or, as I shall indicate, a non-practice.

The Data Protection Act 1984 (DPA)

In the literature of political science there is a phrase which describes the rationality crisis when the State can no longer cater for all the tasks which its regulation has created. This is known as 'administrative overload'. The Data Protection Act might be described as Parliament's first step to deal with 'information overload'. The Act is only concerned with personal information or data.

It has to be emphasised that computerised information is subject to the same control and availability as manual information, except to the extent that it is available under the DPA. If within a government department there is computerised data covered by the Official Secrets Acts and not exempt from prosecution by virtue of the DPA, unauthorised disclosure could result in prosecution.[99] If it is a question of Parliament being informed of the data held by Government or its agencies, whatever limitations apply to Parliament's ability to obtain information from the Government will apply here also.[100] Data constitutes property, although the complexities involved in the legal classification of concepts conveying appropriate rights and protection have caused, and will cause, legal disputation of a more than usually complex nature.[101]

The DPA was passed primarily to incorporate into British law the provisions of the European Convention on Data Protection 1981.[102] Had the Convention not been incorporated, the flow of data into the UK from other signatory states might well have been prohibited.

Section 1 of the Act defines 'data' and related terms. 'Data' means information recorded in a form in which it can be processed by equipment operating automatically in response to instructions given for the purpose. 'Personal data' means data consisting of information which related to a living individual (the subject) who can be identified from that information (or from that and other information in the possession of the data user), 'including any expression of opinion about the individual but not any indication of the intentions of the data user in respect of that individual'.[103] Section 2 establishes the Data Protection Principles which can be added to, or modified, to add additional safeguards to personal data on racial origin; political opinion or religious or other beliefs; physical or mental health or sex life and criminal convictions. Schedule I contains the principles.

Information in personal data shall be obtained and processed lawfully and fairly and must be held only for *specified* and *lawful* purposes. It shall not be used or disclosed in any way which is incompatible with those purposes. It must be adequate, relevant and not excessive in relation to the purpose(s) specified, and be accurate and where necessary kept up to date, nor must it be kept for longer than necessary for those purpose(s). Further, an individual 'shall be entitled – at reasonable intervals and without undue delay or expense' to be informed by any data user whether he holds personal information about him and, if so, he must have access to such data. Where appropriate, the individual shall be entitled to have such data corrected or erased. Data users[104] must take appropriate security measures to prevent unauthorised access to, alteration, disclosure, destruction or accidental loss or destruction of personal data. The Schedule[105] contains some details on the interpretation of the principles. These state, in relation to obtaining data fairly and lawfully, for instance, that 'regard shall be had to the method by which it was obtained, including in particular' whether any deception or misleading statement was made as to its purpose. Information is to be treated 'in any event' as obtained fairly if obtained from a person who 'is authorised by or under any enactment to supply it'. The 'specified purpose' in relation to the second principle must be described in particulars relating to the data and registered under the Act.

The Act creates the Data Protection Registrar and the Data Protection Tribunal (DPT). Data users holding personal data must be registered with the DPR, who maintains the register. Users had to be registered by 10 May 1986. By January 1987, the DPR estimated that 100,000 data holders, including public bodies, had not registered.[106] The DHSS was the last of the government departments to register.[107] The register of data users was expected to run to about 500,000 pages and is stored on computer at the DPR's central office. A pilot version and a printed index of user names are available on microfiche at local libraries. The budget of the DPR is £2 million, and in April 1987 he had 45 full-time staff. These seem sparse resources to fulfil such an onerous regulatory activity. In a survey conducted by the Registrar, although there was a far greater public desire for privacy, less than one-third of those surveyed had heard of the Registrar.[108] Concern over the legislation has been fuelled by Treasury pressure to charge subjects a 'realistic price' of £40–£50 for a search of a user's systems. This would be greatly in excess of the £3–£8 maximum predicted by the Home Office Minister in the Standing Committee on the Bill.[109]

Each entry on the register has to contain certain particulars: the name and address of users; a description of the personal data and the purpose of holding or using it; a description of the source(s); a description of the recipients; and 'one or more addresses for the receipt of requests from data subjects for access to the data'. Personal data can only be held if registered and in the description specified and for the purposes described. Applicants for registration must specify which category of user they wish to be classified under, viz. data user or computer bureau or both. If an application is rejected, there is a right of appeal to the DPT. Information in the entries in the register has to be available for inspection by members of the public at all reasonable hours and free of charge. The DPR has power to issue Enforcement Notices: to comply with the data protection principles; to rectify or erase the data in certain circumstances. Enforcement notices must contain a statement of the principle(s) which are being contravened, with reasons, and details of rights of appeal.[110] Appeal lies to the DPT on a point of law, on the merits or on fact. The DPR is given powers of search and entry on a warrant from a Circuit judge, though this will not apply to exempt data.

Subjects are given the right to be informed by any user whether the user holds personal data on the subject as well as intelligible copies of such data, and both shall be given after a request in writing with the appropriate fee. Data will not be given unless the identity of the subject is established. Nor will it be given where the identity of another subject will be revealed, unless he or she consents. There are time limits. Court orders may enjoin compliance, including compensation from the user for damage by reason of inaccuracy of the data. Compensation can include an amount for distress. The user may invoke a defence of taking reasonable care in the circumstances to ensure accuracy, or that the data indicates that it is in a form in which it was received from the subject or a third party and it accurately records that information as received or obtained. Any notification from the subject that he or she regards the information as incorrect will have to be entered with the data. Obviously the subject has to know that the data is collected in the first place, and this will often not be the case. Compensation can also be awarded for damage caused by unauthorised disclosure due to loss, unauthorised destruction or disclosure to a non-specified recipient.[111] The subject can ask the court for rectification and erasure where data are inaccurate.

Part IV of the Act concerns the data which are exempt from the above provisions. National security is a ground for blanket exemption under sections 21–24[112] and Part II,[113] and a certificate from a Cabinet Minister, Attorney-General or Lord Advocate that data is exempt for the purpose of safeguarding national security shall be conclusive evidence of that fact. Also exempt from the registration and subject access provisions are data concerned with payrolls, pensions and business accounts, though they may be given to a third party for audit and are subject to other conditions, as well as domestic or household management data.[114] Where data is made public under any other statute[115] it is exempt from registration and subject access. Personal data are exempt from the non-disclosure provisions in any case in which disclosure is required by law, court order or for obtaining legal advice or in legal proceedings by a party to the proceedings or a witness. They may also be so exempt where 'urgently required' to prevent injury or other damage to the health of any person or persons (e.g. on an AIDS victim).

The most important exemption for ordinary individuals under the Act concerns subject access exemptions under Part IV of the Act. Subjects cannot have access to personal data on them which concerns:

(a) the prevention or detection of crime;

(b) the apprehension or prosecution of offenders;

(c) the assessment or collection of any tax or duty,

where access to the information would frustrate the above official duties. The non-disclosure provisions would also not apply where persons engaged in the above tasks would be likely to be prejudiced if they did apply. The Registrar will not exercise his powers in relation to a breach of the first principle – obtaining and processing lawfully and fairly – where enforcement would cause similar prejudice. This means that the lawfulness or fairness of acquisition of information is not, in the above cases, a matter for the Registrar, though it will, or may be, a matter for the courts if there is a suit for civil redress or it is claimed by the defence in a criminal trial that evidence is inadmissible. Information on police computers, including the Police National Computer, that is not information of the above kind, or otherwise exempt, will be accessible to subjects. One can imagine that a broad interpretation will be given to 'prevention or detection of crime'. Where the exemption from subject access provisions applies, not only will subjects not have access to such data, but they do not have to be informed by the user whether he holds information on them.[116] Subject access exemption also covers statutory regulation of financial services if access would prejudice the proper discharge of such regulation, as well as data concerning judicial appointments from third parties and data protected by legal professional privilege. Personal data held for preparing statistics or carrying out research are likewise exempt on certain conditions, although examination marks are accessible, subject to restrictions on the timing of access. 'Backup' copies, e.g. for security against loss, are exempt if they are not processed.

One of the most sensitive areas has been data information relating to the physical or mental health of the data subject. The Secretary of State may by order exempt or modify the provisions in the Act apropos of such information. An order may be made for the same purposes covering what is essentially social work data which is held by government departments or local authorities or voluntary organisations or other bodies designated by or under the order. The DHSS has published circulars on *Subject Access to Personal Health Information*.[117] These circulars sought the views of health authorities, community health councils and family practitioner committees[118] on the question of subject access. The circular adverted to the obvious point that although the legislation only applied to computerised data, their working parties had examined access across the board and 'we recognise that whatever principles of access are adopted in relation to personal health information held on computer, the public expectation will be that similar principles should eventually be applied to manual records'. The working groups believed that access by patients and clients 'encourages openness and can improve the quality of the record by correcting factual errors and reducing misunderstandings'. An absolute duty of disclosure was undesirable, however. The answer lay in an 'acceptable mechanism' through which 'proper discretion' could be exercised by the medical profession. Access would be allowed to the degree judged suitable by the appropriate clinician, with an 'independent' review by another doctor specialising in the same field, with ultimate right of access via the Registrar or the courts if successful. The order would cover 'personal data consisting of information as to the physical or mental health of the data subject originated by or on the instruction of health professionals irrespective of the context in which the data are generated or where, or by whom, they are held'.

The presumption would be that access should be given to as much of the data as possible in all cases. Disclosure should be withheld where 'Knowledge of the data would lead to distress or harm to the patient' or where 'disclosure would be expected to cause actual harm to the physical or mental health of the patient'. The DPR in his *Second Report*[119] expressed his support for these appeal provisions, believing that suitable arrangements could be made as in the case of the police and revenue services where information was not exempt under the subject access provisions. By November 1987, draft orders had been approved by Parliament on medical and social welfare data (HC (87)15 and LAC (87)10 respectively; and SIs 1987, nos. 1903 and 1904).

These exempt from subject access, personal data which would be likely to cause 'serious harm' to the physical or mental health of the data subject or any other person or in addition, for social work records, the subject's or any other person's emotional condition. Also exempt from subject access are data which would be likely to disclose to the subject the identity of another individual (who has not consented to such disclosure). This is where the data relates to that person or shows him or her to be the source of the information, whether this is obviously the case, or where it can be deduced. This exemption would not apply to protect the identity of a health professional nor an 'employee' in social work operating in their official capacity. Decisions will be made by 'health professionals' for health records and 'a member of senior management' for social work records. Widespread consultation with other health professionals etc. may be necessary, but the draft orders do not build in a 'second opinion' safeguard as originally envisaged. As disclosure is seen as the usual order of the day, however, a failure to provide good grounds may lead to challenge before the courts or the DPR, users are advised. For health records, however, the data user 'is not obliged to disclose whether information has been withheld or not', making successful challenge virtually impossible.

Apart from these specific exemptions, section 26(4) of the Act states that the 'subject access provisions shall apply notwithstanding any enactment or rule of law prohibiting or restricting the disclosure, or authorising the withholding, of information'. The most obvious provision covered by these words will be the Official Secrets Act, so that this does not apply to personal data which is not exempt or excluded under the 1984 Act.[120] The Secretary of State may by order exempt the subject access provisions to information which statute has prohibited from disclosure or has restricted if prohibition or restriction ought to prevail over access 'in the interests of the data subjects or of any other individual'.

The DPR is charged with the duty of performing his functions under the Act 'to promote the observance of the data protection principles by data users and persons carrying on computer bureaux'. He considers complaints by persons directly affected by alleged breaches of the Act and the data protection principles, provided they are made without undue delay. He has wide powers to publicise the Act and his functions under it; he reports to each House annually, and he can do so additionally 'if he sees fit'. Self-regulation by the data users is envisaged to the extent that the Registrar, where he considers it appropriate to do so, is under an obligation to encourage trade associations, or other bodies representing data users, to prepare and disseminate to their members codes of practice for guidance in complying with the data protection principles.

This outline of the major provisions of the 1984 legislation shows that it is a particularly tortuous statute. Users had to be registered by 10 May 1986, although the enormous extent of non-registration has been referred to. In the first year of the DPR's existence he received

160 complaints from individuals, although the subject access provisions did not come into effect until 11 November 1987. By the time his *Third Annual Report* was written in 1987, he had received 225 complaints in the relevant year. The travel and advertising trades, and universities, had produced their own codes of practice. His Report criticised the exemption of information on electoral registers from the privacy safeguards of the Act, which meant that electoral officers could sell such information without restraint by virtue of the Representation of the People (Amendment) Regulations 1985. The Home Office refused to impose restrictions. The Registrar also requested Departments of State to publish their rules on exchange of personal computerised information between themselves. He indicated that problems would arise when new legislation failed to take into account the data protection principles.

More fundamentally it has been established that it is quite easy to devise an information retrieval system that only provides an incomplete copy of an individual's record and that the duties under the Act are, in effect, unenforceable under present budget limitations. To guarantee complete retrieval, specialists would have to examine the software systems for retrieval to examine the full contents. At present, the Act places the onus upon the shoulders of the individual data subject to make the running, instead of providing a form of regulation that assesses overall quality of the information. It is an emergency safeguard, and not a full regulatory system.

In the case of manual files, a Bill was presented to Parliament which sought to introduce access by the subjects, and its proponents claim it had overwhelming public support.[121] As we shall see in Chapter 7, it was dramatically reduced in scope. At present, access to manual files depends upon ownership: if you do not own, you cannot see,[122] unless the documents can be obtained by a court order for discovery for litigation purposes. Various educational and health authorities have provided for access to files, but as we shall see later this often depends upon the consent of professionals, and the British Medical Association has voted that access by patients under the DPA should rely upon the consent of the doctor. The discrepancy between computerised and manual data has caused the National Computing Centre to advise its members to transfer 'sensitive' personal information to manual files,[123] where it is not covered by the DPA, unless it is housing or social services information. Surely this discrepancy speaks for itself.

In the area of national security, none of the safeguards advocated by Lindop was incorporated, and we must be content with the say-so of a Cabinet Minister or the Attorney-General. It might, or it might not, be difficult to conceive of instances where one would wish to doubt the sincerity of such a person's word; but the issue is not one of sincerity but of reliability, and this may turn on the information given to the Minister as well as his motivations.

6

Openness, Information and the Courts

The role of the courts, and their part in providing information about the working of Government or in protecting or advancing rights to information, has not been examined in depth so far. Proceedings before Powell J. in the New South Wales Supreme Court, and before Scott J. in the English High Court where the Cabinet Secretary was subjected to detailed cross-examination, suggest the potential for the insights that may be gained into the inner workings of Government.[1] We encountered the courts in Official Secrets Act cases and in relation to aspects of local government administration. We do not possess a rich case law of decisions debating citizens' rights to governmental information, which is not in the public domain, because the common law interprets such claims in terms of property holding and quasi-proprietorial rights; or it interprets the claims in the face of statutory prohibitions, such as the Official Secrets Acts. If you do not own the information, or the documents on which it is expressed or placed, or you cannot claim the protection of confidentiality, you have no claim in law. One has to rely upon release of information at the Government's will to our representatives or to the public at large by the devices we have discussed.

One qualification must be made. Since 1967 the courts have been prepared to assist litigants in dispute with state institutions in England and Wales, to the extent that, on exacting conditions, they will allow access to documents in the possession of state bodies or allow cross-examination of official witnesses. This topic will be discussed in more detail later in this chapter.

When discussing openness and the courts, it must be appreciated that the theme is subject to various interpretations. It may refer to the openness of courts themselves: their being open to the public, their proceedings being in the public domain; their proceedings being open in the style and manner of their argument and the accessibility of their discourse. In a second sense the phrase can refer to the role of the courts in helping to achieve openness or fuller provision of information: by insisting on information being provided as evidence supporting an assertion, or by way of reasons being afforded for decisions which affect our lives, or by giving greater access to those with a right to information as in the case of local government legislation. A further element in this second sense would involve the role of the courts in advancing freedom of speech; protecting and enhancing our civil liberties such as demonstrating peaceably; developing without unjustified interference our intellectual and personal lives.

A third sense of the expression can refer to the role of the courts in resolving disputes between parties over property rights in information or over the use of information acquired in a variety of circumstances. Typically, a confidential relationship creates certain obligations and entitlements over the use of information. While the courts have made some 'progress' in advancing the law of confidentiality,[2] it has remained for the legislature to give fuller definition to the law relating to copyright,[3] patents,[4] and copyright of information held on computers.[5] Our law on intellectual property nonetheless cries out for systematisation. Defamation would also be relevant. I touch on this third sense in this chapter, but my overriding concern is with the first two senses. I will not be able to deal in any detailed manner with freedom of speech or demonstration or censorship. These are detailed topics and are well provided for elsewhere.[6]

The 'Golden Met-wand'

As Harden and Lewis have recently reminded us, publicity for the law, and public information about the rules of conduct of society which are to be implemented through its courts and which may account for deprivation of liberty, property, and until 1965 one's life,[7] are vital components of the Rule of Law.[8] So too is a judiciary free from executive or other interference. Developed markets and commercial and financial enterprise require an extended law of property; contract; corporations law; patents; securities and investment law; and the like. The fact that most of the dispute resolution, guidance through rules or standards, or the establishment of dispute procedures and policy-initiating bodies, does not involve the use of courts, is no denial of the fact that courts are ultimately the final arbiters of law. Unless, that is, Parliament has definitively and successfully excluded the courts from a province of decision-making,[9] or where practice has effectively excluded the courts.[10] Deliberate exclusion by Parliament is comparatively rare, and often jealously scrutinised by the courts.[11] What goes on in the courts is public business,[11a] even if it concerns private parties. And what is said in court is protected by absolute privilege in defamation proceedings.

There is no rule of law that judges must give reasons for their decisions. Nor is there any administrative stricture or exhortation. Yet they operate within a tradition spreading back as far as the common law which *insists* that the reasons for their decisions are, unlike juries, publicly expressed or published. Their decisions have to fit into the body of established precedent and be reasoned to conclusions which will be publicly contested and rigorously analysed in academic work and subsequent judicial proceedings. A good judge feels the pressure of his peers to 'pass muster'. If he does not, his reputation as a lawyer, though not his judicial salary,[12] will suffer. Indeed, the alleged secrecy of Star Chamber proceedings was the cause of one of several vitriolic attacks on that body in the seventeenth century. The attack was politically motivated by common lawyers, but it struck a deep and pervasive chord of sympathy in influential circles.[13] The law must be known after hard argument and testing. Being allowed to utter forth truthfully on the law without a reck as to consequences is one thing and has a centuries' old tradition behind it. Being instructed, on the other hand, that certain matters are reserved issues for politics alone, is another tradition and one that is deeply engrained in our political and legal consciousness. This is why case law has featured so little in our discussions to date. Freedom of governmental information is reserved business. Even when confronted with cases concerning freedom of speech, courts have disclaimed any constitutional dimension to their decisions, holding that the prevention of a meeting or a public address was simply a corollary of the police apprehending a breach of the peace, a concept which has been stretched to breaking point.[14]

Various international declarations seek to protect freedom of expression, opinion and information. The European Convention on Human Rights proclaims that:

Everyone has the right to freedom of expression. This right shall include freedom to hold opinions and to receive and impart information and ideas without interference by public authority and regardless of frontiers.[15]

But the right is subject to qualifications: 'as are prescribed by law and are necessary in a democratic society, in the interests of national security, territorial integrity or public safety, for the prevention of disorder or crime, for the protection of health or morals, for the protection of the rights of others, for preventing the disclosure of information received in confidence or for maintaining the authority and impartiality of the judiciary'.[16] This body of qualifications has to be seen in the context of case law of the European Commission and Court of Human Rights, which has stressed that the restrictions *must be* prescribed in law[17] and are subject to strict interpretation. The restrictions must be predicated by a 'pressing social need'[18] which is proportionate to the means of safeguarding it; in short, the authorities must not engage in overkill.[19] Furthermore, the Convention allows judges to strike a note of fundamentalism which has been largely absent from our judicial tradition. In *Handyside*, for instance, it was noted how:

Freedom of expression constitutes one of the essential foundations of a society, one of the basic conditions for its progress and for the development of every man [sic]. Subject to paragraph 2 of Article 10, it is applicable not only to 'information' or 'ideas' that are favourably received, but also to those that offend, shock or disturb the State or any sector of the population. Such are the demands of that pluralism, tolerance and broad-mindedness without which there is no democratic society.

An absence of a constitutional culture, an absence of government-guaranteed freedom of speech, and a repetitive failure seriously to question executive right, have all helped to ensure that far from questioning *raison d'état*, the British judiciary would afford it, with very few exceptions, every endorsement. It is a matter for considerable regret that the Bill incorporating the European Convention on Human Rights fell at its first Parliamentary obstacle in 1987. It might have prompted from the judiciary a new approach in the defence of civil liberties which *is* surely needed in the United Kingdom, without making them unaccountable defenders of entrenched conservatism, a position encouraged by the closed nature of judicial appointments.[20]

Judicial Appointments

The process ensures that only the 'safe and the sound' will be promoted to the Bench. For an appointment to the High Court, a barrister is expected to have displayed the necessary ambition and dedication not only to have mastered the most difficult briefs, but to have mastered the system. Any injudicious, intemperate or outspoken public statements would doubtless be damning. Boat-rockers do not reach the top. The background of the individuals concerned and the remarkable absence of notoriety among the judiciary, certainly the higher judiciary, testify to that. Data information on judicial appointments is one of the protected items under the Data Protection Act. Judicial appointments follow the cosy informal process of sounding out, so beloved of the British tradition, and individuals are recommended for senior appointment by the Lord Chancellor to the Prime Minister. Circuit judges, who have usually served as Recorders, are recommended by the Lord Chancellor, as are High Court judges.[21] Appointments are by the Crown. Once in office, judges serve under a 'voluntary' code of silence known as the 'Kilmuir Rules', whereby they do not make public utterances on subjects in the media.[22] For our present purposes it says much about the culture of caution and silence and conservatism which can be buttressed by a powerful Lord Chancellor and senior civil servants threatening dismissal and acute shame[23] before their colleagues in the case of Circuit judges and Recorders.[24] 'So long as a judge keeps silent', opined Kilmuir, 'his reputation for wisdom and impartiality remains unassailable.' On his first press conference as Lord Chancellor, Lord Mackay announced that the 'Kilmuir Rules' were ripe for reform. He would encourage more discretion on the part of judges so long as interviews did not prejudice their judicial work.[24a]

What of the openness of the courts themselves? Jury vetting in criminal cases has become an increasing practice and now operates under guidelines issued by the Attorney-General.[25] In Northern Ireland 'scheduled offences' are tried by a judge alone and deal essentially with terrorist crimes.[26] In trials where classified information is to be heard, juries will be given a security vetting and the public and press will not be allowed to attend. Contempt of court protects the 'open and free' proceedings of courts and 'public confidence' in those proceedings.

Contempt of Court

The Contempt of Court Act 1981[27] put most of the law of contempt on to a statutory footing. Conduct which tends to interfere with the course of justice in particular legal proceedings regardless of intent to do so, may be treated as a contempt. This rule of 'strict liability' only applies to proceedings which are 'active' under the terms of the Act[28] at the time of a publication[29] which creates a 'substantial risk that the course of justice in the proceedings in question will be seriously impeded or prejudiced'. A defence is available where 'if at the time of publication (having taken all reasonable care) [the publisher] does not know and has no reason to suspect that relevant proceedings are active'.[30] A person will not be guilty of contempt under the strict liability rule in respect of a fair and accurate report of legal proceedings held in public, published contemporaneously and in good faith.[31] The court has power to order postponement of publication for such periods as it thinks necessary to prevent a substantial risk of prejudice to the administration of justice in those proceedings, or any other proceedings pending or imminent. Knowledge of the order must be proved to establish contempt.[32] A further defence is available under section 5. This protects publication 'made as or part of a discussion in good faith of public affairs or other matters of general public interest'. When 'the risk of impediment or prejudice to particular legal proceedings is merely incidental to the discussion' it is not to be treated as a contempt of court under the strict liability rule.[33]

The Attorney-General's *fiat* is required for issue of contempt proceedings or they can be issued 'on the motion of a court having jurisdiction to deal with the matter'. The Act leaves to the common law publication or behaviour which interferes with the *general* administration of justice[34] and preserves as contempt that which intentionally impedes or prejudices the administration of justice.[35] Section 8 of the Act protects the confidentiality of jury deliberations by making breach of such a contempt.[36] Section 9 of the Act prohibits the use of tape-recorders unless the leave of the court is obtained,[37] although these recordings must not be published in any way. Section 11 allows the court to give directions prohibiting the publication of names or evidence where these were not disclosed in open court. The section does not give instruction on when such matters may be withheld. The widespread use of the section to protect the anonymity of witnesses, decisions which cannot be directly reviewed, has led to challenge in the European Commission of Human Rights. Some statutes allow the names of witnesses and other evidence to be withheld,[38] and courts have a common law power to withhold identity and information where its revelation would frustrate the cause of the action, such as breach of confidence or patent. In *Scott* v. *Scott*[39] it was stated as a general principle that justice should be openly administered, although proceedings in chambers are an exception. This is not to satisfy public curiosity or to stimulate debate, but to keep the 'judge while trying under trial'.[40] Trials concerning prosecutions under the Official Secrets Acts and security-sensitive information have been the obvious occasions where secrecy has been invoked,[41] as are cases where justice itself would be defeated.

The subject headings of contempt have been developed by judicial precedent, and as they are based upon 'the broadest of principles' can occasionally be put to novel and unexpected use. In 1980, a prisoner named Williams sued the Home Office for false imprisonment in the Control Unit in Wakefield Prison. His claim was based on the argument that the Control Unit was established without specific legal authority and in breach of the Prison Rules.[42] The unit concentrated on particularly severe forms of isolation, deprivation and discipline. To help establish Williams's case, the Home Office had been ordered, after an application for discovery, to hand over to Williams's solicitors at the National Council for Civil Liberties documents relating to the establishment and operation of the unit. These constituted a voluminous bundle of documents, many of which were read out and examined in open court. A reporter for *The Guardian* asked Williams's solicitor if he could borrow the documents for a feature article on the case and its background. Without any improper motive on her part,[43] the solicitor allowed sight of the documents which had been obtained on discovery. The Home Office had released the documents by order of the court on the basis that they were used for the litigation and not for other general purposes of the NCCL.

The House of Lords held by a 3–2 majority, upholding the High Court and Court of Appeal, that the solicitor had been guilty of civil contempt by breaking an undertaking to the court.[44] 'The case', fulminated Lord Diplock, 'is *not* about freedom of speech, freedom of the press, openness of justice or documents coming into the "public domain" . . . nor does it call for considerations of any of those human

rights and fundamental freedoms' contained in the European Convention for the Protection of Human Rights and Fundamental
Freedoms. The case was about discovery of documents in litigation,
the compulsory handing over of documents in their possession or
control between the parties in a lawsuit for inspection and copying
and which 'contain information that may, either directly or indirectly, enable that other party either to advance his own case or
damage the case of his adversary or which may fairly lead to a chain of
inquiry which may have either of these two consequences'. It is an
'inroad' into privacy in the name of justice which requires safeguards
against abuse.[45] Had the reporter copied all the evidence given in
court orally as the trial proceeded, no breach of law would have
ensued as long as the public were admitted.[46] He could also have
'bargained privately' to obtain a copy of the mechanically recorded
speeches in court. He was a feature article writer, not a reporter
producing an accurate account of the proceedings for the quality
press,[47] so his sight of the documents was not *de minimis* and a mere
breach of technicality, but a serious contempt, the majority held.

Lords Scarman and Simon believed that once documents had been
read out in open court, the obligation of protection of confidentiality
ceased; potentially inadmissible documents should be filed separately; anything else marked as exhibits should be available for
inspection as part of the public record, as occurs in the USA, whether
read out or not. The documents had become public knowledge, and
after objecting to discovery the Home Office had not subsequently
objected to publication on grounds of 'Public Interest Immunity'.
Lord Scarman favoured the American practice of a judicial record
and a public right to 'complete information' as a common law right.[48]
Per contra, Lord Roskill observed that we have no FOIA in this
country.[49] The decision to hold in contempt the solicitor who handed
over the documents, from which evidence had been given publicly,
seems vindictive. But the story does not end there.

The case was taken to the European Commission of Human
Rights,[50] and in June 1986 the Government announced that it
intended to amend the law of contempt after reaching a friendly
settlement before the Commission, rather than persisting to the full
opinion of the Commission and judgment before the European Court
of Human Rights.[51] The provisional opinion of the Commission and
the terms of the settlement are confidential. A formal report with
detailed findings and opinions is not issued, but a four-page report

which gives outline statements and which is published with little publicity is. In many previous friendly settlements, the press had not noticed the reports that were issued, and the Home Office had not made an announcement about those unnoticed. The Government's increased use of friendly settlements marks an interesting development away from confrontation and towards informally bargained confidential outcomes involving the European Convention. In February 1987, the Lord Chancellor's Department produced a draft memorandum suggesting that judges should have an unfettered discretion to decide whether a document 'given in evidence' in open court should remain confidential.[52] When a claim for an interim injunction is heard in open court as opposed to chambers, the documentary evidence should remain secret. The proposed amendment did not suggest that the discretion be exercised with reference to the principle expressed in Article 10: that freedom of speech should only be restricted where there is a pressing social need or to advance some other important objective. The frequent use of sections 4(2) and 11 of the Contempt of Court Act by judges to prohibit reporting of proceedings caused apprehension *vis-à-vis* the exercise of the proposed discretion.[53]

Protection of Sources of Information in Litigation

Section 10 of the Contempt of Court Act states:[54]

No court may require a person to disclose, nor is any person guilty of contempt of court for refusing to disclose, the source of information contained in a publication for which he is responsible unless it be established to the satisfaction of the court that disclosure is necessary in the interests of justice or national security or for the prevention of disorder or crime.

This section gives an immunity from contempt proceedings to those who do not reveal the identity of a source of information contained in a publication for which they are responsible, unless the person seeking the identity proves to the court that disclosure is necessary for one or other of the stated grounds. At common law, courts may order an individual to reveal the identity of a source of information.[55] The court must exercise a discretion before ordering disclosure and must regard a broad array of factors. Of especial importance is the need to maintain confidentiality of the source of supply, *inter alia*, of information to the police,[56] voluntary societies promoting the welfare of vulnerable individuals,[57] or licensing or regulatory authorities promoting the public interest.[58] Prior to section 10 being enacted, the courts had given no immunity to protect the revelation of a source of information where national security was allegedly involved.[59] Nor had courts given much succour to claims of immunity where the 'interests of justice' *are* advanced by disclosure,[60] though immunity may be given where investigation of crime, or its possibility, is advanced, as in the case of police informers or where information relates directly to law enforcement, e.g. collection of customs and excise revenues, or taxes.[61]

It was the litigation concerning the 'mole' in the *British Steel* case[62] which constituted the leading judicial discussion of immunity from revealing a source of information in the interests of justice. The chairman of the British Steel Corporation had been involved in an industrial dispute with the steel unions over wage levels and redundancies. An employee at the Corporation handed a substantial number of documents to Granada TV, which was making a documentary on the dispute. The thrust of these documents, it was suggested, was that, far from being caused by inefficient workforce practices, the ills of the nationalised industry were more closely related to mismanagement and too much political interference in the Corporation's affairs from successive Ministers. Informed by these documents, the interviewer subjected the chairman of British Steel to a 'disgraceful' and 'unfair' cross-examination for *seven* minutes of prime viewing time.[63] To pursue an action against the unidentified 'mole', BSC required Granada TV, which by its actions had become implicated in the wrong, to reveal his identity. This Granada refused to do, claiming that there was a public interest in informing the public of the behind-the-scenes activity in a major nationalised industry whose fortunes had a direct bearing on the well-being of the national economy.[64] It was urged on Granada's behalf that, by analogy with the 'newspaper rule' which protected newspapers from revealing the source of information that was the subject of possible defamation proceedings, the media should be likewise protected for breaches of confidence which were in the public interest on one or other of various grounds.

Granada's argument was not successful at first instance, nor before the Court of Appeal. Lord Wilberforce in the House of Lords did not think the analogy with defamation was exact, although before the

House of Lords the main argument of Granada turned on technical aspects of their defence and not on whether the balancing of the public interest on either side was required. '[This] brings out the limitations of the reasons we are required to give', Lord Wilberforce believed. Both appeal courts accepted in principle the possibility of an immunity from disclosure, but not on the facts before them. The conduct of the TV producers was reprehensible and unfair in the context of a 'trial' – but this was the first time the documents had been made public, and short of a 'leak' they would not have been made available to the public nor to Parliament. Lord Wilberforce thought there was a public interest in the free flow of information, the strength of which will vary from case to case. In some cases it may be very weak; in others very strong. He did not believe there was 'iniquity' on the part of management or the politicians, and he did not believe the public interest was such that the source of the information should be protected. Viscount Dilhorne did not think the case concerned the freedom of the press,[65] despite 'the resounding rhetoric' to the contrary. This is, quite frankly, baffling, as Lord Salmon suggested in his dissenting judgment. The story of 'woe', he believed, had to be known in the public interest.[66]

This, then, was the background to section 10 of the Contempt of Court Act. The section introduced a rule of law concerning disclosure of sources of information rather than a balancing of judicial discretion as before. The section was considered *in extenso* in the litigation[67] involving the *Guardian* newspaper and the arrival of cruise missiles and, as it transpired, Sarah Tisdall.

A 'secret' memorandum was prepared by the Ministry of Defence relating to the installation of cruise missiles at a Royal Air Force base in the UK. A copy of the memorandum was sent to the Prime Minister, and six copies were sent to senior members of the Cabinet and the Cabinet Secretary. A junior civil servant photocopied the memorandum and anonymously handed it to *The Guardian*, which subsequently published the memorandum. The Secretary of State for Defence was furious[68] and demanded the return of the documents in order to identify the source of the leak from markings on the copy and to take appropriate action. The claim of the Crown was basically that it was their property and they were entitled to its return under the Torts (Interference with Goods) Act 1977 in an undamaged form. Although successful in the lower courts, this point did not succeed in the House of Lords.[69] The Crown also argued that recovery was necessary in the interests of national security. While publication of this particular document was not a security risk, but merely a political embarrassment since its publication warned the Opposition in Parliament of the time of arrival of the missiles, the fact remained that a civil servant in a position of trust and confidence had betrayed a loyalty to the Minister, and this did constitute a security risk for future, more important potential leaks. Section 10 was prayed in aid by *The Guardian*.

The House of Lords established that section 10 places the onus of proof on the party seeking the order of disclosure of identity, viz. the Crown. Identity will remain a secret unless the court is satisfied that 'disclosure is necessary in the interests of justice or national security or for the prevention of disorder or crime'. Lord Diplock was emphatic that the discretion involved in balancing the interests between the public interest in being informed of events of public importance and the public interest in maintaining a confidence did not occur. The immunity applied *until and unless* one of the four grounds of release was established on the balance of probabilities to the satisfaction of the court. This is a question of fact, not a question of discretion nor of 'constitutional right', an evocative phrase which Lord Diplock would repudiate:

if it is intended to mean anything more than that in ascertaining the extent of the rights which it confers the section should give a purposive construction and, that being done, like other rights conferred on persons by statute, effect must be given to it in the courts.[70]

It is important to appreciate that the case came to the Law Lords as an appeal against an interlocutory order, i.e. a preliminary procedural point. By the time the Law Lords had to decide the construction of section 10 and its application to the case, the identity of the 'leaker', Sarah Tisdall,[71] had become an issue of national notoriety. The Court of Appeal and three of the Law Lords thought that the affidavit evidence of the Principal Establishment Officer of the Ministry of Defence, to the effect that disclosure of the document was necessary to discover the source of the leak, was in the interests of national security, together with the affidavit evidence of the editor of *The Guardian*[72] and, for the Law Lords, the notorious events concerning Sarah Tisdall, who pleaded guilty to a charge under section 2 of the OSA, and of which judicial notice could be taken, *just about* established the case for the Crown. As Lord Diplock noted, however, there was evidence in existence *at the time the affidavit from the Principal Establishment Officer was presented to the High Court* which would have put beyond all doubt that it was necessary to establish the identity of the leaker. Two Law Lords, and the judge who heard the application for the order of disclosure, did not think that the Crown had made out their case at the time of the application under section 10. The two dissenting Law Lords did not think that it was permissible to take judicial notice of events subsequent to the application. It is not unknown for judges to give instruction to officials on how they *should have* drafted affidavits to put forward a more plausible case in order to avoid such difficulties in the future.[73] This Lord Diplock obligingly provided,[74] as well as applying 'the necessary mental gymnastics' in order to feel satisfied that the interests of national security required the release of the document to establish the identity of the source. 'The evidence', said Lord Fraser to the contrary, 'may have caused a little political embarrassment to the Government', but it contained nothing of military value. 'Without more information than he had, the judge could not properly have been satisfied that disclosure' by *The Guardian* was 'necessary' – not necessary and expedient, but necessary in the interests of national security. Any other interpretation, agreed Lord Scarman, would not have done justice to the rule which in its structure 'bears a striking resemblance' to the way in which the Articles of the European Convention are drafted, viz. 'a general rule subject to carefully drawn and limited exceptions which are required to be published, in case of dispute, to the satisfaction of the European Court of Human Rights. . . . It is no part of the judge's function to use his common sense in an attempt to fill a gap which can be filled only by evidence.'[75] On the contrary, Lord Bridge's common sense dictated, 'it is surely unthinkable that the Government should have embarked on the present litigation without taking the elementary step . . . of an internal interview' to establish the 'leaker'. And Lord Bridge could infer from his involvement in governmental responsibilities[76] that a lack of urgency in the Government's demand for the document[77] was not due to sloth on its part. Judicial notice could be taken of the fact 'that important decisions in Government are rarely taken without time consuming consultation and deliberation'.[78]

On one point, however, the Law Lords rejected the Crown's arguments, accepted by the judge at first instance and the Court of Appeal by majority, that its right of property in the documents and information thereon defeated *ipso facto* the immunity from disclosure under section 10. The Crown could not use its proprietorial claim to get access to information from the document, thereby allowing it to pursue its contractual, tortious or equitable claims against the 'leaker' in order to pursue the 'interests of justice':

> Having regard to the emphatic terms in which s. 10 of the 1981 Act is cast, I have not found it possible to envisage any case that might occur in real life, in which, since the passing of the Act, it would be necessary *in the interests of justice* to order delivery up of the document. . . .[79]

In more fundamental terms, Lord Scarman declared:

> [Since] it is in the 'interests of all of us that we should have a truly effective press' (per Griffiths L.J.) rights of property have to yield pride of place to the national interest which Parliament must have had in mind when enacting the section.

This would seem to cover the situation in the *British Steel Corporation* case,[80] so that it might well be decided differently today in favour of Granada TV.[81] 'In the interests of justice' meant identifying a source of information to advance the actual administration of justice, and not justice in an abstract sense of vindicating a speculative claim in law or that which is relevant to determine an issue before the court. 'The public interest which s. 10 . . . serves is therefore the preservation of sources of information and ensuring that they come forward.'[82] The House of Lords ruled in December 1987 that prevention of crime meant crime in general, not a specific crime, in denying a journalist the immunity.[82a]

Now we can look at the role of the courts in insisting upon, if not openness, then at least the provision of information. Our first consideration continues the discussion of national security.

The Courts as Guarantors of Openness

National Security
For years before the *Zamora* case[83] and for years afterwards courts accepted unquestionably the sentiments of Lord Parker that

> Those who are responsible for the national security must be the sole judge of what the national security requires. It would be obviously undesirable that such matters should be made the subject of evidence in a court of law or otherwise discussed in public.

In that case, however, the order for angary of a cargo in the Prize Court by the Government failed because the judge did not have evidence before him that the goods were needed in the *national interest*. As evidenced by *Chandler* v. *DPP*, although the courts might not associate ineluctably the interests of the State with the interests of the government of the day,[84] on national security matters they were ready to defer to the judgment of the Crown and would not allow evidence on national security from its witness to be shaken in cross-examination. In the *Hosenball* litigation, deportation of an American citizen in the interests of national security precluded the usual tenets of fair play and knowing the details of the case that one's accusers were making. 'In national security cases,' declared Lord Denning, 'even natural justice must take a back seat.'[85] These are familiar fare to the public lawyer, given added interest by judicial decisions in which the national security blanket has been spread over executive action.

The first such judicial decision concerned the controversy surrounding events at General Communications Headquarters. The Government in January 1984 announced that it was banning trade union membership among civil servants at GCHQ at Cheltenham.[86] There had been minor disruptions through industrial action at GCHQ, the last occasion being in 1981, and for some years the Government had been conscious of the sensitivity of serious disruption in the information-gathering reponsibilities of GCHQ. The Government was studying the possibility of lie detectors (polygraph security screening) on the staff at GCHQ, and the Cabinet Secretary told union leaders, prior to the Government's announcement about banning unions, that there would be further consultation after the results of pilot schemes were known. In the event, the right of the GCHQ civil servants to belong to a trade union was taken away without any consultation with their representatives. On the Government side it was claimed that what was done was performed on the grounds of national security. A contrary belief is that the Prime Minister wished to implement lie detectors without any objection from unions and that the Government had acted under pressure from the US Government. The claim of a threat to national security was not made in substance at the hearing in the High Court when the Council of Civil Service Unions challenged the legality of the Government's action. It was argued on the Government's behalf that consultation upon matters affecting national security would be so circumscribed as to be practically useless. Glidewell J. rejected this, holding that the decision was one that should be taken fairly, and that the failure to consult rendered it unfair and a denial of a legitimate expectation of consultation because of the serious implications involved in depriving an individual of union membership.[87] The Court of Appeal accepted the Government's claim that consultation *could* have interfered with the interests of national security, and so did the House of Lords,[88] holding that, on the facts, consultation was not necessary as a matter of law.

In the House of Lords much attention was given to the role of the courts in assessing claims involving the invocation of national security. Courts, the Law Lords unanimously believed, were ill suited to assess the national security requirements of state affairs. However, if action affecting individual rights, interests or legitimate expectations were based upon national security, whether in consequence of a statutory or prerogative power, the courts would look for *evidence* to support a claim that the action was, as in the instant case, for the purpose of avoiding disruption injurious to the national security. The court must act on evidence, said Lord Scarman. 'Evidence', reiterated Lord Roskill, 'and not mere assertion must be forthcoming.'

The evidence relied upon was an affidavit of Sir Robert Armstrong, the Cabinet Secretary, sworn on 6 April 1984. His affidavit recorded the apprehension that consultation would have caused disruption. Two months prior to this, the Foreign Secretary, in giving evidence to the Commons Foreign Affairs Select Committee, did not mention this matter, but spoke of the necessity of keeping the activities of GCHQ out of the public eye.[89] Nor was the matter mentioned in legal argument at first instance before Glidewell J. It may be, as Griffith has suggested, that the real reason for banning union membership without warning was one of political expediency and not national security.[90] Certainly, the courts accepted without question the affidavit evidence. It was not tested; it was not probed; it was not examined. The case was an application for judicial review, and this procedure is not meant to be a process for clarifying disputes of fact by allowing cross-examination of the witness – the Prime Minister, the Foreign Secretary, the Secretary to the Cabinet – nor allowing frequent applications for discovery of documents.[91] The courts wanted evidence of a national security risk; the evidence had to be more than a bare assertion; but the court was not prepared to weigh it. Some

evidence was given, and in the circumstances it w
person to predict that disruption injurious to natio
not have occurred had the unions been forew;
suspect the duplicity of the Government, but, a;
would be difficult to come to a conclusion other
one were put into a neutral seat and asked was i
such disruption, and if so would it be likely to affect adversely nat...
security? The argument is not against the outcome of the GCHQ
decision, though the Government's case should have been pressed
more severely; the argument is against the manner in which courts are
structured in Britain to avoid asking the most pressing questions in
cases affecting the public interest, and in which the prerogative of
national security happens to be one example. Should we require
evidence of a clear and present danger to national security? The
argument also concerns the issue of whether we need to give fuller
definition to what the 'national security' actually is. A few more
points on the use of 'national security' to preclude examination in the
courts of matters of public interest are apposite.

A Wright Mess

Peter Wright was a former member of the British security services
who wished to publish his memoirs.[93] In these he made serious
allegations against senior officers of MI5 of treasonable wrongdoing
and criminal activity.[94] The allegations were based on 'confidential'
material gained while in Crown employment. He sought to publish
his book in Australia. The English Attorney-General sought to
restrain publication by commencing proceedings in New South
Wales. He also commenced proceedings against the *Observer* and
Guardian newspapers, which had published details of the affair which
they claimed to have received from other sources as well as the author.
In the English proceedings,[95] the Attorney-General sought injunctions restraining further publication. This is referred to in the
USA as 'prior restraint'. Its use in America is heavily circumscribed;[96] it has a much wider scope in England, where courts are not
so willing to allow publication, while reminding the 'injured' party
that he may sue for damages. The absence of 'prior restraint' may,
conversely, help freedom of speech; it can also be easily abused by a
powerful and irresponsible press.

No one suggested in the case of the *Observer* or the *Guardian* that they
were acting irresponsibly.[97] In fact they gave an undertaking that

would exercise their own judgment carefully before publishing
ything relating to the security service. This would permit, said Sir
John Donaldson, 'the disclosure or publication of information
whether or not in the public domain, about serious criminal
misconduct or other serious wrong-doing by members of the British
Security Services'. This was too much. While accepting that there
was a public interest in knowing of grave malefactions by senior
officers, there was a competing public interest in maintaining a
confidentiality which was not simply a private 'contractual' confidentiality but a confidentiality relating to 'public secrets':[98] 'The
Attorney-General is not personally the beneficiary of the right to
confidentiality which he asserts, nor is the Executive. His claim is
made on behalf of the State, that is the general community.' When
assessing the competing public interests of knowing, and maintaining
a duty of confidentiality by preventing the public from knowing, it
'might lead a court properly to conclude that, in the context of the
confidentiality of the work of the Security Service, the proper
approach is that the conflict . . . should be resolved in favour of
restraint unless the court is satisfied that there is a serious defence of
public interest which is *very likely*[99] to succeed at the trial'. It *was* in the
public interest to discover wrongdoing in the security service, and the
greater the wrongdoing, the greater the right to know; but Sir John
could not agree that, given 'a sufficiently serious *allegation*', publication of the allegation with a view to forcing an investigation[100] 'was
justified'.[101] Sir John reasoned:

Where there is a confidentiality, the public interest in its maintenance has
to be overborne by a countervailing public interest, if publication is not to be
restrained. In some cases the weight of the public interest in the maintenance
of the confidentiality will be small and the weight of the public interest in
publication will be great. But in weighing these countervailing public
interests or . . . those countervailing aspects of a single public interest, both
the nature and circumstances of the proposed publication have to be
examined with considerable care. This is sometimes referred to as the
principle of proportionality – the restraint or lack of restraint proportionate to
the overall assessment of the public interest. Thus it by no means follows that,
because the public interest in the exposure of wrong-doing would justify the
communication to the police or some such authority of material which has
been unlawfully obtained, it would also justify wholesale publication of
material in a national newspaper.[102]

Publication through a newspaper, 'the widest and most indiscriminate' form of publication, was not justified. However, the papers were free to publish accurate reports of legal proceedings in New South Wales (although the House of Lords subsequently enjoined such discussion) or England, or proceedings before Parliament. One matter that was not enjoined was a TV programme by Ms Cathy Massiter which contained an appearance by Mr Wright. No action was taken against Ms Massiter in England, yet it was taken against Mr Wright in Australia. In those latter proceedings, the British Government admitted the veracity of Wright's allegations as a tactical ploy to avoid a confrontation with Mr Wright and Ms Massiter.[103] This left the British Government with the unenviable task of persuading an Australian court that it was in Australia's national interest to maintain Wright's confidence to the Crown. Public Interest Immunity of documents was sought by the Crown for relevant documents in the New South Wales proceedings. This was refused, and the Crown's case was presented in evidence by the Secretary to the Cabinet, who was subjected to rigorous, indeed hostile, cross-examination. His performance was poor. He had to take the witness box a second time to retract a statement alleging that the decision not to prosecute previous 'leaks' of MI5 secrets was taken by the Attorney-General. It was not so, Sir Michael Havers stated in Parliament. The senior civil servant who had performed so adroitly before the Defence Select Committee[104] was made to look implausible and totally unconvincing. The judge refused the injunction sought by the Crown, undermining all the Crown's assertions unequivocally.[105] He also criticised Sir John Donaldson's judgment preventing by interim injunction reporting in newspapers in England of allegations of unlawful conduct. A different view of such matters is taken in Australia.[106] The Court of Appeal of New South Wales rejected the Government's appeal. 'National security' did not allow the Government to conceal that it had acted without honour and capriciously.

In the GCHQ saga, the feeling remains that such a concealment was maintained. More probing, more testing, would have vindicated the role of the courts as guardians of our liberties. Even if it is not for the courts to make decisions on the 'national security', they should convince us that they are not over-willing to be sold the 'dummy pass'. And we all have a right to know what national security means. Is this not appropriate for statutory definition? This would involve judicial supervision of criteria approved by Parliament, not judicial second-guessing.

The injunctions issued against the *Guardian* and the *Observer* were subject to further proceedings when three English newspapers published extracts from Peter Wright's memoirs. Sir John Donaldson in his judgment had warned that other newspapers were not free to republish, and the Lord Chancellor had chipped in with his own warning. In proceedings initiated by the Attorney-General, Sir Nicolas Browne Wilkinson held that a contempt of court for breach of the precise terms of an injunction could only be committed by a party enjoined by the injunction – the *Guardian* or the *Observer* – or by a party who has aided and abetted those bound by the injunction.[107] In the absence of such elements, it would only bind those who were parties to the initial litigation: it operated *in personam* not *in rem*. Sir Nicolas was at pains to dissociate himself from the necessity of the law protecting a public secret as a public right, as Sir John had endeavoured to do. '[T]he basic right protected by the 1986 injunction was exactly the same as the right of a manufacturer to stop an employee disclosing trade secrets or of one spouse to restrain the other from revealing "pillow talk".' It was for Parliament and not the courts to create a public law remedy protecting public rights to confidentiality of state secrets, he believed.

This reasoning did not prevail in the Court of Appeal, which overturned the Vice-Chancellor's decision, paving the way for contempt proceedings against the respective newspapers. However, the judgment of the Master of the Rolls was particularly receptive to some of the Vice-Chancellor's criticisms. The case was not about national security, nor about a State interest (as he had formerly suggested), but about confidentiality protecting an employment relationship, he believed. The Attorney-General was now seeking to protect a right to confidentiality by contempt proceedings against publication which was 'intended or calculated to impede, obstruct or prejudice the administration of justice'. Publication would destroy that most evanescent of rights, confidentiality. The courts, and no one else, would decide to what extent the right should be protected, regardless of who asserted it.[108] This seems understandable in basic principle. But its similarity to a 'gagging writ' should not be overlooked, especially where, as in Wright's case, the publishers allege that the Government acquiesced in prior publication of similar 'confidential' information.

Wright's case became a matter of international notoriety. After publication of his book in the USA, and further publication of extracts in the *Sunday Times*, the Government's attempts to protect the confidentiality of information acquired by its servants appeared forlorn. Government efforts concentrated on seizing the profits emanating from Wright's breach of duty, as well as maintaining the injunction. That such a confidentiality existed was accepted, though it was unclear whether it was a private or public law right. That, however, did not prevent the House of Lords from upholding the interim injunction, and even extending it to cover legal proceedings in New South Wales concerning Wright's allegations.[109] The real motive of the majority of the Law Lords appears to have been the desire to use an injunction against the newspapers to punish Wright and to deter other security officers, rather than to protect a confidence. The public could not read reports of what was publicly available. In further proceedings, the BBC was enjoined from broadcasting a serious discussion on the security services on Radio 4.[109a]

As I have remarked elsewhere, a contract enforceable at common law did not appear to exist between Crown servants and the Crown at the relevant time. That is no reason why an express stipulation of confidentiality and a subjection to vetting of memoirs for approval before publication might not be incorporated into the relationship.[110] The law of confidentiality is not dependent upon the law of contract. As we saw in Chapter 2, CIA agents may publish memoirs, but only after vetting has been performed and approval given. The Government would not have approved Wright's memoirs. A right of appeal to an independent body would therefore be necessary.

Some judicial sanity was restored to these events when Scott J. refused to award a permanent injunction against the newspapers at the suit of the Attorney-General. In a judgment distinguished by its clarity and grasp of legal principle, the judge held that the secret was out and the public interest dictated it be reported upon. Confidentiality was not the same as copyright.[111] The Government appealed unsuccessfully to the Court of Appeal.[112] The court upheld the right of the press to report what was in the public domain. Two judges agreed with Scott J. that the newspapers were correct to publish the initial serious allegations because it was in the public interest that they should be reported. This would seem to go against the thrust of the House of Lords majority judgment in the interlocutory proceedings.

The allegations by Ms Massiter, to which reference was made, led to judicial proceedings in England when representatives of CND[113] sought a declaration that the phone of its deputy director was unlawfully tapped on the authority of the Home Secretary. It was alleged that this was done to gain information to embarrass CND as a Conservative Party ploy prior to the 1983 General Election. The judge required evidence of the 'highest order' to establish these claims and was satisfied that the deputy director's membership of the Communist Party, and Communist infiltration of CND, was a legitimate reason for the tap.[114] However, he rejected the government assertion that, because the Government maintained silence on telephone taps in the interests of national security, the court should do likewise: 'To do so would be to say that the court should never inquire into a complaint against a Minister if he says his policy is to maintain silence in the interests of national security.'[115] The facts of this case emerged before the Interception of Telecommunications Act took effect; but that Act would have made no difference to the outcome, because the tribunal applies judicial review principles to authorised warrants. The case suggested that even in cases involving national security, the courts will not refuse to ask questions. But what sort of answers or reasons do they insist upon to justify the exercise of power?

Reasons for Decisions[116]

Another Australian court has recently upheld the long-standing doctrine of English common law which holds that public bodies are not required to give reasons for decisions in the absence of statutory requirements.[117] It seems strange that we have not witnessed a full-frontal assault on this bastion of inscrutability. Since 1963,[118] the courts have developed a more pronounced sense of fair play in novel institutional settings by extending the concept of natural justice which insists on a hearing before an unbiased decision-maker before being condemned or suffering a detriment. Fair procedure and legitimate expectation in fairness have been significantly extended; and acting unfairly, or acting unreasonably, or deviating unexpectedly from a settled, consistent or promised state of affairs before making a decision, have all been met with censure from the courts and have been regarded as unfair administrative decision-making. A very flexible range of standards and tests has been invoked and developed to protect individuals who face administrative decision-making which might be adverse to their interests or expectations, as well as legal rights. So that, for instance, being forewarned of allegations or accusations,[119] being allowed a reasonable time to prepare one's side of a case or argument,[120] being allowed legal representation as a right *where the circumstances warrant it* because of the difficulty of the charges or proceedings,[121] being allowed to probe the evidence against one, if necessary in a form that maintains confidentiality for the person who gave the information leading to the adverse decision – are considered necessary elements of fair procedure.[122] The move from natural justice in a legal/judicial forum to fair procedure in a broad range of administrative processes has been one of the success stories in the development of our administrative law. But certain irrational limits have been set. If reasons for decisions are not demanded by the courts, then this constitutes a barrier to fairness, an attack on openness, and it helps to pre-empt legitimate challenge to arbitrariness and inefficiency.

In Britain courts are loath to meddle too frequently or to pervasively in public administration. The success with which the autonomy of law has been perceived in a British setting has rested very obviously on judges operating within their allotted areas and not trespassing into politics or into areas of administration for which there is ultimate political responsibility. Too frequent an incursion would arouse suspicion of political bias or at best would result in accusations that judges were setting themselves up as administrators.[123] However, a refusal to insist on giving good reasons for decisions or non-decisions,[124] a general failure to ensure full information about a decision or to allow informed challenge to public decision-making, might be equally political in favour of the status quo and vested interests, a presumption as to the adequacy of existing arrangements for debate or discussion of proposals and decisions, or an assumption that those who make decisions always know best.

The judicial record on these points is not a venerable one. It took Parliamentary legislation in 1958 to reverse the impact of judicial decisions which held that reasons did not have to be forthcoming after an appeal had been made to the Minister in an environmental matter and after an inspector had conducted an inquiry and made recommendations to the Minister. Nor was the appellant allowed sight of the recommendations.[125] It was the 1958 Act which imposed a statutory duty to give reasons for decisions on a range of scheduled tribunals and ministerial decisions following public inquiries.[126] The courts have settled for an approach which would suggest that for tribunals which are under an obligation to give reasons for decisions, a failure to give reasons, or adequate reasons, is not *per se* a reason for allowing an appeal for an error of law from the tribunal.[127] The failure to supply a sufficient reason would appear bad enough, but to provide *no* reason would seem to fly in the face of the requirement that reasons shall be given.[128] The arguments in favour of this restrictive approach centre around the proposition that the appellant must show that the process of decision-making itself was vitiated by erroneous legal reasoning. Keeping a decision record to a minimum, and giving exiguous reasons, would make successful challenge less than likely, and probably deliberately so. In *Crake* v. *SBC*, Woolf J. adumbrated a test which, while not automatically stating that a failure to give adequate reasons is conclusive proof one way or the other on whether a tribunal has erred in law, suggested: 'in practice I think that there will be few cases when it will not be possible, where the reasons are inadequate, to say one way or another whether the tribunal has gone wrong in law.'[129] Courts, he felt, are now more readily persuaded that inadequate reasons, or reasons which show a failure to consider relevant factors, may lead to an *inference* that a decision was bad in law. If it is impossible to make this inference but doubt exists, the court can remit the case to the tribunal for reconsideration. When considering the reasons, the court will have the benefit of the chairman's notes in deciding whether, although the reasons are inadequate, the decision-making process was itself sound. Where it is impossible to discern from the surrounding evidence what the reasons for the decision of the tribunal are, and where the subject-matter of the decision is important, e.g. it involves the liberty of the subject,[130] or severe physical injury,[131] the court may be more willing to quash the decision for an error of law inasmuch as the decision does not comply with the statutory duty to give reasons.[132]

It is possible to see, however, that the courts might impugn failure to give adequate reasons where they construe that the duty is a part of the *condition* for the exercise of power and Parliament intended it to be such a condition. This appears to be the case in planning and environmental cases where a traditional right of property is being interfered with or effectively restricted. Here, because the property-owning developer needs to be informed of the reasons for an adverse decision so that he may amend a future application to the planning authority, failure to provide adequate, intelligible reasons has been fatal.[133] Indeed, the courts have gone further, holding in some cases that a failure to provide factual support for the reasons given could also prove fatal to the legality of the decision.[134] It is difficult to know how to reconcile these decisions,[135] although one can point to the fact that the tribunal cases generally refer to statutory rights of appeal,[136] whereas the environmental cases involve a statutory application to quash.[137] But not all distinctions are thus explicable. Distinctions on procedural points are the stuff of law in any system, but it is lamentable that such important issues of principle are obscured by an over-technical debate.

As mentioned earlier, where statute is silent on giving of reasons, the problem of interpretation does not arise. Social Security Commissioners, for instance do not, under statute, have to give reasons for decisions when refusing leave to appeal to them from local tribunals.[138] The Court of Appeal recently ruled[139] that reasons for decisions for refusing an appeal do not have to be given. It may be admirable in the interests of justice that they be given, but there is no duty in statute or common law to do so. Expedience and the expertise of the tribunals on questions of fact were the obvious reasons in Parliament's mind when it legislated to exclude the Commissioners from a duty to give reasons.[140] Any judicial encouragement to give reasons *de facto* would, it was felt, create more problems than it would solve, and should be deprecated.[141] The court should assume that Social Security Commissioners acted on good grounds, *unless* the appellant can prove to the contrary. But without reasons. . . ?[142]

In other circumstances the courts have not insisted on the giving of full reasons by the Parole Board, chairmen of local review committees, or the Home Secretary, in cases involving refusal to grant licence or in decisions recalling a prisoner on licence.[143] While these decisions may be explained by the authorities on the basis of the confidentiality of reports from medical officers and others and the seriousness of the crime involved, one is unhappy that the authorities do not have enough confidence in their decisions to give public justification for them – absenting the identity of officials or others where risk to their safety is involved. The European Court of Human Rights, in *Weeks* v. *UK*, has found the UK in breach of Article 5(4) when a prisoner on parole did not have the benefit of full disclosure of adverse information in the possession of the Parole Board on decisions affecting recall or review. British sensitivity has been centred on public security, crime prevention and confidentiality. No such considerations apply to a line of cases recently decided in the Court of Appeal and the House of Lords which reveal a questionable over-sympathy for administrative expedience at the expense, it is felt, of human dignity.

The decision of *ex p. Swati*[144] concerned the refusal of entry to this country of visitors – essentially those from the New Commonwealth. Briefly, such visitors had, via the intercession of relatives or friends who were already in the UK, sought to delay their removal by invoking the assistance of an MP[145] or applying for leave for judicial review. The Home Office responded to the former practice by restricting the opportunities to contact MPs. The Court of Appeal dealt with the latter practice by holding that the standard reason for refusing leave of entry was a sufficient *ex facie* reason to refuse entry. This allows the officer to state baldly that he or she is not satisfied that the visitor is 'genuinely seeking entry for the period of the visit as stated'. To go any further, Parker L.J. believed, was to seek 'not reasons for refusal, but the reasons for the reasons for refusal'. If such a reason is *ex facie* good, leave will not be given to apply for judicial review unless the applicant has further information that the officer's decision is unlawful. If the officer does not have to give a reason of any more substance than the above, the applicant will have nothing to shift the burden of proof from his shoulders.

The second case is a House of Lords decision which suggests that, in cases where local authorities are challenged by individuals claiming various rights under the Housing (Homeless Persons) Act, the decisions of fact are for the local housing authorities, and courts should be reluctant to interfere with their decisions and decision-making processes. Their decisions should be viewed with latitude, and a loose framework, i.e. no safeguards, should not be taken to mean that improprieties existed on the authorities' part.[146] In these circumstances, individuals are going to find it virtually impossible to substantiate allegations of unfairness or abuse of discretion. It is a decision which echoes the sentiments of Lord Denning's 'presidency' of the Court of Appeal, when he suggested that welfare legislation should not become the 'happy hunting ground of lawyers'.[147] When the courts want to keep out, they can easily allow processes to remain closed. When they wish to intervene, they can construe a duty to give reasons strictly or establish that findings are unsubstantiated by the facts.[148] Too often, predictability is reduced to a guessing game.

There are judicial dicta that might have encouraged a rationalising tendency. In *Padfield*, Lord Upjohn suggested that a failure to give reasons for a decision *could* lead a court to presume that no good reasons in law existed for the decision, which would then be invalid and subject to possible redress in the courts.[149] Such a piece of *obiter dicta* was bound to be interpreted by later courts as a momentary lapse from judicious caution or simple exaggeration.[150] A second's thought would make one realise what a preposterous notion this was, and the unreasonable burden under which it would place the administration! It is sobering, therefore, to consider that in France it has been a presumption of law in *droit administratif* that no reasons for a decision constitutes 'bad reasons' for a decision in law.[151] French public administration works in a very different manner and cultural framework from our own, but surely there is a lesson to be learned. And from a common law jurisdiction, the right to have a decision, or rules expressing policies based upon 'reliable, probative and substantial evidence', under the Administrative Procedure Act (APA) of the USA has helped to promote the expectation of fully reasoned decisions as a matter of course. The requirement has assisted in cutting down the use of administrative procedures as opportunities for closed bartering between regulatory overlords and powerful regulated interests.[152] The fact that FOIA legislation was required testifies to the fact that the APA was not, in itself, a panacea for closed or cosy brokerage between powerful groups but – and this is the important point – the US legislation and judicial interpretations of it have shown an awareness and insight of the realities of administrative and commercial power which have, as yet, been denied to our law and lawyers, even if a period of retrenchment has existed in the USA latterly.[153]

What is required in a British setting is a greater provision of statutory duties to give reasons which stipulate the consequences of failure to comply, and which specify the items which should be addressed in the reasons. The failure of British judges this century to adopt a more vigorous approach to the giving of reasons for the exercise of discretionary power bears sad testimony to their lack of appreciation of the requirements of constitutionality. This is all the more regrettable considering the judiciary's extra-judicial support for such constitutional safeguards, and their tendentious application of them in practice.[154]

Foreclosing Discussion

In a way, some of these arguments are thrown into greater relief by looking at challenges to administrative decision-making which are not centred on individuals being given reasons for decisions, but which are attempts to put an alternative view to those who make decisions which will have a pronounced impact upon the collective weal. We therefore find in relation to public inquiries that, while obtaining reasons for a decision is important for a property holder whose land is affected,[155] when we come to broader-ranging inquiries where a policy proposal is more obviously in issue, limiting the issues on the agenda is as crucial and as important as the giving of reasons, if not more so. The courts, for instance, have ruled out the necessity of any discussion of the policies or merits of a proposal to build a road, for example, at an inquiry. Furthermore, discussion of the factual basis supporting a proposal, e.g. the traffic flow predictions for future years, has been held to be an unsuitable topic for discussion at a public inquiry.[156] These matters are better suited to discussion within the department, and between the department and local authorities, rather than being debated in public.[157] For broad policy concerns the Minister can answer to Parliament.[158] Rules for inquiries invariably stipulate that where a representative of the Minister is obliged to appear, he or she will not answer questions on the merits of policy. The inquiry is into objections, not the merits of proposals.[159] Nothing prevents a department opening up a large inquiry to debate the need and merits for a proposal if it so wishes, and the Sizewell 'B' Inquiry into the Central Electricity Generating Board's proposal to build Britain's first pressurised water reactor at Sizewell is a case in point. The Department of Energy, but not other departments, allowed questions on the merits of policy.[160] However, although the Department of Energy allowed a pressure group to use 'misappropriated' internal documents, it refused their requests for more up-to-date figures which might have thrown light on that document; nor would the same department reveal 'as a matter of practice . . . internal departmental working documents'.[161]

The difficulty with inquiries into major proposals is that it is often impossible to discern where policy begins, and pure fact or details behind the proposals end. The House of Lords decision in the 1980 *Bushell* case is illustrative of such a problem.[162] It was also evident in litigation where the Department sought to exclude the question of the *principle* of levying tolls for the Severn Bridge from the scope of the inquiry into objections against a proposal to raise the tolls.[163] Objections on the specific application of the policy had been made at the inquiry, but had not formed part of the inspectors' recommendations. The department argued that the principle of raising tolls *per se* involved government economic policy.[164] At first instance, the judge disagreed, holding that this was not a matter which was unsuitable for discussion. While Ministers had power to remove from discussion matters that were not suitable for an inquiry, it was not simply a matter of their *ipse dixit* but depended upon whether the Minister would be assisted by discussion,[165] or whether he was already committed *lawfully* to a policy which could only be upset at the cost of considerable disruption.[166] That was not the case here, since the objectors wished their views on the *specific application* of policy to be raised in the inspector's report. The Court of Appeal unanimously overruled the judgment to quash the Secretary of State's decision.[167] The inspector had been perfectly correct not to allude to the policy objections, because they related to 'general policy matters' and his views would be of no more significance than those of any other 'member of the public'. Furthermore, the court was satisfied that the Secretary of State *had* considered the gravamen of the objections on policy in his department, deciding nonetheless to increase the tolls. All in all, fairness had been achieved.[168]

An inquiry has to be fixed into a continuing time process through which new information will emerge. It was clear in *Bushell* that where such information emerges from *within* the sponsoring department *after* the inquiry, natural justice does not dictate that this has to be presented to the objectors at a new inquiry. Inquiries Rules under statute[169] only provide for the position where, after the inquiry, new evidence or facts[170] are considered and *as a consequence* the Minister is minded to disagree with the inspector's recommendations. This rule seems to have been given a strained interpretation recently when an inspector was unhappy about environmental safeguards surrounding an application to build an aerodrome in the London dockland. He recommended conditions to be attached to the grant of permission. The Secretary of State took evidence from another department *after* the inquiry and gave permission for development without reopening the inquiry. The court held that the Minister had not disagreed with the inspector's recommendations, merely amplified and clarified them,[171] so therefore the safeguard in the rules was not triggered.

One final point concerning the restriction of the agenda, and the effect this restriction has on information provision, concerns the Transport Users Consultative Committee and closure of passenger railway lines. Public hearings must take place before the TUCC. These hearings cannot examine the economic case for closure. At the hearings into the prospective closure of the Settle–Carlisle railway line, counsel for British Rail accepted that the economic case was the sheet anchor of their case, but the hearing was precluded from discussing this item. The Committee's report criticised this exclusion vehemently.[172] The Court of Appeal has, moreover, held that the procedure at these truncated hearings is at the chairman's discretion, so that he was within his powers to refuse cross-examination of BR witnesses or to allow final submissions from counsel for the objectors.[173] The body was making recommendations, not determining a justiciable issue. This is a lame excuse if *fairness* is not seen to be done. It is a question of balance, and too often the balance is heavily weighed in favour of administrative convenience.

Information and the Conduct of Legal Argument

In January 1985, an Australian Royal Commission under the chairmanship of another Australian High Court judge began the first day of its sitting by lambasting the British Government for its refusal to hand over information concerning the testing of nuclear weapons by the British Government in Australian deserts and the Christmas Islands in the early 1950s. The papers covered medical reports and monitoring the effects of the explosions, including the effects on servicemen who took part.[174] Many of these claimed they had been exposed to radiation with inadequate protection. The Government released over a period of time three and a half tons of documents. These revealed that such monitoring had been taken at the time but had remained secret.

Technically, the Government was not bound to give any information to the Commission. The episode is interesting because of the robust manner in which a judge criticised government secrecy, and for the fact that a considerable degree of evidence was forthcoming eventually. When it comes to the crunch, what will a British court insist on a British public body disclosing? This has to be seen in the context of the adversarial process, which is the method adopted by British, and common law, courts to establish facts and obtain information. It is to be compared with the inquisitorial process, which is the method of inquiries, commissions and civil jurisdictions. The distinction between the two has been explained by Lord Devlin:[175]

The essential difference between the two systems – is apparent from their names: the one is a trial of strength and the other is an inquiry. The question in the first is: are the shoulders of the party upon whom is laid the burden of proof, the plaintiff or the prosecution as the case may be, strong enough to carry and discharge it? In the second the question is: what is the truth of the matter? In the first the judge or jury are arbiters; they do not pose questions and seek answers; they weigh such material as is put before them, but they have no responsibility for seeing that it is complete. In the second the judge is in charge of the inquiry from the start; he will of course permit the parties to make out their cases and may rely on them to do so, but it is for him to say what it is that he wants to know.

The courts provide, in an adversarial system, on the surface at least, a forum within which an equal debate can take place. It is up to the parties involved to present their cases as fully and completely as possible. The judge can then adjudicate. It is a contest which operates within procedural restraints imposed by the rules of evidence and the rules of procedure, as well as substantive restraints. These latter are contained in the law itself. To give a simple example, a tenant facing eviction at the suit of an allegedly rapacious landlord may see his 'problem' relating to a whole series of social, economic and possibly political factors. These could be unemployment, indigence, the favouritism or otherwise shown to property-holders over the propertyless. The law cuts down the substance of these issues by asking does, or does not, the landlord have a legal right to possess the property? Everything else is irrelevant in law. Law narrows the range of debate. The procedure narrows the issues which are legally relevant by insisting that they be presented in a particular way, i.e. that only admissible evidence is entered and that hearsay evidence is not.[176]

The received tradition of the adversarial process, then, is of a two-cornered fight between the parties before the judge.[177] In public law cases, it is difficult to justify this approach when the 'public interest' or constitutional issues are involved. The courts may recognise such an interest, although there is frequently a reluctance to describe matters involving individuals as constitutional, as opposed to legal.[178] The restraints of law, both substantive and procedural, will ensure that courts will not, in a British system, be used to prise open closed government or widen the debate about political right against our governors. Unlike the situation in the USA, the British courts are not sympathetic to extended *amicus curiae* briefs or class actions.

When parties are involved in litigation, the court does not give them an unbridled right to invade each other's privacy. Questions can be asked before and during the proceedings which are relevant to those proceedings. In a trial between private parties, discovery of documents in the possession, custody or power of either may be ordered to the other.[179] In some circumstances, the courts may even award an *Anton Piller* order where, if there is a danger that relevant documents will be destroyed, the court will allow the other party to enter the relevant premises to seize them for the purposes of the litigation for 'such relatively short period' as is reasonably necessary to copy them.[180] It is hardly surprising that the subject of discovery of documents should have spawned a wide-ranging body of case law on the extent of third parties to disclose documents to a party in litigation;[181] being allowed to use a skilled co-ordinator who was a third party to collate and conduct discovery in an action involving over 1 million documents requiring a multiplicity of scientific skills;[182] whether documents discovered in one action may be used against the same party in other litigation;[183] the extent of the immunity of legal professional privilege, especially where the party claiming it has accidentally allowed access to such 'privileged' documents;[184] and how far down its corporate hierarchy a company must go to establish the existence of documents which have to be handed over on discovery.[185] Our pressing concern is with Public Interest Immunity.

Public Interest, Immunity and Information

A public body[186] may wish to withhold documents, or not to have officials answering questions in a court, because the public interest demands that the information should not be made public. A claim used to be made, misleadingly, for Crown privilege.[187] The Crown possessed a prerogative immunity at common law against orders for discovery of documents. This was abolished by section 28 of the Crown Proceedings Act 1947, subject to two provisos: any rule of law survived which authorised the withholding of information in the public interest because disclosure would be injurious to that interest;[188] and disclosure of the very existence of a document was not to be enforced if in the opinion of the Minister it would be injurious to disclose whether it existed.[189] The first proviso related to the doctrine of Crown privilege, which was given extensive definition by a unanimous House of Lords in 1942,[190] whereby, having regard to the contents of the particular document(s), or if the document belongs to a class which, on the grounds of public interest, must as a class be withheld from production, they should be withheld. The judgment of the Minister sufficed.[191]

Administrative concessions were made by the Government, and in 1968 the House of Lords overruled the wider aspects of *Duncan* v. *Cammell Laird* in *Conway* v. *Rimmer*.[192] Against the claim of the Crown that the candour[193] of communications between officials required protection, the Law Lords maintained the court's right to inspect the documents for itself; to make its own judgment on whether they should be privileged; and if not, whether they should be disclosed to the other party if relevant. The decision was regarded as epoch-making, albeit daunting. Judges were to be the arbiters of the public interest in what could be highly sensitive areas of official confidentiality. Professor de Smith thought that if 'There are some things that English judges are poorly equipped to do', this was certainly one of them.[194] Examination of the judgments shows how cautious the Law Lords were. Cabinet documents were excluded, as were diplomatic dispatches and even papers coming before junior Ministers concerning advice and formulation of policy at a low level. 'The business of government is difficult enough,' opined Lord Reid, 'and no government could contemplate with equanimity the inner workings of the government machine being exposed to the gaze of those ready to criticise without adequate knowledge of the background and perhaps with some axe to grind.'[195]

On the contrary Lord Keith, in the *Burmah Oil*[196] decision, believed such an opening up might lead 'not to captious or ill-informed criticism, but to criticism calculated to improve the nature of that working [of Government] as affecting the individual citizen'. In *Burmah Oil*, the House of Lords held that a certificate from a Secretary of State that the documents were of a high-policy content, and related to ministerial discussions with senior officials,[197] was not conclusive. The courts could balance the public interest of preventing harm to the State or the public service by not ordering disclosure, and the public interest of doing individual justice in the courts by ordering discovery if that would assist a litigant to vindicate his claims in law. If necessary, the court could examine the documents if they appeared likely to be relevant to the cause in action.[198] The case extended the principle of *Conway* v. *Rimmer* and was doubtless influenced by case law in Australia and the USA.[199] The Law Lords' insistence that courts had a power to review the certificate of the Minister concerning documents of a 'high policy content' in the highest levels of Government, subject to national security or considerations of an equally important dimension,[200] is quite startling, albeit welcome. The impact of this approach can be seen in a case such as *Williams* v. *Home Office (No. 1)*,[201] where discovery was ordered to a former prisoner of discussion documents between high-level officials and a Minister on the merits of the Control Unit at HM Prison Wakefield. The plaintiff did not win his eventual action, but the documents revealed a clash at the highest level on the merits and propriety of the form of punishment implemented within the unit, and confusion in the aims of penal policy.

But *Burmah Oil* was perhaps too emphatic. The grounding of the argument by some of the judges in terms of the rhetoric of constitutional principle could not remain unamended.[202] A 'more considered' approach characterised the majority ruling in the *Air Canada* litigation.[203] Air Canada and other airlines complained of the exorbitant landing and user charges at Heathrow Airport. It was claimed on their behalf that the charges imposed by the British Airports Authority were *ultra vires* inasmuch as they were not exacted for the purposes contained in the statute,[204] but to pursue an ulterior governmental economic policy of reducing public sector borrowing.[205] On general discovery[206] the Minister refused to disclose documents which comprised communications passing between government Ministers and the preparatory drafts used by Ministers of their meetings, and which related to the formulation of government policy regarding BAA and the limitation of public sector borrowing. Public Interest Immunity was claimed. At first instance the judge ordered production, subject to his inspection, even though the documents might not assist the plaintiff's case *because* the information 'would substantially assist the court to elicit the true facts regarding the plaintiff's case' and would thereby affect the court's decision. This was a sufficient public interest justification for their discovery, subject to judicial inspection. This decision was overruled in the Court of Appeal and by majority in the House of Lords.[207]

The majority decision of the Law Lords held that, before a judge exercises a discretion to examine documents for which Immunity is claimed, the plaintiff must establish that they will assist his case or damage his adversary's, and that they are necessary for disposing fairly of the case or saving costs. Not only is the onus on the applicant to convince the judge that they will assist the applicant, but he will also have to convince the judge as to *how* they will assist. If he cannot be precise on this point, stating with conviction and specificity what they will contain, then the danger is that his arguments will appear speculative and part of a fishing expedition. In cases against a public authority, Fox L.J. held in the Court of Appeal, a plaintiff must have prima facie evidence of his own without the aid of discovery, 'save in the most exceptional of cases'. The 'interests of justice', the majority held in the House of Lords, meant that the task of the court was to decide the case fairly on the evidence before it, and 'not to ascertain some independent truth by seeking out evidence of its own accord'. The minority felt that the court could inspect where disclosure *might* assist the plaintiff, or defendant, *or the court*, in determining the issues, with the onus of proof on the applicant for discovery. If this onus is discharged, then there is strong authority to suggest that even Cabinet documents can be inspected by the judge to establish whether disclosure to the applicant is necessary.[208] Without a doubt, the onus on the applicant to get the judge to inspect is a very heavy one. The more probing a judicial inquiry is, the more likely it is that there will be material to establish *ultra vires* or unlawful considerations or action. Courts are not there to inquire, they are there to decide on the basis of what the applicant can give them. This is especially true of judicial review cases, which are meant to be speedy and expeditious and, save in rare circumstances, a review on the affidavits as filed and not by way of discovery and cross-examination of witnesses.[209]

John Griffith has asked that as judges are required 'to make policy decisions in the public interest, they should equip themselves with the means to gather all the relevant information. That is an indispensable necessity for all decision-makers.'[210] His comment came after a critique of the pusillanimous approach of English courts to testing Ministers' claims that they were acting in the interests of national security, or in judicial interpretation of complex statutes affecting social policy without referring to White Papers, policy documents or debates in the House explaining the intention of the legislators.[211] Arguments have been advanced before for a British equivalent to the Commissaire du Gouvernement in France, who has access to the files within public authorities and who enters into public law cases to argue for the 'public interest' as identified by a non-combatant where that interest requires to be represented. As Sir Harry Woolf has said:

The position of the public in general must be taken into account [in judicial review] since . . . public law is designed to protect the public as a whole as well as the individual applicant. The public has a very real interest in seeing that litigation does not necessarily and unduly interfere with the process of government both at a national and a local level.[212]

In judicial review cases, Sir Harry said, the court is not concerned with a fact-finding exercise and 'in practice applications for discovery and cross examination are very rare . . . I have no doubt . . . that justice is served by the present approach'.[213] Nevertheless, he had misgivings about the adversarial approach in the combat, even in judicial review cases, and suggested a Director of Civil Proceedings for public law litigation, sufficiently independent of, but answerable to, a Minister of the Crown or the Attorney-General. The Director would take references from the public and would proceed where he thought necessary in the public interest, assuming the expense and responsibility.[214] He would monitor cases before the court on judicial review,[215] and would intervene with an argument on behalf of the public which is not catered for by the parties before the court. The initiative would be with the Director not the court, 'and would depend upon the special expertise which the Director would build up as a result of his ability to consult the relevant Government Departments and special interest groups'.[216] He would have access to the papers and books of public bodies,[217] as the Ombudsman does. The Ombudsman, as we saw, is not allowed access to Cabinet documents. This barrier ought not to apply to the Director, although Sir Harry was silent on the point, especially as he envisaged the Director advising the courts on discovery of documents and we have seen that these might include Cabinet documents.

In cases that do not raise issues close to the governmental bosom, the courts have suggested a possible liberalisation of the test for discovery on judicial review, aligning it with the same test for private law actions.[218] So where a prisoner contested the conditions of his confinement, discovery of all medical and psychiatric reports was allowed.[219] A decision of the Court of Appeal[220] could have a bearing on giving of information and reasons for decisions by public bodies. The court accepted that public bodies who are challenged over the matter of the exercise of a discretion or power can expect that the burden of establishing a case will be upon the applicant; however, once the case is accepted for hearing, it becomes the duty of the respondent council 'to make full and fair disclosure'.[221] It is, said the

Master of the Rolls, 'a process which falls to be conducted with all the cards face upwards . . . and the vast majority of cards will start in the authority's hands'. It won't do for the authority to assert that it acted within the law and that the applicant must prove to the contrary:

> If the allegation is that a decision is prima facie irrational and that these are grounds for inquiring whether something immaterial may have been considered or something material omitted from consideration, it really does not help to assert boldly that all relevant matters and no irrelevant matters are taken into consideration without condescending to mention some at least of the principal factors on which the decision was based.[222]

The authority should set out fully and fairly what is required to meet the challenge by way of explanation.[223] Having promised so much, the court then backed down entirely and did not allow review even where such explanations were not forthcoming. If courts do not go all the way, they should not tease. When the courts do decide to go through the books of public authorities on application for discovery, they will inevitably find what they are looking for if they wish to intervene. In the Fares Fair litigation,[224] which involved the pursuit of a manifesto pledge to reduce fares on the London Transport system by increasing public subsidy financed by a rate increase, while Griffith attacked the courts for failing to examine the background information on urban transport enterprises and systems,[225] it is clear that the Court of Appeal and House of Lords went through the internal documents of the Greater London Council with a fine-tooth comb to establish procedural and substantive errors in the decisions of the GLC. This is particularly apparent in the influential and pivotal judgment of Oliver L.J.: 'In the GLC's bundle of documents there is *another* significant document. . . . It is a report of a transport policy committee running into over 100 pages.'[226] In a discussion, a lawyer working for the GLC informed the present writer of the extent of the order of discovery against the authority and his surprise at its ambit. When the judges wish to intervene, they know the weapons: get reasons and insist on fuller information. In themselves, these are desirable objectives of a democratic and civilised government; it is therefore regrettable that the judicial record has been so inconsistent and often pusillanimous.[227]

One final area of concern involves police investigations into complaints and/or incidents surrounding the subject-matter of a complaint against an officer. Clearly, a complainant who could obtain the investigation report with police statements would be in a strong position to launch proceedings in the courts if the evidence indicated that a crime or tort had been committed. Complaint investigation reports are protected by Public Interest Immunity in subsequent litigation to protect the candour of those supplying statements, especially police officers.[228] The Court of Appeal has recently held[229] that where the *preponderant* cause of the investigation was not a complaint, but the desire of the police to establish the events and facts behind an incident, the Immunity will not automatically apply on a class basis, but might on a contents basis.[230]

However, it has also been held that, while a complainant cannot see the complaint report since this is protected, his complaint itself is not, so the officer complained against may commence a defamation action over the complaint.[231] Where an officer is sued after a complaint, it is common for the officer's counsel to have the statements of the complainant, but not vice versa. Indeed, the chairman of the Police Complaints Authority has complained of the unfair use by the police of witnesses' statements to the investigating officer, which the chairman cannot publicise other than in anonymous summary form. The Home Secretary and the police are not so restricted.[232] The chairman would like to have powers to make full publication, subject to the legitimate needs of confidentiality.[233]

Judges and Confidences

The law recognises a duty to maintain a confidence which has arisen from a contractual relationship, or in circumstances where information is acquired and from which an obligation of confidence can be inferred. In the absence of an express or implied contractual undertaking, most common in employment and trade secrets cases, the law looks for some relationship where it would be inequitable not to protect the confidences or 'secrets' which exist within a relationship.[234] The fact that information is stamped 'confidential' does not make it so for legal purposes, nor is every secret protected by the law.

In the Crossman diaries litigation[235] it was held that the law of confidentiality could protect by injunction not only domestic or trade/commercial secrets, but 'public' secrets, that is information emanating from State or public business, not information which has been made public.[236] The case concerned Cabinet and Cabinet

Committee discussions, which are buttressed by the convention of Ministerial Collective Responsibility, a convention which the court saw it as its duty to maintain to protect the confidentiality owed in law to Cabinet discussions and details of decisions. The period of time for which it had to be maintained was a matter of judgment on the facts of the individual case. The litigation involved the diaries of the former Cabinet Minister, which revealed information about Cabinet business while in office obtained from other Cabinet Ministers and civil servants. The Crown was seeking to restrain publication by injunction – by prior restraint. On the facts, an injunction was not necessary, because the events happened over 10 years before the litigation.[237] As we have seen, the concept of public secrets was extended in the Court of Appeal decision prohibiting the publication of memoirs by Peter Wright, the former MI5 official,[238] to protect the confidentiality of the 'public secrets' attaching to operations of the security services. We saw how later proceedings sought to play down the public law element while extending the concept of confidentiality.

Confidentiality is a protean but uncertain concept protecting information. When the courts are concerned with relationships between individuals and a legal remedy is sought to protect confidentiality, the courts are on more familiar territory where they can assimilate the concept with property – though this can be taken too far. This is especially important for trade secrets and freedom of trade, and for secrets acquired in Crown service.[239] The law is on more difficult ground where it seeks to protect confidences arising from relationships when breach would be inequitable. Confidentiality alone is insufficient reason to withhold information where the interests of justice require its release.[240] In sex and race discrimination cases the tribunal chairman can examine papers on other employees to assess whether discrimination has taken place against the plaintiff in promotions or appointments.[241]

The courts have held that the 'public interest' may justify a leak which would constitute a breach of confidence or copyright, and a defence to an application for an injunction could be made by establishing that it was in the public interest for the public to know, for instance, that the police were using unreliable instruments to assess the level of alcohol in motorists' blood, as in *Lion*.[242] However, to be protected, one has to show that the breach was in the public interest and not merely interesting to the public, and that the chosen method of publication is appropriate. Illegal or other wrongdoing which is effected by a breach of confidence may be more appropriately published by informing the police or respective authorities, rather than by detailing the contents of a conversation, obtained by an illegal tap, in the national press.[243] Donaldson M.R. has insisted that there should be a 'moral imperative' to publish openly, rather than informing the authorities before an injunction restraining publication would be refused. In *Lion*, the Court of Appeal believed that plaintiffs seeking an injunction prohibiting publication would have to establish that the defendant could not show that there is a serious defence of public interest which *may* succeed at the trial. In *Lion* the plaintiffs could not establish this, so the injunction was refused.[244] Where a defence of public interest can be raised, the courts can involve themselves in a familiar balancing act of weighing the public interest in maintaining confidentiality, against the public interest of informing the public of matters of *real* public concern. In the *Spycatcher* case, Scott J. believed it was of real public concern that there should be reporting of allegations of serious misconduct by MI5 officers.

The law will protect a confidential, original and commercially promising idea. There can be no breach of copyright in a creative idea unless it is reduced to material form and used without permission. It is beyond the scope of a work such as this to describe the emerging law relating to intellectual property, copyright and patents.[245] Judicial law is inadequate to provide appropriate protection to such ideas and information and has given way to a succession of unsatisfactory statutes.[246] A White Paper of April 1986 proposed a Patent Office which will be a non-Crown, non-departmental body, appointed by the Secretary of State.[247] An advisory group, the 'Whitehall Liaison Group', will be established to improve the Government's knowledge and understanding of intellectual property. The Patent Comptroller and Performing Rights Tribunal will be given extended jurisdiction over disputes. As well as incorporating relevant European Conventions, further proposals cover employee inventions; industrial designs; levies on blank audio tapes; restrictions on educational broadcasts; the addition of perpetual copyright and the introduction of lifelong 'moral rights' for authors; boosting of criminal sanctions against bootleggers and formalisation of civil remedies. In 1985, the Copyright (Computer Software) Act was passed.[248] Computer software piracy ran to about £150 million in 1984, a figure readily extendable because of the ease with which computer programmes can be broken into and copied. The Act extends the 1956 Copyright Act to computer programmes with necessary 'adaptation' of program(mes) and to include storage within a computer as forms of 'reproduction in . . . or reduction to a material form'. Many key terms and phrases, e.g. 'Computer', 'Computer program(me)', are not defined.

By December 1987, the Copyright, Designs and Patents Bill had been introduced in the Lords amid fears that it would unjustifiably extend authors' proprietorial rights in a manner which would substantially interfere with freedom of speech.

7
Conclusion – How Nigh is the End?

What we know helps to make us what we are. The information we are able to use and build upon constitutes our past, our present and our future. It is small wonder that the protection and dissemination of information has attracted so much political and legal attention, for it is concerned with power and possession, wealth and influence, success and failure. It has as much relevance to the process of government as to our most intimate secrets. Very different kinds of information have been examined in this book. In some areas, for instance protection of private secrets by the law of confidentiality, the courts have occasionally adopted some sensible approaches in establishing where the protection of a private confidence ends and a public right to know begins. The extension by the courts of confidentiality to protect without reservation 'public secrets' has a less happy aspect in its application, however much the courts might declare that they are merely giving fuller articulation to the general principles of the law of confidentiality, and not confusing it with the law of copyright. The progress of the law in this direction until Scott J.'s judgment in the *Wright* case in December 1987, was reminiscent of erstwhile judicial attitudes which saw an extension of information about the operations of Government as undesirable and unnecessary. The judicial extension protects the 'arcane mysteries' of Government which we spoke of in general terms in Chapter 1, the development of which we saw in Chapter 3 and the contemporary practices of which we explored in Chapter 4. Protection of an individual's confidentiality and privacy are often necessary to protect that individual's integrity and identity. Over-protection of governmental information can be destructive of integrity and identity. Taken to extremes, over-protection will not only prevent more participatory forms of democracy, it can undermine democracy itself. So much seems to have been present in the warnings of Lords Bridge and Oliver, Browne-Wilkinson V.C. and Scott J. in the *Spycatcher* litigation.

In Chapter 5 we examined how Government has to give information in order to observe certain democratic promises. Courts have
sometimes assisted in a limited fashion in helping litigants to have
these promises fulfilled. And it is true that the courts have insisted
that private litigants be more open in all stages of litigation to save
time and costs. But where information cannot be conceptualised in
proprietorial or quasi-proprietorial terms, the courts lack the
resources to foster 'communicative competence' between Government and governed in the absence of constitutional principles of good
and responsible government which they could invoke.

How far would the creation of a property right in information
protect personal interests which at present are inadequately
protected? Imagine that we accepted a legally protected definition of
privacy as 'the claim of individuals, groups or institutions to
determine for themselves when, how and to what extent information
about them is communicated to others'.[1] Would we create more
problems than we solved? We would be able to insist that whenever
we gave information about ourselves it could only be used for the
purposes for which we gave it. Otherwise, information about me
cannot be used unless it has come into the public domain through my
own choice or my actions. Even if we agreed that there are good
grounds for invading privacy where a clear and identifiable public
interest exists, e.g. the prevention of crime or disorder, much
investigative journalism as we know it would cease if such a definition
were accepted. At present a rather lame Press Council, without
enforcement powers, hears complaints from those who feel that
journalists have overstepped the bounds of responsible or acceptable
reporting. Many who are forthright in their support of a free and
independent press are equally critical of an irresponsible press.
Making information about oneself a property right could create
enormous restrictions on our freedom of speech. Abusive invasions of
privacy are probably best settled by responsible self-regulation in the
absence of a breach of private law. The Press Council has not shown
itself equal to the task of such regulation, which to be effective
probably needs legislative support.

In a way, we do accept that information is a property right.
Information in my possession does not have to be given to anyone
else. Not even, as we have just noticed, when it concerns them.
Providing I do not break any laws in possessing it, using it or
communicating it, such information is mine to do with as I will. I

cannot prevent others using the information they possess about me, except in those circumstances where they are not complying with the law. I have no general duty to let others know what I hold. Here, we come back to the points raised in Chapter 1, where we debated the implications of privileged access to information by powerholders.

Allowing others to determine exclusively the means by which they collect, use or disseminate information gives them the greatest of managerial prerogatives. As with all prerogatives, they are potentially inimical to shared responsibility, accountability and democratic values. Certain anaemic statutory provisions on disclosure cover national and multi-national companies, but otherwise they are regarded as private commercial enterprises with a variety of somewhat exiguous duties[2] to actual or prospective creditors and shareholders[3] but few to the public at large. The benefits of 'efficient' and closed management of public institutions were seen when water authorities were no longer caught by the Public Bodies (Access to Meetings) Act and their meetings were withdrawn from the public. This was justified by the responsible Minister on the grounds that water authorities were no longer operating like public corporations, but more like private companies under the Companies Act, with executive and business responsibilities. The true democratic nature of much of our public affairs may be weak, but privatisation runs the risk of diminishing it further. Openness at all costs can lead to indecision and folly. Efficiency at all costs, without any balancing values such as openness, can lead to tyranny.

Trade unions have often complained about the inadequate nature of information from managements employing their members concerning management proposals for future developments affecting the company and employees. The British tradition has seen a voluntarist and 'soft law'[4] approach, but one which has meant that management most of the time is afforded enormous latitude. Since our entry into the EEC, an increasing number of directives have sought to create the machinery for consultation and participation in commercial enterprises, as well as providing information in advance of decisions.[5] The *Vredeling Directive* attempted to achieve an effective and genuine flow of information from employers to employees, although 'sensitive information' as defined need not be disclosed. Confidential information should go no further than the employee representatives. There was nothing of significance to prevent the information being slanted in the employer's favour, and the provisions were watered down at the request of the European Parliament before the draft directive fell. The British provisions that do exist on employee involvement have been largely ineffectual.[6] The draft directive only applied to groups or undertakings employing 1,000 or more employees, and was only to exist in such groups where employee representatives were recognised for bargaining purposes and were certified as independent, i.e. a trade union. Participation based on employee share ownership is more popular, as a limited democracy based upon a property stake is acceptable whereas a democracy based on notions relating to human dignity and respect for individuals because they are individuals is a more difficult proposition.

Closely related to managerial confidences are professional confidences. We have looked at these in the course of the book.[7] Through control of information, the professions can enhance their monopoly of control, regulation and practice as well as their position *vis-à-vis* the communities they serve. The Law Society has, since October 1986, opened its meetings to its membership and has given limited press access to its meetings.[8] These seem likely to deal with the most routine and uncontentious of business. The concession came at a time when solicitors through the Law Society reluctantly accepted a more 'independent' element in their client complaints procedures. As we noted, accountants are being actively pressurised by the Government to reveal information to the Bank of England, thereby breaking the confidentiality which they owe to their clients.[9] To seek a breach of similar confidence for lawyers would interfere with legal professional privilege. The compliance of the accountants' governing bodies has ensured that the Government will not impose the duty by legislation, but by a voluntary self-regulatory code. Further spin-offs could be a far closer relationship between the profession and the State, as exists on the Continent.

The medical profession is probably under attack more than any other over its secretive administration. A complex web of arguments envelops this profession. Firstly, people do want greater access to those medical files that their doctor or health authority holds on them. The Access to Personal Files Bill originally included 'health records' of authorities, hospitals and practitioners, subject to exemptions, including that where disclosure 'would expose the applicant to a risk of serious physical or mental harm' access will be deferred for six months pending a second opinion. The Government insisted that health records were excluded from the Act. Doctors' associations[10] claimed that if patients were allowed access to files, and if independent inquiries were conducted into medical practice, these developments would only encourage those who were hell-bent on litigation.[11] Confidentiality helps to protect the professional status of doctors. This is one of the important issues at stake.

The Access to Personal Files Act 1987

The original Bill which was proposed as a Private Member's Bill included social security, employment (private or public), immigration, and health records of individuals, as well as housing, education (including university[12]) and social services records. The Bill attended to many of the more pressing problems associated with abuse or inaccuracy of manual records, but it was not a Bill regulating the use or manner of collection of information.[13] Nor did it create a registrar or register, nor a mode of enforcement apart from access to the courts when seeking amendment if the record was inaccurate or irrelevant to the purpose of compilation, and compensation for damage or distress.

However, the Government forced the proponents to accept an eviscerated Bill which left the duties and extent of the obligations to disclose to be finalised in regulations. The Government are not under a legal duty to make the regulations, and they only have to consult with local authority interests in preparing their drafts. Housing and social services manual files alone are covered, i.e. the Act was restricted to local government. The Government undertook to make regulations for education by exercising powers under the Education Act 1980, section 27. The power had not been exercised between 1980 and 1987. Draft regulations were published in October 1987. These do not cover independent schools, nor will they apply to teachers' personal notes. Children under 18 will not be entitled to access, only their parents. References were not to be covered unless there was an overwhelming consensus in so doing.[13a] The requestor may add comments to the record if he or she disagrees with it.

The regulations under the 1987 Act will specify the duties upon authorities to allow access to 'accessible' personal information by the subjects. Exemptions will be drafted. The duties will not apply to information collected before the regulations come into effect, unless access is necessary to make accessible information intelligible.

It is likely that regulations will protect the privacy of others,[14] prevent exposing another person to physical or mental harm, and prevent disclosure that would reveal information relating to criminal investigation or tax collection and legal professional privilege.[15] National security is unlikely to be relevant to housing or social services files. It is probable that where access might cause distress, or expose the applicant to serious physical or mental harm, there will be safeguards to be followed[16] involving second opinions. It is hoped that reasons for refusal will be given in writing and that any communications of records will have to be recorded with the information.[17] The Act speaks of rectification and erasure of inaccurate[18] information, but not *irrelevant* information as did the Bill.[19] It is hoped that bodies covered by the Act will have to keep adequate indexes of personal data held and that explanations of all coded or abbreviated expressions will have to be given. It was acknowledged in the course of the Bill that there was nothing to prevent the keeping of a secret file behind the accessible file. 'Accessible personal information' and 'personal information' are defined in the Act. Fees for access are not to exceed a prescribed maximum. Details of access procedures, review and other procedural points will be provided in regulations.[20]

Information relating to social workers' clients has been available to clients since 1983 under a DHSS circular, subject to restrictions.[21] Failures on the part of social workers to be informed, to understand the information they have, to co-ordinate it properly or to ignore it, have all been highlighted in the last dozen years or so as root causes of failure to appreciate serious child abuse. How to obtain, use and assemble information is a problem pervading the whole of institutional structure, whether in the public or private spheres.[22] But abuses of information-holding are, as with other professions, common, especially in the case of child abuse and 'at risk' registers of children in danger of abuse.

It must be emphasised that before the Access to Personal Information Bill was presented to Parliament, the British Association of Social Workers, the National Council for Voluntary Organisations, individual authorities, education authorities and schools had supported or accepted voluntary access procedures. Some hospitals carry out an informal practice of notifying patients of the contents of their files, and an unexpected consequence is that doctors' notes are more carefully written, honest and straightforward. However, the British Medical Association[23] voted in June 1986 to maintain the confidentiality of doctors' files, consultants showing themselves especially protective of confidentiality. The Government hopes to agree a 'voluntary practice' of disclosure with doctors. The BMA also pressed for reversal of the General Medical Council guidance that broke the complete confidentiality owed by doctors to their patients. This concerned girls under 16 seeking contraception, after the Court of Appeal ruling in the case of *Gillick* held that doctors must notify the parents.[24] When an inquiry into an alleged medical malpractice is held in public, the GMC has warned participants not to use confidential files on patients in evidence in public, but only *in camera*. This was the GMC ruling even though it seemed that patients were happy to have the evidence examined in public.[25] The inquiry was held in public at the request of the person investigated to avoid a 'cover-up', although usually such inquiries are internal. In other circumstances inquiries into tragedies, such as child deaths, have been roundly condemned *because* they were heard in public.[26]

This was so in the inquiry into the Jasmine Beckford case in 1986. At a local authority inquiry into the death of another battered child,[27] the Home Office refused to hand over reports about the child's father made by the Inner London Probation Service. In July 1986, the Home Office announced that criminal records of any potential and some existing employees or volunteers working with children would be open to local authorities, the health service and independent schools and voluntary bodies.[28] It often appears to be a hopeless situation. More inspection, more collection of information, and we witness more complaints about an over-intrusive State. More deaths and child abuse: more recrimination and censure of officials and social workers for not knowing or heeding the warning signals. We need to know when vulnerable interests are at risk; we must improve the necessary co-ordination of information; we must train the staff in the necessary skills; and we must spend what is necessary to fulfil a fundamental social commitment.

To recapitulate: what protection should be afforded to private personal information? To allow *all* personal information to be protected by the law of confidentiality would be going too far. It would undermine a genuine public interest in knowing. Conversely, our laws on subject access in relation to manual files are seriously deficient. Once the principle of subject access had been accepted with the Data Protection Act, it seemed unnecessarily cautious to restrict access by individual subjects to manual files containing personal information about them. The use of misleading, inaccurate or irrelevant personal information by wielders of power and influence, whether professional bodies or employers or institutions, is a widely documented abuse of power. The provisions in the original Access to Personal Files Bill were a far greater safeguard against abuse than those that seem likely to appear under regulations. But even the Bill did not provide for registration of data holders; nor a specific process of enforcement along the lines of the Data Protection Act; nor, like that Act, that information should be collected, and its use regulated, according to acceptable criteria. The original Bill sought to draw the balance between access by individuals to their records and protection of the privacy of third parties, legitimate public needs such as national security, the enforcement of crime or the protection of the vulnerable by way of second opinions before they were granted access. It is to be hoped that the burden of justifying a refusal will be placed on the record-holder. As it is, many of the areas which have witnessed the greatest abuse of personal information-gathering are not covered.[29]

Government and Information

As a general premise, the law should only protect government information where a risk of a breach of national security, which itself must be defined in specific terms, is clearly established, or where a clear and present danger would exist by disclosure of an identifiable public interest, such as economic security, or where there would be an unjustifiable invasion of an individual's privacy. The ability of Government to abuse information is limitless. The initial Russian secrecy surrounding the Chernobyl nuclear disaster in the spring of 1986 met with pervasive political criticism in this country and in the West generally. The history of our own nuclear industry is a stunning indictment of secrecy and deceit practised by both major political parties when in power, a practice which had left its mark on public scepticism long before the publication in 1988 of the papers, under the thirty-year rule, on the Winscale accident cover-up. No one can deny that legitimate limits can be placed on the public's right to know, especially the timing of their right to know. The usual exempt areas are: national security; investigation of crime; diplomatic relations; the budget; and the economy. Government, however, is too important and powerful to be taken completely on its terms. The tradition of government in this country has persistently demanded that we take it on total trust. It has been found wanting too frequently. An FOIA is a necessity if we are to have an adequate account of stewardship. An FOIA by itself will not be adequate, however, as we must consider major changes in government and administrative institutions.

The past is not encouraging. The Fulton Report of 1968 registered the lack of openness in British government and administration.[30] The Labour Government responded in 1969 with *Information and the Public Interest*.[31] The incoming Tory Government of 1970 as part of its election manifesto appointed Franks to examine section 2 of the Official Secrets Act. The 1974 Labour Party manifesto implied the possibility of legislation along the lines of Sweden or the United States. Under the stewardship of Prime Minister James Callaghan, a secret Cabinet Committee was established to discuss the subject of secrecy, while Home Secretary Merlyn Rees published a document on secrecy which was silent on the topic of public access. In 1977, the initiative to release more information as a result of administrative exhortation under Lord Croham's Directive was originally leaked to *The Times*, and only then made public officially. Between 1977 and 1979, there were four Bills on FOI, and Clement Freud's Bill had finished its second reading in the House and was at committee stage at the time of the fall of the Callaghan Government which had published its own White Paper on reform of section 2.[32] The Croham Directive was effectively eviscerated by the Whitmore letter,[33] and in 1979 the Protection of Official Information Bill was presented by the Government to the Lords. In many respects it was more restrictive than section 2, and only the acute embarrassment resulting from the Blunt affair caused the Government to withdraw the Bill.[34] Since then there have been several unsuccessful attempts to introduce Private Member Bills on freedom of information, the most recent being that drafted by the FOI Campaign and presented by the Rt Hon. David Steel MP. There was also the Shepherd Bill of January 1988 which I examined in Chapter 3, and which sought to reform section 2 of the OSA. The campaign has tasted success, for we have noted elsewhere the passage of the Local Government (Access to Information) Act, but we have suggested the disingenuous motives of the Government in accepting that legislation. On its own position, the Government seemed intransigent. In its reply to the Defence Committee's *Westland plc* report,[35] the Government in a tone of bored censure indicated that all necessary explanations of the leaking of the Solicitor-General's letter had been given through Parliamentary statements, Questions, and debates. As far as it was concerned, the basic principles on accountability are: ministerial responsibility to Parliament, and a civil servant's responsibility to the Minister.[36]

The Government's reply continued with some fine examples of obscurantism. Select Committees' powers of inquiry existed by virtue of ministerial responsibility to Parliament. They did not result from Parliamentary supremacy. Civil servants appear before them only on the sufferance of Ministers, and they remain accountable to their Ministers for the evidence they give on their Ministers' behalf. Under standing orders, a Committee has power to send for papers and persons as it chooses:

it does not, and in the Government's view should not attempt to, oblige a civil servant to answer a question or to disclose information which his Minister has instructed him not to answer or disclose, or which it is contrary to his duty of confidentiality to answer or disclose.

If a civil servant does not answer a question because of ministerial instructions, then the Minister should be summoned. If the Committee cannot get information out of the Minister, they should not summon the civil servant, thus in effect exercising 'an accountability to Parliament separate from and overriding his accountability to his Minister'.[37] An erring servant should be brought to account via the Head of Department, not the Select Committee. A civil servant is likely to feel constrained by pressure of confidentiality from giving evidence, and a Select Committee is not a 'suitable instrument for inquiring into or pressing judgment upon the actions or conduct of an individual civil servant'. The civil servant would have no protection, especially if an inquiry was politically motivated.[38] The Government was to instruct civil servants appearing before Select Committees not to give evidence or answer questions directed towards their conduct or that of fellow civil servants.

This is a striking appeal by a government to official obscurantism. A civil servant will not answer for what he has done. If he has behaved improperly at the Minister's behest, it is up to the Minister to come clean. If he does not, that is the end of the matter unless the public is informed by other means. The Government reiterated its view that the dual capacity[39] of the Cabinet Secretary was not problematical. It is quite sobering to realise that if the Government's spokesmen are not actively regurgitating the platitudes of good government of the 1930s, then they seem to have learned little since the pre-Fulton days of 1968. The words of Sir R. Armstrong in his *Note of Guidance on the Duties and Responsibilities of Civil Servants in Relation to Ministers* reverberate through the reply:[40]

[T]he civil servant's first duty is to his or her Minister. Ultimately the responsibility lies with Ministers, and not with civil servants, to decide what information should be made available, and how and when it should be released, whether it is to Parliament, to select committees, to the media or to individuals.

That civil servants' first duty is owed to Ministers is unexceptional. Official publications, however, do little to counter the view that duties are owed *exclusively* to the Government of the day, even when Ministers are seriously abusing their trust.

In December 1986, the chairman of sixteen Select Committees (through the Liaison Committee) called on the Prime Minister to withdraw her plans to issue guidance to civil servants not to answer MPs' questions on their conduct and action when appearing before them.[41]

The Establishment Officers' Guide for civil servants proclaims the need for greater openness in the work of Government, subject to the overall control of the appropriate authorities.[42] Institutionalised 'leaks' from senior civil servants are well documented. One such that is not commented upon relates to the First Division Association of Civil Servants. Technically, much of the information received by the FDA would be in breach of section 2, although the Government did not appear unhappy at civil servants using the FDA as their spokesman to the press. Interestingly, the FDA and Sir Douglas Wass do not believe an FOIA by itself will make government significantly more open, or in the latter case, that it will make very little difference to Minister/civil servant relations.[43] What is important, the FDA believed, was knowing what existed and how to get hold of it.[44] How, then, would an FOIA help? It will help to look at the Bill that was drafted by the Campaign for Freedom of Information. I have misgivings about some of its details which I shall spell out. However, the Bill has the support in principle of Opposition parties, and I shall use it as a basis to discuss the ideal reforms. As of writing in late 1987, FOIA involving central government does not appear as a likely candidate for the statute book. But access legislation has been given a significant momentum since 1984, and time does not stand still. Not even for a Prime Minister.

However, the possibility of the reintroduction of a Bill along the lines of the Protection of Official Information Bill 1979 should not be overlooked, especially following the disrepute of section 2 and the uncertain parameters of the law of confidentiality. By the end of 1987, there was widespread discussion of the possibility of a statutory duty on civil servants of a life-long duty of confidentiality, enforceable by criminal law – section 2 with a vengeance.

FOI Bill

In the words of the Prime Minister in 1986, an FOIA is 'inappropriate and unnecessary'. Ultimate decisions would be transferred to the courts. Although there is widespread if not universal agreement that FOI is an idea whose time has come, it is ambitious to expect legislation before the 1990s.[45] Even assuming a future government committed to FOIA, if the necessary groundwork has not been set in motion well before the presentation of a Bill, it is possible that the complexity of the issue and the politics involved could mean repeal of section 2 of the Official Secrets Act alone, a more 'liberal' replacement of section 2 but a deferring of an FOIA until the issues are clearly sorted out. In November 1987, this appeared as a possibility, although as we noted in Chapter 3 the reform of section 2 was unlikely to be liberal, in spite of Government assurances. The Labour Party has pointed out that an FOIA would cost little, and it would therefore expect the Act to be popular inasmuch as it would be seen as a major constitutional innovation, would not be financially onerous and would go down as a significant political achievement. Yet no one should doubt the power of inertia. FOIA has support from sections of all parties, the support of all the civil service unions and more than 50 major national organisations –yet it still has not taken root in Whitehall. Government, quite simply, controls the agenda.

The 1984 FOI No. 2 Bill had some useful objectives which require development. Its stated purpose was: 'to establish a general right of access to official information for members of the public subject to certain exemptions; to establish the machinery for enabling the right of access to be exercised by members of the public, to make new provision for the protection of official information and articles. . . .' It was a revised version of earlier Bills excluding the Protection of Official Information Bill. The Bill established a right of access for all persons, and no reason requiring access had to be stated. Access was to documents (access was to information in the form in which departments held it) belonging to or possessed by departments and agencies as scheduled, unless 'exempt'. Departments would have to publish indexes of the documents they hold as well as Codes of Guidance describing how to apply for, inspect, copy and correct the information. Departments had 30 days to respond. If a department granted access, the document, etc., had to be made available for copying and inspection as soon as practicable. A refusal had to be accompanied by written reasons. The unsuccessful applicant had to be informed of his right to complain to the Information Commissioner who was to be established by the Act. A subsequent review could take place before the Information Tribunal. These provisions built upon those obtaining in Australia, Canada and New Zealand. The Bill did not cover a Minister's correspondence dealing with his constituency or party political matters. Exempt information was that which, if disclosed, would seriously impair the defence of the UK or related territories; foreign or diplomatic affairs; law enforcement and criminal investigation or crime prevention, the disclosure of which would endanger the life or safety of any person; information protected by legal professional privilege; financial/commercial information where disclosure would give an unfair advantage to the competitors of the party concerned or impair the ability of the department or authority to obtain similar information in future; information the disclosure of which would amount to an unwarranted invasion of privacy; information which if disclosed would reveal information in the nature of, or relating to, opinion or advice or recommendation tendered by any person in the course of his official duties for the purpose of the formulation of policy within a department or authority to which the Bill applies. The Bill should stipulate that the onus is on the Crown to *prove* that exemption is justified, albeit by evidence *in camera*.

An Information Commissioner would take up complaints of refusal of access or unreasonable delay or unreasonable charges. He would have power to grant access, subject to an appeal to the Tribunal. He would have more extensive powers of investigation than the Parliamentary Commissioner for Administration. The Tribunal was modelled on the Data Protection Tribunal, although it could hear appeals from applicants and the Government. Third parties seeking to establish that information was exempt as commercially confidential on privacy grounds would have the onus of proof on them. The Tribunal would only sit *in camera* where exempt information is the subject of the application. 'It is likely that a large part of the Tribunal's work will involve *ex parte* representation, and hearings and deliberations *in camera*.' The length of time needed to process appeals would make it likely that the Tribunal's emphasis would be on establishing precedents rather than resolving individual disputes. The Commissioner can present cases before the Tribunal and it can see whatever documents it wishes.

Several possible roles for the Commissioner have been suggested: for instance that of overseer of public records and their administration; or auditor of a department's practice in providing access to information, especially where there are going to be highly variable workloads on departments and sections within departments. A final role would be that of constitutional arbiter between Ministers and civil servants in cases involving a difference of opinion or crisis of conscience, although this would be a role requiring a sensitive touch.

Part II of the Bill was to replace section 2 of the OSA. It limited the range of information the unauthorised disclosure of which would lead to criminal prosecution. The provision followed Franks in insisting on 'serious' injury to defence, security and intelligence and international relations. The Protection of Official Information Bill of 1979 would have applied to *all* information on security or intelligence.

Classification procedures, as in Shepherd's 1988 Bill, would be laid down by the Minister and approved by Parliament. *Certification was not*, as Franks required, *conclusive evidence* for a court of law of the possibility or actuality of serious injury. Shepherd's Bill provided for a Privy Council judicial committee ruling on certification. The FOI Bill provided that a jury would have to be convinced of appropriate certification before returning a guilty verdict.[46]

The Bill offers a Public Interest Defence to those who have knowingly disclosed protected information in contravention of the Act where –

(a) it tended to prove the commission of a crime, misfeasance or abuse in public office or misuse or other unlawful or improper use of public funds;[47]
(b) it established a person's unfitness to hold public office;
(c) the information related to a matter of justifiable public concern and disclosure was made to a person having a public duty in respect of the matter.

'Public duty in' is obviously phrased with MPs in mind, especially if addressed to a member of an appropriate Select Committee, though clearly much is left to judgment. It is vital therefore that these terms are left for the interpretation of juries, and not judges, given the history of section 2 of the Official Secrets Act, nor the Executive. The onus of establishing a defence will be on the defendant.

Other Disciplinary Action

The immunity only covers, as in Shepherd's Bill, criminal prosecution; it does not cover disciplinary actions such as dismissal or civil actions for breach of confidence. The law may protect an employee from an action for breach of confidence *vis-à-vis* his employer where the breach has taken place to advance, or in the cause of, the public interest,[48] and the Law Commission has produced a report arguing for extension of the public interest defence.[49] As regards defences against dismissal for breach of contract, or claims of unfair dismissal after confidential information has been divulged in the public interest, the position is not so clear.[50] The nature of confidentiality flowing from an employment contract may well justify a dismissal pre-empting any right to damages against an employer.[51] In unfair dismissal claims, the employee will complain about the *fairness* of dismissal; if a dismissal follows a serious act of misconduct, e.g. divulging confidential information albeit in the public good, then, providing the proper procedure is adopted, the dismissal may be fair. Whether a dismissal was justified by all the factors that were relevant will not be examined.

[T]his is a perfectly simple, straightforward case of a man bound by a contract to behave towards his employer with the same degree of confidence and trust as he is entitled to expect of them . . . the real gravamen of the employer's complaint which they found to be thoroughly reasonable and justifiable was that by sending the letter to *The Guardian* . . . he was in breach of trust to his employers.[52]

If a complaint is made internally about an employer's or superior's conduct and not divulged externally to the press, the industrial tribunal may well take a more sympathetic approach to the employee.[53]

Civil servants do not, as of writing, have a contract of employment enforceable through the courts although the Government intends to create a contractual status by legislation for limited purposes. They do have the protection of unfair dismissal legislation,[54] and certain public law rights.[55] The case has been made out for a general protection of public-spirited employees who divulge confidences in the public interest, as in the US Civil Service Reform Act. The proposed Bill would, as indicated above, protect civil servants from criminal prosecution, but not from dismissal. The Information Commissioner could not be invoked by a civil servant wishing to use him to challenge a classification under Part II, although he could be used by a citizen wishing to challenge a decision that information is exempt.

The Bill sought significantly to reduce the information which is protected by the criminal law, while making all other information available if it was not exempt. In order for a prosecution of a Crown servant, government contractor or other person to take place, the Minister and the Attorney-General would have to certify that the information was properly classified in accordance with the classi-fication procedures under the Act and its regulations. Depending upon the offence, the permission of the DPP or Attorney-General would be required for prosecution. Shepherd's Bill provided likewise.

An interesting provision is clause 14(1) and (2), which stated that an authority shall grant access to documents containing exempt information where disclosure would be in the public interest on grounds including, but not limited to, the protection of public health, public safety or the environment, and where such public interest clearly outweighed in importance any prejudice to the competitive position of the party whom the information concerns, or where public interest in disclosure clearly outweighs any invasion of privacy. No such provision as this could be passed in the American FOIA.

The Tribunal was to have the power to award costs at its discretion where applications under certain sections have raised an important issue of principle. Otherwise costs are to lie where they fell unless the Tribunal directs otherwise. There is no provision for appeal on a point of law or otherwise, and nor was judicial review precluded.

The onus was to be on the applicant to be specific in a request. Although the applicant can refer to a class of documents, the request could be refused if the compliance would cause unreasonable difficulty for the department concerned in locating materials, etc. A department may refer a request to another department 'more closely connected with the information'. Such a phrase may create a game of ping-pong in which the applicant is the ball. Clause 10 allows someone to apply for correction, supplementation or expunging of incomplete or inaccurate material where a file document had been provided and the information relates to him or her. Could this be used for collateral attack of public decisions by disgruntled individuals, natural or artificial? It does not relate to personal files alone, it should be noted, as the files may contain other information.

The Bill does not refer to documents created before the Bill came into force unless the applicant requires them for understanding documents to which he or she has access. There should be provisions to allow 'prior documents' to be inspected by periodical extensions of, e.g., three to five years.

How much will the Bill cost if enacted? In 1984, UK government press and information services cost £27 million.[56] I have looked in Chapters 1, 2 and 5 at the cost factor. The most commonly expressed apprehensions concern the enormous cost in financial terms of indexing, filing and systematising record holdings. There will then be the vast numbers of applications to be processed. The debates on the Access to Personal Information Act rehearsed these arguments. The Minister emphasised the numbers of manual files on individuals and expressed his concern over workload. We looked at cost figures for the American FOIA in Chapter 2. In Australia, a 1985 report by the Attorney-General on the operation of the FOIA in 1983–4 provided the following figures on estimated and actual requests:

Department	Estimate of no. of requests that would arise	Actual no. of requests received 1983–84
Department of Health	16,000	249
Department of Housing	1,000	70
Department of Immigration and Ethnic Affairs	103,700	1,069
Department of Employment	100,000–200,000	166
Australian Electoral Office	86,000	19
Attorney-General	3,000–5,000	163
Treasury	600	32
Prime Minister and Cabinet	2,000	36

The total number of requests actually received in 1983–4 was 19,227.

Sir Douglas Wass has argued that one benefit of FOIA is that it will force departments to file records coherently. This has been one of the benefits of the open government policy adopted by some local authorities, e.g. Bradford city before the 1985 legislation affected local authorities.

What might we expect from FOIA? I have looked at the operation of such laws in Chapter 2. However, the following provide interesting examples.

In the USA a tax analyst obtained previously undisclosed tax rulings issued by the Internal Revenue Service in response to letters from individuals and corporations. Congress changed the law to ensure that such rulings were published. A company used the Act to show that a competitor had used false information to secure a contract from a government department. It has been used by Honeywell Information Systems to obtain details of the Department of Defense's procurement regulations. New Mexico used the Act to obtain details of the Federal Government's compliance with environmental regulations applying to the disposal of nuclear waste in the state. A pharmaceutical industry trade body regularly uses FOIA to request copies of enforcement decisions of FDA inspectors. These are published by the industry in a newsletter as a guide to standards currently being required and as a check on arbitrary decisions – but it is only published internally *vis-à-vis* the industry. FOIA had shown that defence contractors were trying to claim entertainment expenses on procuring contracts from the Federal Government.[57]

Exception of Policy Advice

The Bill has many interesting and useful aspects. But it also has drawbacks which were forced upon the proponents by officials in order to secure their support.

Civil service organisations have generally welcomed the FOI proposals. But they have insisted on an exemption for policy advice: 'information in the nature of, or relating to, opinion or advice or recommendation tended [*sic*] by any person in the course of his official duties for the purpose of the formulation of policy within a department or authority to which this Act applies'. The First Division Association (FDA), representing leading civil servants, justified this exemption in the following terms:

that while the Association wished to enhance the quality of public debate by better informing the public about Government operations by timely provision of factual material, policy-making in a gold-fish bowl was not to be welcomed.

The FDA has been adamant that identification of individuals will lower the quality of decision-making and could frequently have an adverse effect on the career prospects of the individuals concerned. Identification would cause civil servants to be more compliant with the wishes of Ministers, rather than offering independent advice, since they would not wish to be publicly out of step with their Ministers. But this is precisely the charge that is made against various senior civil servants today: that they are not sufficiently independent in their advice, they are the PM's people and the present conditions of anonymity help to conceal this. In Canada, policy advice, although it has wide protection, is not totally exempt, and the consequences so far have not undermined officials' neutrality or efficacy.[58] In other countries, a distinction has been drawn between the deliberative process of decision-making and the post-decision stage. In New Zealand, an exemption protects the confidentiality of advice tendered by Ministers and officials and the 'free and frank expression of opinions' *unless* the public interest in knowing outweighs the confidentiality.

The FDA justify the exemption in terms which are redolent of Sir Robert Armstrong's Memorandum upholding the confidentiality of the relationship between Ministers and their servants. The Bill's prime interest must be in facts and reliable information. Policy advice and alternatives to proposals must be open in order to inform and improve public debate, unless publicity would harm the proposal to such an extent that its purpose would be defeated *and* the public interest thereby injured. This is a question of the timing of release to avoid the defeat or frustration of legitimate plans. The question of identity should not be fundamental,[59] unless a person possesses the necessary information which will assist an inquiry into government practice. At that point the veil of confidentiality needs to be broken, and a Select Committee is the appropriate body to investigate. In the nature of British government such matters are likely to involve an abuse of power, a breach of governmental trust, an untruth or high-handed exercise of public power. Only rarely are these matters susceptible to legal examination before a court of law.[60]

I have no doubt that pressure for FOI will increase. Although it is unlikely that legislation involving central government will be forth-coming in the immediate future, attitudes and climates can change very quickly in politics. From 1984, we have had significant developments in the access to information legislation. When the lessons are learned, and the legislation is not seen to be crippling administrative efficiency, calls for reform in central government will increase. Therefore a potential abuse of the Bill as drafted could arise where policy advice was interwoven with factual and analytical information.[61] The FDA point to the impact of the Croham Directive, which exhorted the publication of background material and its compilation in such a way that it was easily publishable and separate from policy.[62] The short-lived exercise showed that this was possible, and also confirmed how evanescent the practice of open government is, unless the duty to publish is enforced by legislation.

The exemption goes too far and is a major weakness. What should be missing is the name of the advice giver alone. As the exemption stands, it protects not only the identity, but also the content. It should be noted that the exemption only applies to advice tendered by a person, so presumably an advisory committee's report would not be protected. What of an 'outside adviser' who is not a Crown servant? If formally commissioned, are they engaged in official duties?[63] It would appear so.

The Practicalities

Access to information should include access to information in documentary form or in a computer or other memory store. Computer print-outs as well as papers should be available. An FOI office should be established with the necessary staff and facilities. Sir Douglas Wass has suggested[64] that each department would have one FOI office (rather like Companies House of the DTI at present), where general or policy papers could be requested. Personal papers would be kept separately at a local office level, if maintained in that form, or centrally on a single department main-frame computer. Applications for information could be made personally or by post.

Sir Douglas anticipated that the field of 'policy' or 'general' papers would create problems regarding the degree of specification involved in identifying them. A request for documents on the Channel Tunnel would cover thousands of documents in the Department of Transport alone. Two suggested alternatives are:

(1) An FOI officer to establish precisely the information being sought – favoured by Australia and Canada.

(2) A sophisticated system of cataloguing papers and the
unrestricted access to the catalogues so that each document
could be identified by its file number.

The problem with option 1 is that it is subject to possibly subjective
interpretation and it might allow 'unofficial' exemptions of materials
which the applicant will not know about. 'If he does not know, his
right of appeal to some independent arbiter against the withholding of
information becomes a cypher.'[65]

The second option is more expensive and would take some years to
implement fully. It would require comprehensive cataloguing by a
department of all its papers and files, like catalogues of Company
House, which would be available to the public in the FOI office. 'At
present departments do not maintain satisfactory catalogues. Indeed
the standard of cataloguing, indexing, registering and entitling of
papers in government departments falls lamentably below the
standards of even moderate librarianship.'[66] Sir Douglas goes so far
as to say that current practices are a bar to efficient administration,
and the suggested improvement would be a 'boon to departmental
efficiency'. Option 2 would create a 'new discipline in relation to new
documents' producing a decent filing system with cross-referencing.
If this were introduced, the questions would then be: how is the
request met? How are requests for exempt information dealt with?

The FOI officer, Sir Douglas suggests, would inform the appropriate division of the request and it would examine the file to see
whether exempt information is present. If it is not, the file would be
released to the FOI officer, who would inform the applicant of the
cost of reproduction. Help would be given to identify which portions
he requires. If exempt, the file would have the exempt categories
clearly identified and marked, and the applicant would only be
allowed to examine the unexpurgated portion. Sir Douglas thought
the best way to deal with exemption would be to categorise
documents when they are requested, rather than created, unless
presumably they are otherwise classified as 'Top Secret', etc., under
Part II.[67] Categorisation criteria can change, and documents should
not be marked exempt initially and perpetually.

Appeals could be made to the Information Commissioner, who
would have access to the whole file and whose decision would be
binding, subject to appeal to the Tribunal. Exemption decisions
would be made at divisional level unless the information was

politically sensitive, in which case it would be referred to higher authority.

If files contain material from outsiders, e.g. other departments or individuals, their views must be sought prior to release to ascertain whether they consider that the material may be exempt. Last of all, Sir Douglas believed that certain files may be kept off the catalogue, where their very existence would reveal a process of sensitive policy formulation which it was not timely to publicise, e.g. Budget proposals, or foreign relations.

Is FOIA Enough?

The answer to this question depends upon what objectives one has in mind in promoting on to the statute book an open government Act. Open government is a more demanding objective than freedom of information. Freedom of information lobbyists inevitably, if not exclusively, operate on the basis that the more information that is made available, the better and/or the more democratic the process of government will become. Open government places its emphasis upon the opening up of the channels of government decision-making, and provision of information is one feature of open government. Other features, equally important, include the opportunity for wide debate before the Government's proposals are finally confirmed or rejected. Not only the public, but inevitably MPs and Parliament, are left out of this process until the decision is firmly concluded, and discussion of alternatives is really quite idle. Many of the major inquiries of recent years bear witness to this weakness of participatory democracy.[68] So too does the refusal to discuss the policy behind a proposal of a government agency affecting national or regional interests. Also involved is the giving of adequate reasons, full information about proposals and allowing for timely discussion of these. With a subject-matter that is inevitably complex, the provision of brute information is not adequate in itself. One needs to see 'outside' personnel with a sufficient degree of skill, expertise and independence assessing the information. Sir Douglas Wass made a plea for such a body in his Reith Lectures in 1983.[69] The Outer Circle Policy Unit advocated a format for 'Big Public Inquiries' in which a two-stage process would investigate the issues, obtain the necessary evidence, provide Parliament with the fruits of its research and then allow more locally specific inquiries to assess more particular points of objection.[70] A former chief scientific adviser to the MoD has written that a permanent council of independent-minded scientists should be established to encourage Ministers to challenge costly projects promoted by vested interests and to pierce the secrecy surrounding Britain's nuclear affairs.[71] These opinions inevitably come from 'former' senior or leading officials or politicians – rarely do they seem to occur when they are within the charmed circle of executive power. The council would advise the Cabinet on projects put forward by departments.

Here we move inside the government machine. As we noted in Chapter 4, the Westland saga supplied ammunition to those who advocate reform in our central government structure and culture.[72] A primary aim is for efficient internal administration at the higher levels of our government apparatus. We have spoken of the Financial Management Initiatives and MINIS which are concerned with devolving responsibility and initiative down the management line. The Treasury and Civil Service Committee in its report on the relationship between Ministers and civil servants heard a considerable amount of opinion in favour of establishing a French *cabinet* system in each Ministry which would comprise senior civil servants and outside specialists to inform the Minister more expertly on departmental and inter-departmental business.[73] Since the abolition of the Central Policy Review Staff (CPRS), there has been no co-ordinating body to appraise the overall impact of departmental or government policies from within while rising above the temptations of special pleading and inter-departmental bickering and bartering. The Prime Minister's Policy Unit has provided an initiative on policy assessment and development for the PM – but not for the Government as a whole. This, it might be explained, is to make politics rational.

The prize of success in British politics and administration is too great to give away. Any attempts to foist a co-ordinated system of appraisal of departmental programmes, and to assess priorities in programmes such as those relating to the Public Expenditure Survey Committee's activities in helping to formulate spending priorities for the Expenditure White Paper, have failed. Programme Analysis and Review (PAR)[74] or CPRS[75] are clear examples. The reasons for the failures embrace a complex variety of factors such as government scepticism, civil service jealousy, inadequate grasp of detail by the bodies concerned, and a less than thorough approach in their method of appraisal. No one can demand that our Government be omniscient; what is required is an improvement in the information flow between the higher ranks of government and the administration, and the public. Improvement in information flow has a cost in relation to the investment of effort and the reduction of effective prerogative in Government. An independent assessment of major proposals, or reviews of government priorities and programmes, would have to be published, and the Government would have to account for its reasons for not complying with or accepting the recommendations.

Government is not big enough, it would seem, to do that. What is the best information about proposals and performance that is available?[76] How can the information be best understood and best utilised? What is there to stop the information being utilised in its best form and timeously? How do we increase our stock of knowledge and information? How do we assess the viability of different methods for interpreting information to appreciate it more fully? How do we collate information in the most complete form that is humanly possible? How do we ensure that our methods for selecting information and data are not partial, or not overly partial? That we have not, in other words, rejected good information because of subjective value preferences? I can see no compelling reasons why it would be contrary to the public interest to publish the vast bulk of such information. Indeed, it would be a positive asset. This would be equally true notwithstanding any reform of government departments into smaller policy units and the hiving-off of routine administrative tasks to governmental agencies.

We saw in Chapter 5 how we rely upon Parliament to be informed and to impose accountability upon Government, and how inadequately equipped Parliament is in its powers to extract information from a reluctant Executive.[77] Recent events have brought this home rather dramatically. However, the most prestigious of Select Committees, the Public Accounts Committee, has frequently complained of its inability, and government departments' inability, to obtain the necessary information. The community has to rely upon others to wield the tools of accountability. On some issues our society is structured in such a manner that we can only allow representative forms of government and accountability to act on our behalf. I have referred to instances and examples of how greater openness could help fuller accountability and a better-informed society. Nor should we forget the role of the US Sunshine Act and Federal Advisory

Committees Act which I examined in Chapter 2 and which opened up the meetings of federal agencies and advisory committees to the public.

This brings us to FOIA. It is a necessary safeguard – a boon to isolated individuals beset by all-powerful Government. They will know and will have a better hand in playing Government at its own game. We should not be oblivious to the fact that the market might operate to ensure a supply of information brokers whose services will be used by those intent on exploiting a relatively new commodity. I have no doubt that the means to access is important. But unless the FOI movement is accompanied by a wide-ranging change in constitutional culture, institutions and practices, it must be question-ed whether it will be of lasting utility to all but powerful organised interests who have the resources to use it; to a few academics; to journalists; and to the occasional public-spirited individual.

To provide safeguards against this happening, programmes of education should be provided to give guidance upon the existence of the legislation, how it works, what it does and how citizens can best use it. The Information Commissioner in Canada has argued for such programmes and she has been fully supported by the Standing Committee on Justice and Solicitor-General.[78] No one should expect that an FOIA will change the nature of government or the behaviour of the governed overnight. Much work, effort, goodwill and education will have to be provided. Progress and democratic development will take time. They are worth striving for. Unless, however, there is a change in attitude and ethos in our public administration, FOIA by itself will be something of a confidence trick. It is an inescapable development in democratic and responsible government. But an FOIA must be accompanied by more widespread changes in attitude if we are to be better informed and more open. Those are the necessary conditions to help reduce the abuse of power.

Notes

Chapter 1: Persistent Themes and Novel Problems

1. R. Berger, *Executive Privilege* (1974), p. 3.
2. *Sidaway* v. *Board of Governors of the Bethlem Royal Hospital etc* [1985] A.C. 871.
3. *Gillick* v. *West Norfolk and Wisbech A.H.A. and the D.H.S.S.* [1985] 3 All E.R. 402 (H.L.), concerning contraception for girls under 16.
4. Resulting from a leak by the Queen's Press Officer: *The Times*, 28 July 1986.
5. H.C. Debs. vol. 110, col. 1172 (20 Feb. 1987). In Standing Committee C for the Access To Personal Files Bill, it was stated that Government Departments hold 12 million linear feet of records, half the files being on individuals (25 March 1987, col. 5).
6. J. Halton, 'The Anatomy of Computing', in T. Forrester (ed.), *The Information Technology* (1985). See *Information Technology Futures* (NEDC, 1987).
7. Cmnd. 7341 (1978), following *Computers and Privacy*, Cmnd. 6353 (1975).
8. *New Statesman*, 4 March 1982.
9. *The Guardian*, 7 January 1987.
10. H.C. Debs., 2 July 1985 (Written Answers); for numbers of 'accesses' and entries on the P.N.C. and the audit and logging procedures, see H.C. Debs. 9 July 1986 (W.A.).
11. H.C. 307 (1985–6), para. 3.14 and *The Guardian*, 18 June 1986. In 1984, it was stated that there were 25 million subjects on the PNC.
12. Legal Aid Act 1974, s.22.
13. And see *Police Computers and the Metropolitan Police* (G.L.C. 1985); *Techno-Cop: New Police Technologies* (Free Enterprise Books 1985).
14. *The Times*, 14 February and 9 September 1977.
15. *Information Technology in the Civil Service, No. 9* (1985).
16. *Computer Security in Government Departments* (N.A.O., H.M.S.O. 1987).
17. See A.V. Lowe and C. Warbrick (1987) 36 *I.C.L.Q.* 398. The refusal of the Department of Trade and Industry to safeguard British subjects has led to applications for judicial review.

18. H.C. 312 (1985–6), p. 32. The 'Local office project' will link social security offices into a national network starting in 1988–9, H.C. Debs., 7 March 1985 (W.A.).

19. Ibid., pp. 12 *et seq.*

20. Ibid., p. 18.

21. Lindop, op. cit., chapter 23. In cases of disagreement about the handling of personal information, a code should be approved by Parliament, he recommended. In Sweden, codes are negotiated between the Authority and the Police. The European Court of Human Rights has recently held that there was no breach of Arts. 8 or 10 of the Convention on Human Rights when the Swedish Government refused access to a register containing personal information relating to national security.

22. *Oxford* v. *Moss* [1978] 68 *Crim. Ap. Rep.* 183; *R.* v. *Absolon, The Times*, 14 September 1983. Printing or other infringement is an offence under the Copyright Act 1956, and dealing may involve a conspiracy to defraud; cf. *Rank Film Ltd* v. *Video Information Centre* [1982] A.C. 380. On computer 'hacking': *R.* v. *Gold and Schiffreen* (1987) *The Times*, 21 July.

23. J. Habermas, *Toward a Rational Society* (1971), esp. chapters 5 and 6, and *Communication and the Evolution of Society* (1979). See Prosser, 'Towards a Critical Public Law' (1982) 9 *J.L.S.* 1.

24. 'Discursive examination' free from domination, *per* Prosser. op. cit.

25. *Communication etc.*, p. 205.

26. As well as actions for wrongful invasion of privacy developed after the seminal article of Warren and Brandeis, 'The Right of Privacy' (1890) 4 H.L.R. 193. See the Younger Report on Privacy, Cmnd. 5012 (1972).

27. S. Bok, *Secrets* (1984). Bok's work has numerous references to theoretical works on secrecy.

28. Cited in Bok, op. cit.

29. J. Bentham, 'On Publicity', *Works of J. Bentham* (1843, ed. J. Bowring), 2, pp. 310–17; see also *The Collected Works of J. Bentham: Constitutional Code*, vol. 1 (1983), ed. F. Rosen and J.H. Burns, esp. pp. 162–8, 283–93; and F. Rosen, *Jeremy Bentham and Representative Democracy* (1983), esp. chapter VII.

30. Rosen, op. cit., notes how the *Code* stipulated that no one could be a Member of the Legislature who had not been admitted and successfully examined in the system of education prescribed for judges and senior civil servants.

31. C.B. Macpherson, *The Life and Times of Liberal Democracy* (1977).

32. A. Gewirth, *Reason and Morality* (1978), p. 20. See generally J.S. Mill, *Considerations on Representative Government*.

33. J. Rawls, *A Theory of Justice* (1971).

34. See R. Dworkin, *Taking Rights Seriously* (1977), chapter 6.

35. Rawls refers to this as 'publicity', op. cit., p. 133. Bernard Williams calls it 'transparency' in *Ethics and the Limits of Philosophy* (1985). See also

A.M.S. Piper, 'Utility, Publicity and Manipulation' (1978) *Ethics* 88, p. 189.

36. Williams, op. cit., p. 102.

37. See L. Fuller *The Morality of Law* (1969), pp. 185–6 on 'communication'.

38. *Communication etc*, op. cit., p. 186.

39. *Ibid.*

40. The Frank Field revelations in 1976.

41. H.C. Debs., 25 July 1986.

42. H.L. Debs., 30 March 1987 – the controversy surrounding the alleged suppression of the Health Education Council's Report *The Health Divide* on poverty and sickness, two hours before it was due to be published.

43. *Occupational Morality: The Registrar-General's Decennial Supplement for Great Britain 1979–80/1982–83 Part II.* It consists of microfiche tables.

44. Freedom of Information may be seen as wider insofar as it covers, potentially, all information in the public and private domain. The phrase 'Open Government' refers to the openness of processes, as well as documentation and may concern private institutions insofar as they are used as a surrogate for governmental decision-making.

45. K.G. Robertson, *Public Secrets* (1982).

46. Cf. *R.* v. *Secretary of State etc. ex p. Ruddock* [1987] 2 All E.R. 518.

47. On the role of the judiciary, see pp. 186–9 below.

48. For a history, see C. Andrew, *Secret Service: The Making of the British Intelligence Community* (1985). Recent escapades involve the activities of Blunt, Prime, Aldridge, Bettaney and Oldfield.

49. MI5 is the Security Service. MI6 is the Secret Intelligence Service. MI5 was established in 1909. The 'arms and legs' are provided by the Special Branch and MI5 has 'close relations' with Chief Constables. It has been reported that, in 1984, MI5 had six branches and nine regional networks. The Security Service and the Special Branch are co-ordinated at the top levels through the Home Office – N. Davies and I. Black, *The Guardian*, 17, 18 and 19 April 1984; G. Zellick (1985) *Public Law* at 300, for works on the Security Service; D. Campbell, *New Statesman*, 19 November 1983, pp. 8–9, on the committee structure. The Defence Intelligence Staff assess, among other things, defence commitments.

50. Statute Law (Repeals) Act 1978, s.1 and Sched. 1, Part II. Accounts of expenditure vary widely. For Supply Estimates, see those for 1983–4, H.C. 237 II (1982–3); see also P. Hennessey, *The Times*, 10 April 1984 (£125 million p.a.); R. Norton-Taylor, *The Guardian*, 1 August 1986 (£1 billion p.a.); and R. Cook, *New Statesman*, 13 December 1986. Formally speaking, the Service is not known by common law and has no executive powers. The Comptroller and Auditor General has suggested the suitability of his office to oversee expenditure of the security services.

51. As evidenced by the alleged RUC 'Shoot to Kill' policy in Northern Ireland, H.C. Debs., 25 January 1988.

52. H.C. Debs. Vol. 59, col. 187 (1 May 1984).

53. 'A branch of the civil service' whose main functions are to ensure the security of the UK military and official communications and to provide signals intelligence for the Government.

54. Cmnd. 2152. He described its functions as 'the Defence of the Realm, from external and internal dangers arising from attempts at espionage and sabotage' or actions 'subversive of the State'.

55. The P.M. threatened to break this convention in December 1986, H.C. Debs., 2 December 1986.

56. Cmnd. 8540 – a Government *Statement on the Recommendations*. A procedure to 'purge' communists and fascists from vital security-sensitive operations was revised in 1957: H.C. Debs., vol. 563, cols. 152–6 (W.A.) (29 January 1957). The 'Three Advisers' may advise the Secretary of State and hear the civil servant, though s/he will not be allowed to cross-examine Government witnesses. 'Positive vetting' was introduced to confirm the reliability of a candidate for a post involving access to 'Top Secret' information in 1952: see H.C. 242 (1982–3) and the Memorandum from the MoD. Except for those under 21, P.V. is reviewed every 5 years. Criteria for clearance are non-involvement with 'treasonable, seditious, espionage, sabotage or terrorist activities against the State'; 'membership of or sympathy with a subversive organisation', 'character defects' inducing unreliability or exposure to blackmail by a foreign intelligence service; 'defects of circumstances', e.g. 'communist country origin'. See Cmnd. 8540, pp. 4, 7–8. Appeal provisions exist. See further the Trestrail case, H.C. 59 (1982–3) and the Prime case, Cmnd. 8876. The Government has introduced polygraph (lie-detector) security screening, H.C. Debs. vol. 42, cols. 431–4 (12 May 1983); cf. *C.C.S.U.* v. *Minister for the Civil Service* [1984] 3 All E.R. 935 (H.L.).

57. H.C. Debs., 3 December 1986. The Bettaney report is Cmnd. 9514. See also H.C. Debs. vol. 78, col. 897 (9 May 1985). No reference was made to Sir Maurice Oldfield.

58. See Drewry (1984) *Public Law* 370, for references.

59. *At the End of the Day* (1973), p. 434 and cf. Drewry (1984), op. cit.

60. Cmnd. 2152. There is a responsibility of the Foreign Secretary for the operation of MI6 and its Director-General reports to the former. In the Zircon Spy satellite débâcle, an alleged rescue mission was launched by the Foreign Secretary and the Home Secretary for a programme ostensibly within the responsibility of the Defence Secretary (*The Guardian*, 24 January 1987).

61. Op. cit., note 58.

62. As evidenced by the Anthony Blunt affair: see generally C. Pincher, *Too Secret Too Long* (1984); and J. Callaghan M.P., H.C. 92 II (1985–6) p. 223.

63. Erskine May, 20th edn (1983), p. 343.

64. Drewry, op. cit., p. 374, note 11 for 'guarded P.M. written answers'.

65. See pp. 112–13 below.

66. See note 56 above.

67. 22 January 1987. An unsuccessful application for a ruling had been sought from the High Court.

68. H.C. 365 (1986–7).

69. 'My Country Right or Wrong', *Att.-Gen.* v. *BBC* (1987) *The Guardian*, 18 December.

70. See note 112 below.

71. Especially the 'inconsistent' failure to restrict publication of C. Pincher *Their Trade Is Treachery* (1982) and *Too Secret Too Long* (1984) and Channel 4's programme, *MI5's Official Secrets* (1985).

72. H.C. Debs, 2 November 1987 (W.A.) and 3 November 1987.

73. The 'mystery' surrounding the resignation of Harold Wilson is often cited.

74. H. Wilson's comment on the P.M. and national security in *The Governance of Britain* (1976) consisted of one page of text!

75. N. West in *GCHQ: The Secret Wireless War* (1986) claims there is a '95 per cent exchange of information' and an exchange of staff.

76. And note the 'Irangate' episode and Congressional committees of inquiry into the role of the President, his advisers and the National Security Council. The Congressional Committee's majority report of November 1987 recommended direct notification by the President of covert actions to the Congressional Committees, and the appointment of an independent Inspector-General for the CIA. See C. Andrews (1977) 53 *Int. Affairs* 390.

77. P. Stiff, *See You In November* (1986).

78. H. Young, *The Guardian*, 18 March 1986.

79. Below, Cmnd. 9438.

80. The terms of reference were 'whether authorised interceptions since 1970 had been approved by Ministers according to the rules'.

81. Merlyn Rees MP

82. Cmnd. 283. The Prime Minister has given a reassurance that MPs' phones will not be tapped (H.C. Debs., 10 December 1986).

83. [1979] Ch. 344, Sir Robert Megarry V.C. And see Cmnd. 7873; and authorisation by the Foreign Secretary for the purposes of national security and economic well-being, Cmnd. 9438, p. 5.

84. Eur. Court H.R., Series A, vol. 82, Judgment of 2 August 1984.

85. *The Times*, 6 March 1985. See I. Cameron (1986) *N.I.L.Q.* 126.

86. H.C. Debs. vol. 75, cols. 156–60. The Younger Committee Report on Privacy, Cmnd. 5012 (which could not propose legislative reform for invasion of privacy by public bodies), listed the technical surveillance devices it had encountered – see chapter 19, especially p. 154.

87. In 'urgent' cases, and following statutory conditions, a senior civil servant may issue the warrant.

88. 'External' interceptions are far broader than 'internal' ones, cf. note 76 above.

89. The first commissioner was Lloyd LJ.

90. In his First Report, Cmnd. 109 (1987), the Commissioner noted that the Special Branch and Customs and Excise had been granted permission to increase their quota of phone-taps. While satisfied that all counter-subversion warrants were within the law, he was critical of certain practices.

91. Although it applies 'the principles of judicial review' in examining authorised leaks, it is unlikely to dig too far beneath the surface. See the Ruddock litigation, below, for judicial review.

92. This emerged from the revelations of Ms Massiter.

93. S.9 and exclusion of evidence of taps in any other civil proceedings. The tribunal is the *exclusive remedy*. It has access to the files of all persons holding office under the Crown (Sched. 1, para. 4).

94. I.J. Lloyd (1986) 49 *Mod. L.R.* 86. See P. Fitzgerald and M. Leopold, *Stranger on the Line: The Secret History of Phone Tapping* (1987).

95. Lloyd, ibid, who asks whether Art. 13 of the ECHR is thereby satisfied: an 'effective national remedy' for breaches of the Convention? See further *Klass* v. *Federal Republic of Germany* (1978) 2 EHRR 214.

96. Fitzgerald and Leopold, note 87.

97. Eur. Court HR, Series A, Judgment of 18 January 1978. Cf. The Bennett Report, Cmnd. 7497 (1979).

98. The Calcutt Report, Cmnd. 9781 (1986), found no evidence of 'deep interrogation' i.e. sleep deprivation, hooding, sensory deprivation: see Lord Gardiner in the Parker Report, Cmnd. 4901 (1972). See also Cmnd. 9923.

99. A.W. Bradley (1986) *Public Law* 363.

100. See Prevention of Terrorism Act 1984. 59,481 people were subject to searches under that Act in 1986 (*Annual Report 1986*, Chief Inspector of Constabularies).

101. Journalistic material would cover broadcasting tapes such as those seized in the Zircon episode from the BBC studios in Glasgow under s.9 of the Official Secrets Act 1911. The Police and Criminal Evidence Act does not apply in Scotland, however.

102. It would cover 'non-confidential' journalistic material. See Sched. 1.

103. *Ex p. Bristol Press and Picture Agency Ltd* (1986) *The Times*, 11 November; cf. *R.* v. *Central Criminal Court ex p. Adegbesan etc* (1986) N.L.J. 704; *R.* v. *Central Criminal Court ex p. Carr* (1987) *The Independent*, 5 March; *R.* v. *Crown Court at Leicester ex p. D.P.P.* [1987] 3 All E.R. 654. Nb. Contempt of Court Act 1981, s.10.

104. M.D.A. Freeman, *Current Law Statutes*, Annotation of PACE, 1984.

105. S.20(1).
106. J. Benyon and C. Bourn (eds.), *The Police: Powers, Procedures and Proprieties* (1986).
107. *R.* v. *Praeger* [1972] 1 All E.R. 1114.
108. See, however, on s.78, *R.* v. *Mason* [1987] 3 All E.R. 481.
109. See below.
110. Ibid.
111. Ottawa: Minister of Supply, 1981. The Report was in three volumes; see A. Goldsmith (1985) *Public Law* 39; I. Cameron (1985) *Mod. L.R.* 201.
112. America has seen Congressional oversight, via sub-committees, of the CIA since the mid 1960s – one of the reasons why the National Security Council sprang into prominence was because it did not have such supervision. Australia has established an Inspector-General of Intelligence and Security, and in November 1986 the Federal Parliament established an All Party Committee to monitor the Australian Security Intelligence Organisation.
113. Which directs the Service to 'collect, by investigation or otherwise, to the extent that it is strictly necessary, and analyse and retain information and intelligence respecting activities that may on reasonable grounds be suspected of constituting threats to the security of Canada'.
114. Note 57 above.
115. The present definition could be improved: 'activities which threaten the safety or well-being of the state and which are intended to undermine or overthrow Parliamentary democracy by political, industrial or violent means'. In Australia, subversion is related to violence or a reasonable apprehension of violence.
116. If an MP is not given a security clearance, is there not a case for the public knowing this much about a public representative once appropriate methods of challenge had been exhausted by the MP?
117. Note 112 above.

Chapter 2: Freedom of Information – Overseas Experience

1. Sweden and France will be referred to briefly: for a fuller analysis of civil law systems, see K.G. Robertson, *Public Secrets* (1982) – on Sweden – and James Michael, *The Politics of Secrecy* (1982). See also generally N.S. Marsh (ed.), *Public Access To Government-Held Information: A Comparative Symposium* (1987).
2. The Housekeeping Statute of 1789. The Administrative Procedure Act 1946 allowed inspection unless 'good cause' required confidentiality. This provision was widely invoked by agencies.

3. Many have their own FOI laws.
4. E.O. 12356 (47 F.R. 14874 – April 1982). In 1983, there were 17,141,052 derivative classification decisions made: this is the act of incorporating, paraphrasing, restating or generating in a new form classified source information.
5. The National Co-ordinating Committee for the Promotion of History believed E.O. 12356 had caused a 'massive' restriction on previously available information.
6. There were 3,945 such requests in 1983.
7. See *Chrysler Corp.* v. *Brown* 99 S.Ct. 1705 (1979).
8. The 1974 Act provided for internal disciplinary measures where refusal was arbitrary or capricious.
9. *Vaughan* v. *Rosen* CA D.C. (1973) 484 F. 2d 820.
10. See B. Braverman and F. Chetwynd, *Information Law* (1985) for a copious treatise; R.G. Vaughan, *Explanation of Federal FOIA etc* (1981). See also K.C. Davies, *Administrative Law Treatise* (2nd edn, 1978), vol. 1, Ch. Five and 1982 Supplement.
11. Under Administrative Procedure Act 1946, s.10.
12. S. Dresner, *Open Government – Lessons from America* (1980).
13. By 'information brokers' for example, seeking commercially confidential information.
14. US Dept. of Justice, *FOIA Update*, vol. VII, No. 4, 1986; and vol. VIII, No. 1, 1987, for details.
15. S.552(7)(c) – 'live proceedings' and informants.
16. For the exemption to apply the documents must be protected from discovery in civil suits: *Federal Open Market Committee* v. *Merrill* 99 S.Ct. 2800 (1979). In *N.L.R.B.* v. *Sears, Roebuck* 421 U.S. 132 (1975) the Supreme Court drew a distinction between post-decision documentation (not protected) and pre-decision documentation (protected).
17. Ehlke and Relyea (1983) *Fed. Bar News and Journal*, vol. 30, No. 2, p. 91.
18. Recent examples covered documents relevant to the Sizewell 'B' proposals for a P.W.R. nuclear generator. See incidentally '*de Zeven Provincien*' [1986] 3 All E.R. 487 (H.L.) and use of American courts in English proceedings to get pre-trial discovery of information.
19. H. Relyea, 'A Comparative Review of the Access to Information Act (Canada) and the U.S. FOIA' (1986, unpublished paper).
20. *Gulf Oil Corp.* v. *Brock* 778 F 2d 834 DDC (1985).
21. Relyea, op cit., note 19.
22. Ibid.
23. The Attorney-General's estimate for 1981 was $45 million.
24. Relyea, op. cit.
25. B.W. Tuerkheimer, 'Veto by Neglect' (1975) 25 *A.M.U.L.R.* 53; Vaughan, op. cit., note 10.
26. H.R. Rep No. 1731 91st Congress, 2d Sess. 14–15 (1970).

27. S. Rep. No. 1098 92nd Congress, 2d. Sess. 6 (1972).
28. 378 F. Supp. 1048, DDC (1974).
29. For meetings of these officials, see 'The Sunshine Act' below.
30. Tuerkheimer, op. cit.
31. Civ. No. 73–707, DDC, 24 June 1974.
32. *Nader* v. *Baroody* Civ. No. 74–1675, DDC, 23 June 1975.
33. OMB had stated that 15 days' notice of meetings was adequate, whereas the courts had ruled that 30 days was the requisite period. OMB works under an Executive brief.
34. Vaughan, op. cit., note 10.
35. E.g. Treasury, Labor, Defense, Interior, and Food and Drug Administration.
36. It does not cover information owned or possessed by private institutions, it should be noted, unless it is held by a federal body covered by the Act; cf. The Data Protection Act 1984 and the UK.
37. Report by Library of Congress, CRS 20 September 1985.
38. Enjoining access, amendment, and damages for 'improper maintenance' of the contents of records or for other breaches of the Act or regulations adversely affecting the individual.
39. E.g. where records are used internally by employees of the agency in performance of their duties; 'routine' use; or where it is required and is not exempt under FOIA.
40. If they have not been, the records may be subject to the PA. If discretion to exempt is exercised, only a few of the Act's safeguards apply.
41. Right of Financial Privacy Act 1978; Foreign Intelligence Surveillance Act 1978; Intelligence Identities Protection Act 1982 (USA), which punishes disclosures which the authorities *have reason to believe* would harm US intelligence operations by naming officials.
42. House Committee on Government Operations: H. Rep. 98–455 (1983).
43. Vaughan, op. cit., note 10.
44. H. 401–59 (1983).
45. This is also a vexed issue in the UK.
46. Though it did run to 5 volumes.
47. See *New York Times Co.* v. *U.S.* 403 US 713 (1971) and the First Amendment protection of freedom of speech and the press; although see *Snepp* v. *U.S.* 444 US 507 (1980), where the Supreme Court held that an agreement by CIA employees not to publish *any* information acquired as an agent without specific prior approval was judicially enforceable *vis-à-vis* classified *and* non-classified information, and all profits accruing from publication were held on constructive trust for the CIA, and see *U.S.* v. *Marchetti* 446 F 2d 1309 (1972). Cf. *Reading* v. *Att.-Gen.* [1951] A.C. 507; and *Haig* v. *Agee* 453 US 280 (1981) *inter alia*. See generally E. Barendt, *Freedom of Speech* (1985).
48. Unlike the CIA, the National Security Council had escaped Con-

gressional oversight, see chapter 1, note 112 above. The War Powers Act 1973, as amended, required prior Congressional notification of military action or covert activity.

49. R. Berger, *Executive Privilege* (1974).

50. 418 US 683 (1974). In *Nixon* v. *Administrator of General Services* 433 US 425 (1977), the Court upheld as constitutional a congressional statute requiring the former President to hand over his Presidential papers to an executive agency prior to their eventual disclosure to the public. Burgher C.J. and Rehnquist J. dissented.

51. *U.S.* v. *Nixon* above, the Watergate tapes. There was an uncanny familiarity to that event when the Royal Ulster Constabulary refused to hand over their tapes recording events surrounding the shooting of two youths in Armagh in 1982 to the investigating officer, John Stalker. When pressurised into giving access, it was announced by the RUC that they had been lost. A written transcript would be made available, but only on the condition that it was not used for any report. Unlike the Special Investigator, Stalker never got his tapes! See J. Stalker, *Stalker* (1988).

52. R.L. Claveloux (1983) *Duke L.J.* 1333.

53. Berger, op. cit. A famous example involved President Eisenhower's refusal to cede to the demands of Joseph McCarthy who was inquiring into the army's loyalty and security programme.

54. *Senate Select Committee on Presidential Campaign Activities* v. *Nixon* (C.A.D.C.) 498 F. 2d 725 (1974).

55. See *Nixon* v. *Administrator of General Services*, note 50 above.

56. *U.S.* v. *House of Representatives of the U.S.* 556 F. Supp. 150 (1983). See *Congressional Quarterly*, 'EPA Document Agreement' (1983) 26 March, p. 635.

57. A claim of privilege was made over the recent appointment of W. Rehnquist as Chief Justice. The claim was withdrawn on the understanding that only Senators, and not their staff, might see the relevant documentation.

58. A.B. Morrison (1986) 99 *Harv. L.R.* 1059, who argues that agencies are placed in a strait jacket and the rules that do satisfy OMB tests are more easily attacked in the courts. See, ibid. p. 1075, for OMB staff reply.

59. H. Relyea (1986), note 19 above. The Canadian Bar Association was very proactive.

60. Ibid.

61. See R.B. Stewart, 'Reform of American Administrative Law: The Academic Agenda vs. the Political Agenda' (unpublished paper for Conference on Comparative Administration and Law, 1984).

62. Canada Act 1982; Wade and Bradley, *Constitutional and Administrative Law* (10th edn 1985), pp. 730–3, for a pithy and lucid account.

63. See *Information Commissioner* v. *Minister of Employment and Immigration* in

Annual Report: Information Commissioner (1984–5), p. 124, for a bizarre interpretation of this provision.

64. *Or* if the *decision* was made at least four years before a relevant request, or if the papers have been in existence for more than 20 years.

65. Trade secrets are specifically referred to.

66. Of 17 cases commenced in Federal Courts until 1 May 1986 alleging unjustified refusal, 6 were commenced by the I.C. 60 per cent of all cases commenced relating to the Act (47 in the overall total) concerned third-party proceedings.

67. 1983–4: 150 complaint files – 46 completed investigations; 1984–5: 188 complaint files – 167 completed investigations; 1985–6: 321 complaint files – 235 completed investigations.

68. Especially the existing 'confidentiality' clauses in existing statutes (about 30 have such); *Main Brief to H.C. Standing Committee on Justice and Legal Affairs*, Office of I.C. (May 1986).

69. H. Janisch in J. McCamus (ed.), *FOI – Canadian Perspectives* (1981).

70. McCamus (1983) 10 *Govt. Publications Review* 51.

71. Janisch (1982) *Public Law* 534.

71a. *Open and Shut: Enhancing the Right Know and the Right To Privacy* (March 1987). See specifically chapter 3 on Exemptions.

72. *Att.-Gen. for NSW* v. *Butterworth and Co. (Aus.) Ltd* (1938) S.R. NSW 195; and Report by the Senate Standing Committee on Constitutional and Legal Affairs on the FOI Bill (1978), chapter 4.

73. See chapter 6 below, pp. 189 *et seq.* This concerned publication of his book *Spycatcher*.

74. See, for instance, the *Annual Reports* of the Administrative Review Council; and M. Partington in P. McAuslan and J. McEldowney (eds.), *Law, Legitimacy and the Constitution* (1985), pp. 199–207.

75. *FOIA 1982 Annual Report by the Att.-Gen.* (Aust. Govt. Publishing Service, 1983).

76. Ss. 32–47.

77. *Re Rae and Department of Prime Minister and Cabinet* (1986) *Admin. Review* 136.

78. As from 1 January 1987.

79. Different departments have taken different attitudes on the same documents as to whether exemption should be claimed: *Re Dillon and Department of Treasury* and *Re Dillon and Department of Trade* (1986) *Admin. Review* 113. Under the Act, the AAT cannot insist on access to exempt information.

80. A Minister has responsibility for administering the FOIA, and he has access to all necessary documents. *Quaere* collective responsibility?

81. One such request was granted in 1983–4.

82. The 1983 Amendment Act allows the AAT to make a recommendation for payment of a successful applicant's costs to the Attorney-General.

83. In that period, the Commonwealth Ombudsman resigned.
84. *Kavvadias* v. *Commonwealth Ombudsman* (Nos. 1 and 2); see CO *Annual Reports* (1983–4), pp. 30–2 and (1984–5), pp. 165–8. Requests come mainly from former complainants.
85. *Kavvadias* has not been followed by Victoria State *vis-à-vis* its own FOIA and their Ombudsman.
86. Unless a certificate under s.9(3) of the Ombudsman Act 1976 is issued. Strangely, the CO does not have access where he represents an applicant before the AAT under s.52F: A.R.C. *Tenth Annual Report* (1985–6), pp. 75–8.
87. *Tenth Annual Report*, para. 76.
88. *Re Burns and Aust. N.U.*, 1 Feb. 1985; cf. *Sankey* v. *Whitlam* (1978) 142 CLR 1.
89. *Public Services Board of N.S.W.* v. *Osmond* 21 Feb. 1986.
90. Kirby J. (1986) *Admin. Review* 102–3.
91. *Re State of Queensland and Dept. of Aviation* (1986) *Admin. Review* 138.
92. *Report of the Chief Ombudsman*, Wellington NZ (1984) and *Murtagh* v. *Commissioner of Taxation*. See *Commissioner of Police* v. *Ombudsman* [1985] 1 N.Z.L.R. 578, on a challenge to the Ombudsman's powers.
93. Following various security-sensitive leaks.
94. J. Michael, *The Politics of Secrecy* (1982), chapters 7 and 9.
95. K.G. Robertson, *Public Secrets* (1982), pp. 183–4.
96. Ibid.
97. N. Brown and J. Garner, *French Administrative Law* (3rd edn 1983).

Chapter 3: Government and Information – An Historical Development

1. As first drafted, it was entitled Breach of Official Trust Bill.
2. Elton, *The Tudor Constitution* (2nd edn, 1981), p. 59; cf. J. Bellamy, *The Tudor Law of Treason* (1979).
3. Elton, *loc. cit.*
4. 13 Eliz. I, c. I (1571).
5. Elton, op. cit., though see his *Policy and Police* (1972).
6. Elton, *The Tudor Revolution in Government* (1953).
7. Op. cit., p. 4.
8. See chapter 3 of Elton, *The Tudor Constitution* for a discussion of the seals.
9. The fine for disobedience was £10 – half to the Crown and half to the informer.
10. Elton, op. cit. note 6 above, pp. 316 *et seq.*
11. Ibid., p. 355.
12. Neale, *House of Commons* (1949), pp. 416 *et seq.*
13. Cited in D. Englefield, *Parliament and Information* (1980).

14. Englefield, op. cit. Nb. C. Parry, 'Legislatures and Secrecy' (1954) 67 *Harv. L.R.* 737.

15. The House still maintains its right to secure the privacy of its debates, e.g. in wartime. The Parliamentary Papers Act 1840 gave the protection of absolute privilege to parliamentary papers. For the position of Command Papers, see H.C. 261 (1969–70); and Cmnd. 5909, p. 55. Press and broadcast reports are protected by qualified privilege: see P. Leopold on 'live' broadcasting (1987) *Public Law* 524.

16. H.C. Debs., 22 January 1987 and 26 January 1987. See D. Campbell, *New Statesman*, 23 January 1987, on the Zircon satellite intelligence system. For the report from the Committee on Privileges, see H.C. 365 (1986–7).

17. My emphasis.

18. *Troilus and Cressida*, I, iii, 109.

19. Although events as far back as 1215 testified to the view that the King could do wrong, see Art. 61 of *Magna Carta*

20. C. Roberts, *The Growth of Responsible Government in Stuart England* (1966), chapter 1.

21. The Watergate and Irangate, or Snoozegate, episodes, for instance. See R. Berger, *Impeachment* (1973).

22. Roberts, op. cit., p. 9.

23. Ibid., p. 118.

24. Ibid., p. 153.

25. J.P. Kenyon, *The Stuart Constitution* (1st edn 1966), p. 479.

26. Bill of Rights, I Will and Mary Sess. 2, ch. 2.

27. William Pitt, II Parl. Hist. England 1009 (1741), cited in Berger, *Executive Privilege* (1974). Berger believes that Parliament asserted an unqualified right: 'it is our duty', said Pitt, 'to inquire into every step of publick management, either abroad or at home, in order to see that nothing is done amiss' (pp. 169–71). Berger's own choice of examples do not support this, see p. 170.

28. *Howard* v. *Gossett* (1845) 10 Q.B. 359 at 379–80, *per* Coleridge J. Unqualified acceptance of this dictum by Berger seems a little incautious.

29. *Complete Prose Works of John Milton*, vol. II (Yale U.P. 1958), p. 159.

30. The Stationers' Company owned a monopoly of book publishing in England.

31. Note 29, op. cit., p. 163.

32. Holdsworth (1920) 29 *Yale L.J.* 841. For censorship and obscenity law, see G. Robertson, *Obscenity* (1979).

33. J.H. Plumb, *The Growth of Political Stability in England 1675–1725* (1967), p. 47.

34. Plumb, *Sir Robert Walpole*, vol. I (1956), p. 348.

35. Ibid., vol. II (1960), p. 41.

36. Ibid., p. 330.
37. Ibid., p. 234.
38. Sir Norman Chester, *The English Administrative System 1780–1870* (1981). I am indebted to Chester's work for information on the following four pages.
39. Ibid., p. 99.
40. Pelican edition (1976), vol. I, p. 349.
41. 27 Geo. III, c. 13.
42. E.g. the numbers employed by public departments and in public offices, as well as their salaries, 50 Geo. III, c. 117: Chester, op. cit., p. 100.
43. Ibid., pp. 102–3.
44. Ibid., pp. 107–9.
45. These were despatches between the British Government, its embassies and foreign governments. I am grateful to Bernard Porter for this information.
46. S.H. Beer, *Modern British Politics* (1982).
47. Chester, op. cit., p. 108.
48. E.g. Society for Supporting the Bill of Rights, the Society of the Freedom of the People (1792), the London Corresponding Society (1792).
49. Beer, note 46 above.
50. Chester, op. cit., p. 158.
51. Ibid., pp. 282 *et seq.* The Colonial Office in 9 months in 1775–6 used 2,000 pens when it employed 9 officials!
52. Ibid.
53. The Home Secretary was responsible for prisons, the police in a general sense, poor relief, factory conditions and local government.
54. Chester, op. cit., p. 312.
55. Ibid., p. 315.
56. The Vice President of the Privy Council; Chester, p. 318.
57. Chester, p. 320.
58. See Robertson, *Public Secrets* (1982), chapter 4.
59. Chester, op. cit., p. 320.
60. See Robertson, op. cit., p. 46, note 14, for examples from the public records.
61. D.G.T. Williams, *Not In the Public Interest* (1965). The civil law of confidentiality was in an elementary state: *Prince Albert* v. *Strange* (1849) 1 Mac. and G. 25.
62. Robertson, op. cit., pp. 53 *et seq.*
63. Ibid.
64. Ibid., p. 61. Hitherto, the Treasury allowed no publication of materials after 1759; the War Office after 1830; and the Home Office after 1778.
65. Williams, note 61 above.
66. A sub-committee on Foreign Espionage of the Committee of Imperial Defence conducted the investigation.

67. There were 47 allegations of espionage or suspicious activities by Germans in 1908, and 31 in the first three months of 1909, Robertson op. cit., p. 64; see also D. French (1978) 21 *The Historical Journal* 355.

68. Cmnd. 5104, vol. I (1972), para. 53.

69. Ibid., para. 50.

70. The Radcliffe Report found that substantial amounts of documents were over-classified and should be downgraded, Cmnd. 1681. See C. Turpin, *Government Contracts* (1972), p. 296, note 187 and contractual clauses specifying secrecy.

71. S.6 of OSA 1920.

72. [1964] A.C. 763; and D. Thompson (1963) *Public Law* 201.

73. Duncan Sandys MP and H.C. 101 (1938–9) and H.C. 173 (1937–8). See an interesting note by A.I.L. Campbell (1985) *Public Law* 212. According to Middlemas, Lloyd George was threatened in 1932 for using a Cabinet document in Parliament – (1976) *Pol. Q.* 39, citing CAB 63/45.

74. D. Hooper, *Official Secrets: The Use and Abuse of the Act* (1987). Atomic Energy has special provisions under: the Atomic Energy Act 1946, ss.11, 13; Atomic Energy Authority Act 1954, Sched. 3, s.6(3), covering prohibited places and nb. Civil Aviation Act 1982, s.18; Nuclear Installations Act 1965, Sched. 1, and European Communities Act 1972, s.11(2), covering Euratom institutions. For specific statutory provisions prohibiting the disclosure of information acquired from citizens, see App. V of Franks, Delbridge and Smith, *Consuming Secrets* (1982), p. 235 and Cripps (1983) *Public Law* 600 at 628–31, updated at H.C. Debs. vol. 108, col. 560 (21 Jan. 1987).

75. It covers any secret official 'code word, pass word or, sketch, place, model, article or note or other document or information which is calculated to be or might be or is intended to be directly or indirectly useful to an enemy' (s.1(1)(c)). The analysis has benefited from R. Thomas, note 81 below.

76. This includes an employee of a local authority working for the police: *R. v. Loat* (1985) *Crim. L.R.* 154.

77. The following five offences do not require *mens rea*. For s.2(1), see *R. v. Fell* (1963) *Crim. L.R.* 207. The absence of high judicial authority on any aspect of s.2 is amazing, although see *R. v. Galvin* [1987] 2 All E.R. 851 below.

78. J. Aitken, *Officially Secret* on *R. v. Aitken and Others*.

79. C. Ponting, *The Right to Know* (1985). He was responsible for the 'Crown Jewells', which were Top Secret documents setting out the details of the events leading to the sinking of the *Belgrano*. Inclusion of this information meant that the jury had to be vetted.

80. The Committee reported in July 1985 and, while critical of the Government's reticence, it did not think the Government had sought to mislead it.

81. See R. Thomas, H.C. 92, II, App. 26, for an informative analysis.

82. Cf. Ponting, note 79 above.

83. (1985) *Crim. L.R.* 318.

84. [1964] A.C. 763.

85. R. Thomas, op. cit., at p. 371. And see N. MacCormick in P. Wallington and R. Merkin (eds.), *Essays in Memory of F.H. Lawson* (1986).

86. 5 U.S.C., ss.1206–1208, 2302. See Cripps (1983) *Public Law* 600; cf. use of the Espionage Act in the USA.

87. Four of the law lords, but not Lord Devlin, so believed in *Chandler*.

88. Or a communication or attempted communication with a foreign agent.

89. *R.* v. *Fell* (1963) *Crim. L.R.* 207 and the ABC trial in 1978 – *mens rea* not required. See *R.* v. *Aitken and Others*, note 78 above, and the Home Office Memo. to Franks (1972), vol. II. pp. 109–10, that *mens rea* was required for s.2(1)(a).

90. Unless he proves receipt was contrary to his desire. For the views of Sir Michael Havers on a third party receiving from a person who has received unlawfully, see Michael (1986) *New L.J.* 1153–4.

91. Bernard Ingham, the PM's press secretary, opined that he hoped a 'severe' Judge would try the case!

92. *The Times*, 12 February 1985.

93. (1670) 6 St. Tr. 999.

94. See notes 89 and 90 above.

95. Apart from s.2(1)(aa).

96. Chapter 6, pp. 189 *et seq.*

97. Suspicion has attended both Labour and Conservative Government interference: see Ponting, op. cit., chapter 6 and Nicol (1979) *Crim. L.R.* 284. For breaches of confidentiality proceedings and the Attorney-General's role, see H.C. Debs., cols. 619–620 (1 Dec. 1986).

98. Sir Robert gave evidence that the decision not to prosecute Chapman Pincher for revelations in *Their Trade is Treachery* was taken by the Attorney-General. Sir Michael Havers took no part in the decision.

99. Especially on unjustified invasion of privacy.

100. Of which there were seven categories of information.

101. *Per contra*, the FOI Bill, see Chapter 7 below, pp. 225 *et seq.*

102. See the Memorandum of the Cabinet Office; Franks (1972), vol. II, p. 9.

103. The DPP would deal with cases of corruption where official information had been traded for private gain (Franks, p. 102, para. 277). The courts have taken a strict line on information under the OSA still being secret, although in the public domain: A. Nicol, note 97 above; *R.* v. *Crisp and Homewood* (1919) 83 JP 121, though Canadian cases differ: *Boyer* v. *R.* (1948) 94 CCC 195, *per* Marchand J. and *R.* v. *Toronto Sun Publishing Ltd* (1979) 47 CCC (2d) 535. However, the Court of Appeal has quashed a conviction where a jury was not asked to consider the defence of prior dissemination of information which might have authorised its use: *R.*

v. *Galvin* [1987] 2 All E.R. 851.

104. Many section 2 cases are tried by magistrates.
105. And *Chandler*.
106. I am grateful to the Attorney-General's office for the following figures.
107. Of the 1920 Act which deals with attempts, incitement etc.
108. H.C. Debs., 9 February 1983.
109. See note 106, and H.C. Debs, vol. 108, col. 13 (12 January 1987).
110. R. Pyper (1985) 56 *Pol. Q.* 72.
111. See Caulfield J's memo. to Franks, vol. II, p. 350. On the Act's effects upon civil servants, see Franks, op. cit. vol. I, p. 17; Ponting, note 79 above, pp. 36–42; see also J. Ward (1986) *Pub. Policy and Admin.* 11; and L. Chapman, *Your Disobedient Servant* (1979).
112. H.C. Debs. vol. 73, col. 181 (12 Feb. 1985) and Cmnd. 9841, respectively.
113. Though cf. the City of London (charter of incorporation).
114. Birkinshaw, *Open Government: Freedom of Information and Local Government* (1986).
115. And their Scottish equivalents. See Widdicombe, Cmnd. 9797 and his interim report (1985).
116. *R.* v. *ILEA ex p. Westminster City Council* [1986] 1 All E.R. 19; and see *R.* v. *GLC ex p. Westminster City Council, The Times*, 22 January 1985.
117. Cf. *Meek* v. *Lothian Regional Council* (1983) S.L.T. 494
118. Patrick Jenkin MP.
119. H.C. 92 II, p. 129 (1985–6).
120. D.G.T. Williams, *Not In The Public Interest*, p. 121.
121. Only where they had referred powers: *Wilson* v. *Evans* [1962] 1 All E.R. 247.
122. Birkinshaw, op. cit. See Birkinshaw, 'Open Government – Local Government Style' (1988) *Public Policy and Administration* 46.
123. Ibid.
124. P. McAuslan, *The Ideologies of Planning Law* (1980).
125. N. Lewis and I. Harden, 'Law and the Local State' (1982) *Urban Law and Policy* 65.
126. P. McAuslan, *Land Law and Planning* (1975).
127. N. Lewis and R. Livock (1979) *Urban Law and Policy* 133.
128. *The New Local Authorities: Management and Structure* (1972).
129. Widdicombe, op. cit., note 115 above.
130. Birkinshaw, op. cit., note 114 above.
131. To what extent were the views of those constituencies under-represented in the representative model? Nb. the special position of police committees (with JPs) and education committees (with teachers).
132. Birkinshaw, op. cit., note 114 above.
133. *R.* v. *Hampstead B.C. ex p. Woodward* (1917) 116 L.T. 213.
134. Ibid., and *R.* v. *Clerk to Lancs Police Committee ex p. Hook* [1980] Q.B. 603.

135. Ibid.
136. *R.* v. *Birmingham D.C. ex p. 'O'* [1983] 1 A.C. 578.
137. *R.* v. *Hackney L.B.C. ex p. Gamper* [1985] 3 All E.R. 275, subject to veto in exceptional instances. Cf. *Ex p. Chadwick* below.
138. *R.* v. *Rushmoor B.C. ex p. Crawford* (D.C./705/81, 27 November 1981).
139. *The Times,* 19 December 1985.
140. Widdicombe recommended that recommendatory committees and sub-committees should be removed from this duty, see Chapter 4 below.
141. *R.* v. *Hyndburn B.C. ex p. Strak* (CO/918/85, 17 December 1985). If operating in a purely advisory capacity, it was doubted whether a right to attend would exist, though surely a 'need to know' may still be established for access to documents.
142. DOE Circ.6/86. See SI 1986, No. 854.
143. And the Islands. It does not cover Northern Ireland. Bodies covered in England include ILEA, Police Authorities, Joint Authorities and Joint Boards.
144. As defined by the Act, not common law.
145. It includes the Data Protection Act.
146. Whose information shows that a criminal offence, breach of statutory duty, a breach of planning control – e.g. s.87(3) of the Town and Country Planning Act 1971 – or a nuisance etc. has been committed.
147. Does this reduce the safeguards available under the 1972 Local Government Act? Standing Orders dealt with urgent business.
148. Including written summaries of proceedings where exempt information is excluded from the minutes and this exclusion prevents a 'reasonably fair and coherent record of the whole or part of the proceedings'.
149. Names and addresses of councillors, rights under the Act etc.
150. Health Service Joint Consultative Committees (Access to Information) Act 1986.
151. Local Government Act 1972, s.270(3).
152. Note 115 above.
153. This power would be vested in the Commission for Local Administration; see Housing Act 1985, s.170; Sex Discrimination Act 1975, s.75; and Race Relations Act 1976, s.66.
154. *R.* v. *Brent AHA ex p. Francis* [1985] Q.B. 869; cf. [1986] 2 All E.R. 273.
155. DHSS Circ. L.A.C. (83) 14.
156. See Chapter 7 below.
157. Chapter 6 below.

Chapter 4: Claims and Counterclaims

1. See Heseltine in *The Observer,* 12 January 1986.
2. H.C. 519 (1985–6), *Fourth Report from the Defence Committee: Westland plc:*

The Government's Decision-Making. It seems he believed he had approval from the PM's Private Office for the leak; the Office certainly knew of the leak.

3. The same classification as the papers leaked by Ponting.

4. These were: the Private Secretary to Leon Brittan; the Chief Press Officer DTI; the PM's Chief Press and Information Secretary; the PM's Private Secretary; and a senior DTI official. To general incredulity, the PM maintained she did not know of the identities involved in the leak until two weeks after it occurred.

5. Far more accomplished than his appearance before the New South Wales court in the Peter Wright case, Chapter 6 below, p. 191.

5a. This statement was made in an interview with Brian Walden on *Weekend World*, London Weekend TV, 12 January 1986.

6. Especially regarding the knowledge of the PM. *World in Action* (30 March 1987) reported that the PM's Private Office positively exhorted the leak.

7. Leon Brittan refused to answer certain vital questions.

8. Marshall (1986) *Public Law* 184.

9. *The Noble Lie* (1986), pp. 110–11.

10. Ibid., p. 112. (my italics).

11. Note 2, para. 100 *et seq.*

12. *Attorney-General* v. *J. Cape* [1976] Q.B. 752; and Cmnd. 6386 on publication by ex-Cabinet Ministers of memoirs. The Cabinet Secretary would have the final say on information relating to national security and international relations. For background restrictions on civil servants, see K. Middlemas (1976) *Pol. Q.* 39.

13. A point which was also made apropos of civil servants' information. The litigation concerned Volume I. No injunction was sought for Volumes II and III after it was refused for Volume I. For non-security-sensitive information, Cmnd. 6386 recommended a delay of 15 years, though in the case of conflict it was up to the ex-Minister what to publish – subject to the possibility of an injunction.

14. D.G.T. Williams, *Not In the Public Interest*, Chapter 2.

15. *Ministry of Defence*, BBC 2, 9 April 1986.

16. Below.

17. H.C. 519 (1985–6), para. 235.

18. Ibid., para. 239.

19. Ibid., para. 240.

20. Ibid., para. 168.

21. See Cmnd. 6386 (1976).

22. *Cabinet* (1986).

23. The most recent available under the Public Records Act. Tony Benn MP withdrew when the Treasury and Civil Service Committee refused to examine his 1976 edition in open session. Mrs Thatcher refused the

committee access to the current edition (*The Guardian*, 11 January 1986).

24. Lord Hunt (1982) *Public Law* 514.

25. Only rarely will a decision be announced as a decision of HM Government.

26. As in the Westland episode itself.

27. Too economical in his own case. This was Sir Robert Armstrong.

28. Note 22, op. cit., p. 31.

29. Nb. Star Chamber to arbitrate on departmental bids for funding before the Expenditure White Paper.

30. Hennessey, *Cabinet*, pp. 102–3, cites Michael Heseltine's report 'It took a Riot' on urban deprivation.

31. Ibid., p. 102.

32. Ibid., p. 11.

33. Cmnd. 4506 (1970), paras. 44–8.

34. D. Howell, quoted in Hennessey, op. cit., p. 112.

35. Wade and Bradley, *Constitutional and Administrative Law* (1985), Ch. 12.

36. A. Robinson in G. Drewry (ed.), *The New Select Committees* (1985); V. Flegmann (1985) *Public Money* 5.

37. John Biffen in D. Englefield (ed.), *Commons Select Committees* (1984).

38. General Notice 80/38, C.S.D. This memo was amended in 1987.

39. See Chapter 6 below, and H.C. 363 (1984–5).

40. Above.

41. Cmnd. 78 (1987).

42. Drewry, op. cit., p. 275.

43. H.C. 555 (1984–5).

44. Ibid. for details, and see Chapter 6 below.

45. The journalist was not punished: H.C. Debs., 20 May 1986.

46. Last used in 1880.

47. And which may cause a conflict of interest where records relate to his own actions as an erstwhile Minister – e.g. Lord Hailsham and the Suez episode.

47a. *The Times* (1987) 1 December.

48. H.C. 92, vols. I and II (1985–6).

49. Ibid., vol. II, pp. 7–9.

50. Ibid.

51. Ibid., vol. I, para. 3.10.

52. Cmnd. 9841. In proceedings before Scott J. in which the Attorney-General sought a permanent injunction prohibiting newspaper reporting of *Spycatcher*'s contents, Sir Robert accepted the possibility, *in extremis*, of a justified leak.

53. The Chief Press and Information Officer at the DTI who effected the leak of the Solicitor-General's letter in the Westland affair.

54. Note 48, vol. II, pp. 43–4. On civil servants who break the law in

performance of their duties, see *Legal Entitlements and Administrative Practices*, C.S.D. (H.M.S.O. 1979).

55. Cmnd. 9841.
56. E.g. US Civil Service Reform Act 1978, and cf. in a breach-of-confidence claim: *Commonwealth of Australia* v. *J. Fairfax and Sons Ltd* (1980) 55 ALJR 45. The 1978 Act establishes the Office of Special Counsel to protect employees and receive 'leaks'. See chapter 1, note 76 and the CIA.
56a. *R.* v. *Civil Service Appeal Board ex p. Bruce* (1987) *The Times*, 22 June; and see Fredman and Morris (1988) *Public Law* 58.
57. See Chapter 7, p. 228 below. The 'public interest' defence will have little scope against a Government's claims to state secrecy and confidentiality.
58. Note 48, vol II, p. 42.
59. See the Memorandum of Nevil Johnson, ibid., p. 169.
60. Ibid.
61. H.C. 92, vol. II, p. 3, and Wass at p. 35.
61a. See *The Media In British Politics*, (ed.) Seaton and Pimlott (1987).
62. M. Cockrell, P. Hennessey, D. Walker, *Sources Close to the Prime Minister* (1984). *Encyclopaedia of Parliament* (1968).
63. See H. Young in *Inside Information* (1982), note 71.
64. *The Guardian*, 9 December 1986.
65. *The Guardian*, *The Independent* and *The Observer* have refused to publish unattributed items of Government information. The Lobby effectively voted for no change in its practices: *The Guardian*, 14 February 1987.
66. This followed the Vassal Tribunal of 1963.
67. Zellick (1987) *New L.J.* 160.
68. H. Young, *The Guardian*, 5 September 1985.
69. H.C. 555 (1984–5), pp. 92–4.
70. Lobby journalists rejected a proposal that each should swear an oath of secrecy, but tied on a proposal that those who broke the confidentiality of Lobby statements should be barred from the Lobby.
71. H. James in A. May and K. Rowan (eds.), *Inside Information: British Government and the Media* (1982).
72. R. Crossman, *Diaries of a Cabinet Minister* (1975), vol. I, p. 497.
73. See *The Protection of Military Information*, Cmnd. 9112 (1983). Self-censorship was emphasised but official censorship was needed, even in limited conflict. False information should be eschewed, but 'sophisticated measures' to deceive an enemy were permissible: see *The Guardian*, 13 August 1986; and D. Mercer etc, *The Fog of War* (1987). See generally on the Press: the *Royal Commission on the Press*, Cmnd. 6433, 6810–6814.
74. Especially but not exclusively in the Westland episode.
75. Home Office, Foreign Office, Ministry of Defence: Cmnd. 5104, vol. II, pp. 241 *et seq.*

76. Vol. II, p. 242.

77. Ibid.

78. See Defence Committee Inquiry H.C. 773 (1979/80); Government Reply, Cmnd. 8129.

79. These were announced by John Nott on 31 March 1982. And see the Defence Committee: H.C. 55 (1982–3).

80. See the Peacock Report, Cmnd. 9824 (1986).

81. Cf. the Cable Authority under the Cable and Broadcasting Act 1984.

82. *Attorney-General, ex rel. McWhirter* v. *I.B.A.* [1973] Q.B. 629; *R.* v. *I.B.A. ex p. Whitehouse, The Times,* 4 April 1985. Cf. *Lynch* v. *BBC* (1983) 6 NIJB.

83. See generally clause 13 of the BBC's Licence and Agreement, Cmnd. 8233, and s.29 of the Broadcasting Act 1981.

84. C. Munro, *Television Censorship and the Law* (1979).

85. Ibid., p. 49; Channel 4 has had particular difficulty with films it wished to broadcast.

86. A Ministerial veto was canvassed.

87. Former Controller at BBC of TV programmes, quoted in Munro, p. 124.

88. *The Times,* 15 July 1986, following *R.* v. *Broadcasting Complaints Commission ex p. Owen* [1985] Q.B. 1153. Cf. the copious scope of review by the Conseil d'Etat over the French Broadcasting Authority (1986) *Public Law* 155.

89. A. Boyle (1986) *Public Law* 562. Nb. s.93 of Representation of the People Act 1983; *X and Z* v. *UK* App. No. 4515/70 (1970) and the European Convention on Human Rights.

90. *The Guardian,* 16 April 1986.

91. And see A. Smith, *Television and Political Life: Studies in Six European Countries* (1979); A. Briggs, *The History of Broadcasting in the UK* (4 vols., 1961–79).

92. And its predecessor, the Independent Television Authority.

92a. Op. cit., note 61a above.

93. See *Wilson* v. *I.B.A.* (1979) S.C. 351.

94. *The Guardian,* 31 August 1985.

95. G. Cumberbatch *et al., T.V. News and the Miners' Strike,* Broadcasting Research Unit (1986). Syndicated tapes are widely used by Government Departments for promotional purposes on local radio.

96. *The Guardian,* 5 July 1986.

97. See Lady Faulkner in *The Listener,* 8 August 1985, maintaining their independence.

98. A. Singer, *The Listener* 8 August 1985.

99. The Home Secretary moved to the Department of Trade and Industry shortly after this fracas.

100. The enforced settlement of a libel action against the BBC brought by

two right-wing Conservative MPs of allegedly 'extremist' views and the attack by the Conservative Party Chairman on BBC's 'left-wing bias': H.C. Debs., 4 November 1986.

101. See A. Davies in A. Barker (ed.), *Quangos In Britain* (1982), chapter 10.

102. Cmnd. 9824.

103. Above, note 80.

104. Cable and Broadcasting Act 1984, s.25, and Public Order Act 1986, s.22; and nb. the Video Recordings Act 1984 and the role of the British Board of Film Censors.

105. With attempts in 1986 and 1987.

106. 'Open Government' in the BBC series *Yes, Minister*.

107. Birkinshaw, Harden and Lewis, *Corporatism and Accountability: The Democratic Dilemma*, forthcoming.

108. Issuing Codes of Guidance, statutory regulations, departmental regulations or by allowing an appeal or complaint to be made by an aggrieved party to the Secretary of State; see Birkinshaw, *Grievances, Remedies and the State* (1985), Chapter 4.

109. See Chapter 5 below, pp. 146 *et seq.*

110. T. Prosser, *Nationalised Industries and Public Control* (1986).

111. Delbridge and Smith, *Consuming Secrets* (1982), p. 22.

112. N.C.C., *Controlling Public Utilities* (1984).

113. *Annual Report 1985,* H.C. 403 (1985–6). After privatisation, B.T. stopped publishing criteria on performance standards, e.g. how many calls go awry. After much pressure, B.T. promised to publish such information.

114. *The Guardian*, 26 February 1986.

115. If it is a private body acting as a surrogate for the State, the courts may hold it susceptible to judicial review: *R.* v. *Panel on Take-Overs and Mergers ex p. Datafin plc* [1987] 1 All E.R. 564; cf. *R.* v. *IBA ex p. Rank Organisation* (1986) *The Times*, 14 March; *R.* v. *NCB ex p. NUM* [1986] I.C.R. 791.

116. P. Nonet and P. Selznick, *Law and Society In Transition: Toward Responsive Law* (1978), p. 112.

117. The responsibilities of the former Select Committee on Nationalised Industries were assumed by departmental Select Committees in 1979.

118. It has agreed to do so. There have been attempts to pass Bills allowing access to registers of those served with Enforcement Notices on environmental grounds.

119. *Health Care U.K.* (1985) CIPFA, A. Harrison, J. Gretton.

120. Ibid.

121. See: *R.* v. *M.M.C ex p. Argyll Group plc* [1986] 2 All E.R. 257; *R.* v. *M.M.C ex p. M. Brown plc* [1987] 1 All E.R. 463, for judicial tests of fairness of MMC procedures. Cf. D.T.I., *Mergers Policy* (HMSO, 1988).

122. *Non-Departmental Public Bodies – A Guide for Departments* (HMSO 1985); I. Harden (1987) *Public Law* 27.

123. Ibid., chapter 8.

124. See note 115 above and *ex p. Datafin*, esp. Donaldson M.R. and Lloyd L.J. The issue of fact and degree of compenetration of public and private will necessitate individual assessment of each institution – see *Law* v. *NGRC* [1983] 3 All E.R. 300.

125. As of the time of writing, it appears that this responsibility is to end.

125a.Section 47 of Banking Act 1987.

126. National Audit Office, *MoD: Profit Formula for Non Competitive Government Contracts* (1985).

127. H.C. 390 (1984/85), para. 26.

128. The MoD has undertaken to publicise details of every major contract just signed or going to tender (*The Guardian*, 29 July 1986). The Minister undertook to notify the Chairman of the Public Accounts Committee of security-sensitive defence contracts in excess of £250 million. He was not informed of the Zircon satellite system, which was estimated at £500 million. The £250 million threshold has been reduced to £25 million.

129. P. West in *Health Care UK 1985*, note 119 above; see H.C. 551 (1983–4).

130. H.C. 551 (1983–4), Chairman PAC.

131. See note 107.

132. L. Hilliard (1986) *Mod. L.R.* 476.

133. Birkinshaw, *Grievances, Remedies and the State* (1985) pp. 152–4.

134. He is not in the analogous position of senior officers who are servants of the authority. Such officers must ultimately work through committees of members, unless power is delegated to them under s.101 of the Local Government Act 1972. Such a conflict between governmental secrecy and local authority pressure to be informed would make an officer's position untenable. See further *R.* v. *Secretary of State etc ex p. Northumbria Police Authority* [1988] 1 All E.R. 556 (C.A.).

135. S.13, Rates Act 1984; and cf. s.6., Education No. 2 Act 1986.

136. As it was put to me by a Chief Housing Officer.

137. (1985) *The Times*, 19 December.

138. See Chapter 3 above, note 137.

139. Ibid.

140. They will also be outside the terms of the 1985 Local Government (Access To Information) Act. This is a difficult issue, as an authority only has formal power to create committees and sub-committees, whether joint or individual. Creation of an ad hoc working party would have to be effected informally and it would possess no executive powers. Even then, its genesis would be looked at with scrutiny to see what it really was: *R.* v. *Eden D.C. ex p. Moffat*, 15 April 1987 (Crown Office List), held that a working party could be established under s.111 of the Local Government Act 1972, but not as an executive body.

141. This would reduce members' rights to information at common law, but would improve pro rata rights of membership of committees.
142. Note 140 above.
143. See *Leicester City Council* v. *D. Auditor for Leicester* (unreported).
144. *R.* v. *Secretary of State ex p. Hillingdon LBC* [1986] 1 All E.R. 810.
145. In the passage of the Local Government (Access To Information) Bill, a city council's assistant solicitor informed a committee that the provision of 'background papers' would cause endless difficulties; he did not inform the members that he had opinions to the contrary from other authorities.
146. Cf. *Ass. Provincial Picture Houses* v. *Wednesbury Corp.* [1948] 1 K.B. 223; *R.* v. *Liverpool C.C. ex p. P.A.T.* [1984] L.G.R. 648.
147. These could be exempt under the 1985 Act.
148. Chapter 7 below, pp. 218–21.
149. Under Education Act 1980, s.27.
150. Cf. Education (No. 2) Act 1986 and school government, and nb. s.62 of that Act.
151. Formerly Housing Act 1980.
152. Birkinshaw, *Open Government: Freedom of Information and Local Government* (1986).
153. R. Skellington (1981) *New Society* 29 January.
154. N.C.C., *Access by Public Sector Tenants To Their Files* (1985).
155. Housing and Planning Act 1986. A tenant will acquire protection under the Rent Act 1977.
156. (1985) 18 H.L.R. 171 (C.A.).
157. See s.6 and Sched. 1 of the Housing and Planning Act 1986.
158. Nor should anyone suppose that nationalisation *per se* is a democratising influence; see Birkinshaw, *Grievances, Remedies and the State*, Chapter 4.
159. From 1980–3, the London Docklands Development Corporation reported only once to Parliament, the G.L.C. alleged.
160. *Annual Report LDDC 1983/84.*
161. Widdicombe; op. cit., pp. 202–3.
162. E.g. Transport Act 1985, transferring passenger transport executives to private-sector companies, or by use of s.137 of the Local Government Act 1972.

Chapter 5: Openness as a Practice or Non-practice

1. Lord Bancroft, H.C. 92 II (1985–6), p. 252. On the time-consuming nature of pressure groups, see D. Hurd, reported in *The Guardian*, 20 September 1986.
2. Public Records Acts 1958 and 1967. See M. Roper in Chapman and

Hunter (eds), *Open Government*. (1987). This legislation does not cover Scottish records.

3. Cmnd. 8787 (1983).

4. Cmnd. 8204, *Modern Public Records: Selection and Access*; Government reply, Cmnd. 8204.

5. *Timewatch*, BBC2, 1 January 1986.

6. See Sir John Donaldson's apprehension on Government apathy: Public Records Office, 26th Annual Report (1985). The Master of the Rolls is chairman of the advisory committee.

7. For such periods as the Lord Chancellor designates.

8. As occurred in 1986–7 *vis-à-vis* Lord Hailsham and Suez.

9. Lord Hunt (1982) *Public Law* 514. Five previous Prime Ministers were consulted in seeking access to documents relevant to Franks' inquiry into the Falklands war. The inquiry had access to all the secret intelligence papers it required. The Cabinet Secretary has access to the papers of a previous administration.

10. A pointed episode involved the allegations of MI5's undermining of Harold Wilson's Government by Peter Wright. The allegations were investigated in 1977 when James Callaghan was Prime Minister. On the conventions just described, Margaret Thatcher denied herself access to the papers. The 'link man' between the Home Office and MI5 at the relevant time was Sir Robert Armstrong, claimed H. Young (*The Guardian*, 19 March 1987). Not so, claimed Sir Robert – the Cabinet Secretary – *The Guardian*, 20 March 1987. The 'link man' was the Permanent Secretary, who was deceased. See Chapter 1, p. 23.

11. Dr W. Wallace and Dr W. Plowden, H.C. 92 II (1985–6), p. 383.

12. Ibid.

13. H.C. 576 (1985–6). See now the PAC Report: 8 April 1987.

14. I.e. headed by a Minister.

15. To call the Metropolitan Police a Government Department begs more than a few constitutional questions!

15a. See 13th Report of Committee of Public Accounts, *Financial Management Initiatives* (1986–7).

16. There are about 350 Command papers each year.

17. C. Bennett and P. Hennessey, *A Consumer's Guide To Open Government* (1980).

18. One reason for insisting that his officers are civil servants. An interesting example of the power of the Commissioner was seen in relation to the NIPCA (Northern Ireland), who took over a complaint made originally to the Fair Employment Agency who were debarred from inquiry because of a ministerial certificate. The NIPCA was not so barred by the certificate and investigated, NIPCA *Annual Report 1984* H.C. 419 (1984–5), para. 19, though cf. Parliamentary Commissioner Act (NI) 1969, Sched. 2(2).

19. H.C. 498 (1974–5).

20. The Head will see the report in draft and will doubtless recommend significant changes, where he feels it is necessary, in the drafting.

21. Cmnd. 9563.

22. D. Englefield, *Parliament and Information* (1980), p. 1.

23. Ibid.

24. Ibid., pp. 20–49.

25. Ibid., p. 28.

26. *Whitehall and Westminster: Government Informs Parliament* (1985).

27. See Erskine May (1983 edn), pp. 331–47; Sir N. Chester in S.A. Walkland and M. Ryle (eds), *The Commons Today* (1980 edn).

28. At December 1984 prices, an hour's search on POLIS cost £55.

29. See Appendix V of Englefield (1985) for a list of Reports and Accounts laid before Parliament and ordered to be printed.

30. E. May, note 27 above.

31. C. Price, *Public Money*, December 1984, p. 26.

32. Ibid.

33. Ibid.

34. P. Luff, *Public Money*, September, 1985, p. 12.

35. See Chapter 4 above, note 36 and D. Wass, *Government and the Governed* (1984).

36. E.g. Bill of Rights 1689, Article 4. Supply procedure is primeval.

37. As well as the Secretary of State.

38. G. Downey, *Public Money*, June 1986, p. 35.

39. Ibid.

40. Ibid., p. 36.

41. National Association of Health Authorities, *Support Services for Members and Chairmen of Health Authorities* (1985), on the patchy information to health authorities. District Health Authorities are also criticised for providing poor information to Community Health Councils.

42. G. Downey, op. cit., p. 37.

43. Ibid. See note 15a above.

44. NICCs (the consumer bodies) cannot get information as of right – it is provided at the discretion of industries. Management corporate plans are still, in some cases, not published and Parliament has had difficulties getting hold of these. The contents of Annual Reports remains very largely a matter of the industry management's discretion.

45. C. Graham and T. Prosser (1987) *Mod. L.R.* 16.

46. H.C. 576 (1985–6); and see the Public Accounts Committee's response: H.C. 98 (1986–7).

47. E.g. numbers of nurses as opposed to amount of expenditure on nurses. The CAG found it difficult to establish the value of assets owned by central departments.

48. See H. Heclo and A. Wildavsky, *The Private Government of Public Money* (2nd edn, 1981).

49. Supplementary Estimates are presented as needed in the summer, autumn or winter.

50. By A. Likierman.

51. See I. Harden and N. Lewis, *The Noble Lie* (1986), pp. 129 *et seq.*

52. *Public Money*, September 1984, and reply, *Public Money*, Dec. 1984, p. 10.

53. A controversy arose when Peter Levene became head of Procurement Executive for the MoD on terms that he dissociate completely from his former employer with the consequence that he could not answer the committee's questions relating to the placement or operation of Government contracts with the company: H.C. 390 (1984–5), p. v.

54. Pp. 124–5. See: National Audit Act 1983, s.8.

55. Royal Ordnance Factories.

56. *Non-Departmental Public Bodies* (HMSO 1985), para. 32.

57. T.J. Cartwright, *Royal Commissions and Departmental Committees in Britain* (1975). The bodies may be seen as expert and pre-eminent, independent and/or representative, a cover for the fact that a decision has effectively been made or a way of putting off a decision, etc.

58. Graham and Prosser, op. cit., note 45 above.

59. If the body in question is considered to be a private body, and not a public one, for instance: see Chapter 4, note 115 above.

59a. See Baldwin and McCrudden (eds), *Regulation and Public Law*, (1987).

60. Cf. *I.R.C.* v. *Rossminster* [1980] A.C. 952; see *Review of Restrictive Trade Practices Policy*, Cm. 331 (1988).

61. *R.* v. *M.M.C. ex p. Elders IXL plc* [1987] 1 All E.R. 451; *R.* v. *M.M.C. ex p. M. Brown plc* [1987] 1 All E.R. 463.

62. *Ex p. Elders plc*, above.

63. *The Guardian*, 2 April 1987.

64. Pp. 72–3.

65. See, inter alia, Financial Services Act 1986 and Building Societies Act 1986.

66. *The Guardian*, 14 February 1986. For the duty of confidentiality owed by a bank to a client, see Chapter 7 below, note 7.

67. Companies Act 1985, ss.352–62; and nb. ss.198–219.

68. Registers are usually kept in a clearing bank.

69. *The Guardian*, 14 February 1987.

70. Financial Services Act 1986, Chapter X; cf. Companies Act 1985, Part XIV – Investigation of Companies.

71. E.g. The National Council for Voluntary Organisations.

72. G. Robertson, *People Against the Press* (1983).

73. See Chapters 3 and 4 above, pp. 88 and 125.

74. *Open Government: Freedom of Information and Local Government* (1986).

75. It will be interesting to see what, if any, response will follow the

publication of a DoE/CLA-sponsored study, *Complaints Procedures in Local Government* (1987) by N. Lewis, M. Seneviratne and S. Cracknell.

76. General Improvement Areas under the Housing Acts.

77. Housing Action Areas, ibid.

78. *Grievances, Remedies and the State* (1985), chapter 3.

79. Abolished in 1985.

80. Op. cit., note 78 above.

81. *Steeples* v. *Derbyshire C.C.* [1984] 3 All E.R. 468; cf. *R.* v. *Sevenoaks D.C. ex p. Terry* and *R.* v. *St Edmunsbury BC, ex p. IICP Ltd* [1985] 3 All E.R. 226 and 234 respectively.

82. Birkinshaw, op. cit.

83. Op. cit., note 75 above.

84. Birkinshaw, note 74 above, chapter 5. Nb. Education (No. 2) Act 1986, ss.30–32. 57 and 62.

85. *R.* v. *South Glamorgan Appeals Committee, ex p. Evans*, 10 May 1984, Crown Office List. The authority must prove to the Committee that the admission of the *single* child in question would cause prejudice to efficient education and not simply that a class of 37 would cause such prejudice. It must then ask whether such prejudice, if established, would outweigh 'parental factors', i.e. their wishes. See J. Tweedie (1986) *Public Law* 407.

86. E.g. *Caught In the Act – A Survey and Handbook*, CSIE, The Spastics Society (1986). Cf. Disabled Persons (Services, Consultation and Representation) Act 1986.

87. Ibid., and see Birkinshaw, op. cit., note 74 above, chapter 5.

88. *The Guardian*, 9 September 1986.

89. Birkinshaw, *loc. cit.*

90. *Charter for Open Government*, A.L.A. (1986).

91. *R.* v. *Newham LBC ex p. Haggerty*, 9 April 1985, Crown Office List. Widdicombe believed legislation should reverse this decision, although a register of interests should be maintained and failure to fill should be an offence: paras. 6.48 and 6.56.

92. Ibid.

93. N.C.C., *Measuring Up* (1986) – on local authority consumer performance indicators.

94. *R.* v. *Eden B.C. ex p. Moffat*, 15 April 1987 (Crown Office List).

95. H.C. 92 II (1985–6), p. 384.

96. DoE 94/75; Scottish Office 95/75, Welsh Office 166/75.

97. And see Cmnd. 5636 and Cmnd. 6524.

98. Cf. the position of MPs, p. 106 above.

99. See Chapter 3, pp. 77–82 above.

100. And the Act only covers personal information.

101. C. Tapper, *Computer Law* (1983); Copyright (Computer Software) Amendment Act 1985.

102. As the text describes, there was also a commercial necessity in the incorporation by the UK Government of the Convention. See Austin (1984) *Public Law* 618.

103. S.1(3).

104. I.e. those holding personal data. See s.1(5) for what constitutes 'holding'. A person who provides other persons with services in respect of data carries on a 'computer bureau'.

105. Sched I, Part II. The D.P.R. has published *Notes* and *Questions and Answers* on the Act.

106. In 1986, it was estimated that there were approximately 300,000 data users in both the public and private sectors.

107. *The Guardian*, 2 January 1987. However, the DPR noted that six departments had not registered by June 1987 (H.C. 33, p. 37). A survey in April 1986 stated that 94 per cent of large firms were ignorant of their duty to register. By that time, the D.P.R. had received 160 complaints. As of writing, he was given no specific guidance on how to deal with complaints.

108. *The Guardian*, 25 June 1987.

109. The National Computer Users' Forum recommended to the Home Office that the fee should be £10–£15. The Home Secretary settled for £10. Regulations provide for a fee of £2 for the supply by the DPR of a copy of the particulars contained in any entry in the Register maintained under s.4; S.I. 1986, 1899.

110. Only 'users' (including bureaus) can appeal to the Tribunal. The D.P.R. may issue 'de-registration notices', or 'transfer prohibition notices' to places outside the UK.

111. Disclosure, possibly destruction, authorised by the data user in contravention of the Act may be a crime but *quaere* non actionable?

112. The subject access provisions.

113. The registration provisions. In other words, there is a *complete* exemption from the Act.

114. Ss.32 and 33.

115. E.g. under the Companies Act 1985. Access by individuals to personal files under the Consumer Credit Act 1974, s.158, is not replaced by the DPA, s.34(3).

116. Part IV and s.26(2) and s.21. This would only cover exempt information.

117. DA (84) 25, which has a useful list of statutes requiring disclosure, and DA (85) 23.

118. For the risk of improper use of GPs' systems, see *Micros in Practice* (HMSO 1986). For the Access to Personal Files Bill and the exemption of medical files, see Chapter 7 below, p. 217.

119. H.C. 493 (1985–6).

120. See also ss.34(9) and 17.

121. See Chapter 7 below, pp. 218 *et seq*.
122. NHS documents are vested in the Secretary of State, but in the inquiry into the conduct of the obstetrician Wendy Savage, the GMC instructed that evidence from former patients was to be given *in camera*: see p. 282 below.
123. H.C. Debs. vol. 110, col. 1183.

Chapter 6: Openness, Information and the Courts

1. *The Guardian*, 14 March 1987; and *Att.-Gen.* v. *The Observer and Others* (1987) *The Times*, 22 December.
2. See p. 189 below and nb. the Law Commission's Report suggesting, *inter alia*, a new tort of breach of confidence, Cmnd. 8388 (1981).
3. Copyright Act 1956.
4. Patents Act 1977.
5. Copyright (Consumer Software) Amendment Act 1985 and nb. *Intellectual Property and Innovation*, Cmnd. 9712 (1986). See generally J. Phillips, *Introduction To Intellectual Property Law* (1986).
6. E. Barendt, *Freedom of Speech* (1985); G. Robertson, *Obscenity* (1979); Public Order Act 1986 *Current Law Statutes Annotation*, vol. 4, chapter 64 T. Gibbons.
7. Though still for treason, certain forms of piracy and some military offences.
8. *The Noble Lie* (1986).
9. *Anisminic* v. *Foreign Compensation Commission* [1969] 2 A.C. 147 is a famous example of the enforced hypocrisy in which the courts engage to insist upon a jurisdiction to review.
10. Especially in the field of government contracts, where even formal arbitration is rare.
11. Note 9 above, but the British Nationality Act 1981 and the Interception of Communications Act 1985 are two recent statutes seeking to preclude the jurisdiction of the courts.
11a. *Re London and Norwich Investment Services* (1987) *The Times*, 16 Dec.
12. Prospects of promotion will doubtless be blighted.
13. Both Elton in *The Tudor Constitution* (2nd edn 1981) and Kenyon in *The Stuart Constitution* (1966) believe that Star Chamber was much maligned and unjustly so: it administered 'the Common Law by means of a different procedure', including written depositions, exchange of evidence and cross-examination of the accused under oath (Kenyon, p. 117). Allegations of secrecy were fabrications. For criticism of the view that it was the Privy Council in another guise, see W. Holdsworth, *History of English Law*, vol. V, Ch. IV.
14. E.g. *Duncan* v. *Jones* [1936] 1 K.B. 218; *Thomas* v. *Sawkins* [1935] 2 K.B. 249; Viscount Dilhorne in *BSC* v. *Granada TV* [1981] A.C. 1096; and

Lord Diplock in *Secretary of State for Defence* v. *Guardian Newspapers Ltd* [1984] 2 All E.R. 601.

15. Article 10(1).

16. Article 10(2). Cf. *Leander* v. *Sweden* (ECHR) (1987) *The Times*, 25 April.

17. Not necessarily statute or statutory instrument, but in a body of *published* rules considered binding: *Silver* v. *U.K.* (1983) 5 EHRR 347 and discussion of the proviso in Art. 8(2); *Sunday Times* v. *U.K.* (1979) 2 EHRR 245.

18. The *Sunday Times* case, above.

19. *Handyside*, E. Court H.R., Series A, vol. 24, Judgment of 7 December 1976; *Silver*, note 115. Is section 2 of the Official Secrets Act 1911 such an overkill? In *Leander*, note 16 above, refusing access to information on a national security register was neither a breach of Article 8 – right to privacy – nor Article 10, the Court held.

20. The Bill was not an entrenched provision and could have been *specifically* overridden by subsequent legislation if enacted.

21. Peer opinion is very important: see *Judicial Appointments: The Lord Chancellor's Policies and Procedures* (Lord Chancellor's Department, 1986).

22. (1986) *Public Law* 384.

23. See Judge J. Pickles, *Straight From the Bench: Is Justice Just?* (1987); one former recorder has threatened the Lord Chancellor with judicial review for failing to renew an appointment; since 1981, 27 expired appointments had not been renewed: H.C. Debs. vol. 107, col. 431 (16 December 1986).

24. High Court judges hold office during good behaviour subject to removal by the Queen on an address from both Houses of Parliament to the Queen, Supreme Court Act 1981, s.11(3)).

24a. *The Guardian* 4 November 1987.

25. First published in August 1980: see H.C. Debs. vol. 72, col. 384 (4 February 1985) for a list of cases in which vetting has occurred; J. Griffith and H. Harman, *Justice Deserted* (NCLL 1979). See Lord Havers on the Criminal Justice Bill, H.L. Debs. (2 November 1987) and jury vetting.

26. Reasons must be given for convictions and an unfettered right of appeal exists – s.7 of Northern Ireland (Emergency Provisions) Act 1978.

27. See *Att.-Gen.* v. *Times Newspapers Ltd* [1974] A.C. 273 and the Phillimore Report, Cmnd. 5794 (1974).

28. Sched. I for 'active'.

29. S.2(1) for 'publication'.

30. S.3. The burden of proof is on the defendant to make out the defence. The distributor is also afforded protection.

31. S.4(1) and *Att.-Gen.* v. *Times Newspapers Ltd* (1983) *The Times*, 12 February.

32. *Re F.* [1977] 1 All E.R. 114 (C.A.) and *Re L* [1988] 1 All E.R. 418; cf. *Att.-Gen.* v. *Leveller Magazines Ltd* [1979] 1 All E.R. 7745 (H.L.).

33. *Att.-Gen.* v. *English* [1982] 2 All E.R. 903 (H.L.).

34. Defaming judges as incompetent or biased.

35. Section 6(*c*). E.g. bribing or intimidating jurors; see also: *Raymond* v. *Honey* [1983] A.C. 1. Nb. *Att.-Gen.* v. *Newspaper Publishing plc and Others* [1987] 3 All E.R. 276.

36. *Att.-Gen.* v. *New Statesman Publishing Co.* [1981] Q.B. 1.

37. Codes of Guidance exist.

38. E.g. Children and Young Persons Act 1933, ss.39 and 49; Administration of Justice Act 1960, s.12; Sexual Offences (Amendment) Act 1976; Magistrates Courts Act 1980, ss.8 and 71. JPs cannot withhold their own identities from the public: *R.* v. *Felixstowe Justices ex p. Leigh* [1987] 2 W.L.R. 380.

39. [1913] A.C. 417; see *Re X* [1975] Fam. 47.

40. *Per* Lord Diplock in *Home Office* v. *Harman*, below.

41. As in parts of Clive Ponting's trial; OSA 1920, s.8.

42. *Williams* v. *The Home Office (No. 2)* [1981] 1 All E.R. 1211.

43. Though cf. Lord Denning in the Court of Appeal [1981] 1 Q.B. 534.

44. *Home Office* v. *Harman* [1983] A.C. 280.

45. It is peculiar to common-law systems.

46. 800 pages of documents were read out. The Master of the Roles, Sir John Donaldson, has exhorted counsel to restrict the length of oral proceedings in civil cases by increased use of written submissions.

47. Which might involve some question-begging!

48. See *Re Application of NBC, USA* v. *Meyers* (1980) 635 F2d 945; *US* v. *Mitchell* (1976) 551 F 2d 1252; *Nixon* v. *Warner Communications Inc.* (1978) 435 US 589.

49. And he made some unsupported assertions that discovery was more widely available (as a practice?) against government departments since *Conway* v. *Rimmer*; but see e.g. Lord Cross in *Alfred Crompton* v. *Commissioners of Customs and Excise* [1973] 2 All E.R. 1169 at 1185 d.

50. After an inquiry by Bingham J. was scuppered.

51. *The Guardian*, 14 June 1986.

52. Supreme Court Rule Committee, 6 Feb. 1987; and see RSC Ord. 24, r.14A.

53. Pannick, *The Guardian*, 6 March 1987.

54. See Y. Cripps (1984) *Camb. L.J.* 266, for the history behind s.10.

55. *Alfred Crompton*, note 49 above, whether or not contained in a publication.

56. *Marks* v. *Beyfus* [1890] 25 Q.B.D. 494; *Neilson* v. *Laugharne* [1981] Q.B. 736; Cmnd. 6542, para. 287.

57. *D.* v. *NSPCC* [1977] 1 All E.R. 589 (H.L.).

58. *R.* v. *Gaming Board ex p. Benaim and Khaida* [1970] 2 Q.B. 417; *Rogers* v. *Secretary of State* [1972] 2 All E.R. 1057.

59. *Att.-Gen.* v. *Mulholland*, and *v. Clough* [1963] 1 Q.B. 477 and 773 respectively.

60. *Norwich Pharmacal Co.* v. *Commissioners of Customs and Excise* [1974] A.C. 133, a case involving discovery against a third party. See, incidentally, Consumer Safety (Amendment) Act 1986, s.1.

61. *Alfred Crompton*, note 49 above.

62. *British Steel Corporation* v. *Granada T.V.* [1981] A.C. 1096.

63. *Per* Lord Denning in the Court of Appeal.

64. *Per* Lord Salmon.

65. Aspinall, *Politics and the Press 1780–1850* (1973).

66. See *Att.-Gen.* v. *Lundin* [1982] 75 Cr. App. Rep. 90, and an acknowledgement by the court of a possible 'public policy' protection of an informer's source of information at common law.

67. *Secretary of State for Defence and Another* v. *Guardian Newspapers Ltd* [1984] 3 All E.R. 601 (H.L.).

68. He had hoped to outflank the Opposition by revealing the information at the last possible moment to Parliament.

69. Griffiths L.J. did not concur on this point with the majority in the Court of Appeal.

70. Cf. Lord Scarman, below.

71. A junior clerk in the registry of the private office of the Foreign Secretary.

72. He destroyed some security-sensitive information.

73. See e.g. Lawton L.J. in *R.* v. *Lemsatef* [1977] 2 All E.R. 835.

74. See pp. 608 h–j and 610 g–h.

75. The evidence of danger to the security system, he believed, was 'meagre and full of omissions'.

76. As Chairman of the Security Commission?

77. The story was published on the 31st October; proceedings were commenced on 22 November.

78. Cf. Lord Bridge's review of telephone taps, Chapter 1 above, p. 27.

79. Emphasis added; see below. Nb. *X* v. *Y* (1987) New L.J. 1062.

80. Note 62 above, where a contractual or tortious claim is pursued.

81. Cf. *Maxwell* v. *Pressdram Ltd* [1987] 1 All E.R. 656 (C.A.). A journalist has been refused immunity from revealing sources of information relating to *fraud* in the City in a DTI inquiry, *In re an Inquiry under the Company Securities (Insider Dealing) Act 1985* (1988) 1 All E.R. 203 (H.L.). The journalist was fined £20,000 for contempt when he refused to identify the 'leak'.

82. *Per* Parker L.J. in *Maxwell*.

82a. *In re an Inquiry etc.*, note 81 above.

83. [1916] 2 A.C. 77, though nb. the comments of Lord Scarman in *Guardian Newspapers* above.

84. Cf. McCowan J. in *R.* v. *Ponting* [1985] *Crim. L.R.* 318.

85. *R.* v. *Secretary of State etc. ex p. Hosenball* [1977] 3 All E.R. 452; the 'Three Advisers' are resorted to: see Chapter 1 above, note 56. Nb: *R.* v. *Secretary of State etc. ex p. Stitt* (1987) *The Independent*, 3 February.

86. For G.C.H.Q, see Chapter 1 above, p. 23. The decision was not announced to the Cabinet.

87. [1984] I.R.L.R. 309.

88. *C.C.S.U.* v. *Minister for the Civil Service* [1984] 3 All E.R. 935 (H.L.). To the limited extent that courts require some evidence of possible injury to national security when action affects individual rights, they have accepted that such issues are justiciable, i.e. susceptible to the judicial process. Usually such topics are catered for and allocated by a constitution: *Baker* v. *Carr* 369 US 186 (1962) esp. Brennan J.

89. See J.A.G. Griffith (1985) *Public Law* 564.

90. Ibid.

91. See below for discovery, pp. 204 *et seq.*

92. The European Commission of Human Rights rejected as inadmissible an application from the union under Article 11(2): App. No. 11603/85, Decision 20 January 1987.

93. See *Att.-Gen.* v. *Turnaround Distribution Ltd*, *The Independent*, 19 December 1986. Approval must be given for publications of memoirs by civil servants. For CIA agents, see *Snepp* v. *U.S.*, Chapter 2, note 47, above.

94. Many details of which had already been published – see Chapter 1 note 71, above.

95. *Att.-Gen.* v. *The Guardian and The Observer* (1986) *The Times*, 26 July. For the European Convention and confidentiality of state secrets, see: App. 4274/69 (FRG) 35 *Recueil* 158, and 9401/81 (Norway) 27 DR 228.

96. E. Barendt, *Freedom of Speech* (1985).

97. Op. cit., note 95. The allegations had also been published elsewhere. *The Independent*, 27 April 1987, and other papers published extracts in defiance of the injunction.

98. *Att.-Gen.* v. *J. Cape* [1976] Q.B. 752.

99. Emphasis in original.

100. Chapter 5, note 10 above.

101. In the N.S.W. proceedings to restrain Wright's book, the British Government accepted the truth of the allegations for *those* proceedings to avoid examination of those issues. This tactical ploy backfired, forcing the Attorney-General and Solicitor-General to make a Press statement – see *The Guardian*, 16 August 1986.

102. *Unlawfully* here means in breach of confidence.

103. Note 101.

104. H.C. 519 (1985–6).

105. See note 1 above. He who comes to equity. . . !

106. *Commonwealth of Australia* v. *J. Fairfax and Sons Ltd* (1980) 55 ALJR 45. See note 107.

107. *Att.-Gen.* v. *Newspaper Publishing plc* [1987] 3 All E.R. 276.

108. [1987] 3 All E.R. at 289. See *In re X* [1984] 1 W.L.R. 1422.

109. The injunction was lifted in the High Court, restored with amendments in the Court of Appeal and extended in the House of Lords in a 3–2 judgment, *Att.-Gen.* v. *Observer Newspaper etc* [1987] 3 All E.R. 316. Cf. the First Amendment to the US Constitution and *New York Times Co.* v. *U.S.* 403 U.S. 713 (1971) and nb. *U.S.* v. *Progressive Inc.* 467 F. Supp. 990 (1979). On prohibition of library loans of *Spycatcher*, see *In re Application by Derbyshire County Council* (1987) *The Guardian*, 22 October.

109a.*Att.-Gen.* v. *B.B.C.* (1987) *The Times*, 18 December.

110. See A. Cavendish, *Guardian*, 24 July 1987, and *Inside Intelligence*.

111. *Att.-Gen.* v. *The Observer and Others* (1987) *The Times*, 22 December.

112. (1988) *The Times*, 11 February.

113. *R.* v. *Secretary of State etc. ex p. Ruddock and Others* [1987] 2 All E.R. 518; see I. Leigh (1987) *Public Law* 12.

114. C.N.D. was not at the relevant time regarded as subversive; it had been when 'communist dominated' in the 1960s. The warrant would have been one of those examined by Lord Bridge, see Chapter 1, p. 27 above, a fact noted by Taylor J. (Leigh, op. cit.).

115. *The Times*, 3 September 1986. Any change in guidelines on tapping should have been publicised, Taylor J. believed.

116. G. Richardson (1986) *Public Law* 437.

117. *Public Service Board of N.S.W.* v. *Osmond* (1986) Admin. Review 114. Nb. s.13, Administrative Decisions (Judicial Review) Act 1977 (Aus.).

118. *Ridge* v. *Baldwin* [1964] A.C. 40.

119. Cf. *Furnell* v. *Whangerei High Schools Board* [1973] A.C. 660.

120. *Lloyd* v. *McMahon* [1987] 1 All E.R. 1118 (C.A. and H.L.).

121. *R.* v. *Secretary of State etc. ex p. Anderson* [1984] Q.B. 778.

122. *Re Pergamon Press* [1971] Ch. 388.

123. See *Grievances, Remedies and the State*, Chapters 1 and 6. Nb. *The Judge Over Your Shoulder* (1987) Tr. Sol. Dept.

124. For a novel judicial recognition of 'non-decisions', see Lloyd L.J. in *Ex p. Datafin* [1987] 1 All E.R. 564.

125. The Franks Report, Cmnd. 218 (1957), and its exhortation of 'openness, fairness and impartiality' for inquiries and tribunals.

126. Now Tribunals and Inquiries Act 1971.

127. *Crake* v. *S.B.C.* [1982] 1 All E.R. 498; cf., for challenge by certiorari, note 222 below; *Mountview Court Props. Ltd* v. *Devlin* (1970) 21 P. and C.R. 689.

128. *Re Poyser and Mill's Arbitration* [1963] 1 All E.R. 612.

129. Note 127. Social Security Commissioners, who hear appeals from local social security tribunals, and other special appeal tribunals, have generally taken a stricter approach on the requirement to provide reasons for decisions (Richardson, op. cit., note 116).

130. *R.* v. *Mental Health Review Tribunal ex p. Pickering* [1986] 1 All E.R. 99,

challenge by certiorari; *U.K.A.P.E.* v. *A.C.A.S.* [1979] 2 All E.R. 478, declaration under private law.

131. *R.* v. *Vaccine Damage Tribunal ex p. Loveday* (1985) *The Times*, 20 April, or where they defer to the expertise of 'experts', *Daejan Properties* v. *Chambers* (1985) 277 E.G. 308.

132. In the area of an individual's liberty the courts have insisted upon *sufficient* reasons being made out to their satisfaction to detain a person on grounds of illegal entry into the UK: *Khawaja* v. *Secretary of State* [1984] A.C. 74; cf. *Bugdaycay* v. *Secretary of State* [1987] 1 All E.R. 940 (H.L.), and *Ex p. Singh* (1987) *The Times*, 8 June. See also *R.* v. *ADHAC etc, ex p. Brough* (1987) 19 H.L.R. 367.

133. *Fairmount Investments* v. *Secretary of State* (1976) 75 L.G.R. 33 (H.L.); *French Kier Developments* v. *Secretary of State* [1977] 1 All E.R. 296.

134. E.g. *Colleen Properties* v. *Minister of Housing and Local Government* [1971] 1 W.L.R. 433; *Prest* v. *Sec. of State for Wales* (1983) 81 L.G.R. 193 (C.A.).

135. See Richardson, note 116, op. cit.

136. Under the Tribunals and Inquiries Act 1971, s.12, on a point of law.

137. E.g. s.245 of the Town and County Planning Act 1971.

138. And also the Attendance Allowance Board.

139. *R.* v. *Secretary of State etc. ex p. Connolly* [1986] 1 All E.R. 998.

140. Ibid.

141. Which is what Woolf J. had encouraged, especially in more difficult cases. How, the Court of Appeal asked, was a distinction to be made between these cases and 'ordinary run of the mill' cases? How full should reasons be, if given? Cf. *Antaios Cia Naviera SA* v. *Salen Rederierna AB* [1985] A.C. 191.

142. And see *R.* v. *Bristol City Council ex p. Pearce* (1985) 83 L.G.R. 711 for a recent refusal to insist on reasons being given.

143. *Payne* v. *Lord Harris* [1981] 2 All E.R. 842; *R.* v. *Secretary of State ex p. Gunnell* (1985) *Crim. L.R.* 105 (C.A.). Cf. *Weeks* v. *U.K.* (1987) *The Times*, 5 March, and *The Guardian* and *Wilson's* case, 28 March 1985.

144. [1986] 1 All E.R.

145. Use of MPs to prevent removal has provoked the Home Secretary to heated comments and various amendments to the procedure, for the latest of which see H.C. Debs. vol. 102, col. 902 (22 October 1986).

146. *Puhlhofer* v. *Hillingdon L.B.C.* [1986] A.C. 484; see Birkinshaw (1982) *Urban Law and Policy* 255; see s.14(2) of the Housing and Planning Act 1986.

147. *R.* v. *Preston S.B. Appeal Tribunal, ex p. Moore* [1975] 1 W.L.R. 624; and *R.* v. *Dep. Gov. of Camphill Prison ex p. King* [1984] 3 All E.R. 897 (C.A.).

148. *Secretary of State etc.* v. *Tameside M.B.C.* [1977] A.C. 1014; *Wheeler* v. *Leicester City Council* [1985] A.C. 1068; and perennial reliance for contradictory outcomes on: *Associated Provincial Picture Houses* v. *Wednesbury Corp.* [1948] 1 K.B. 223.

149. *Padfield* v. *Minister of Housing and Local Government* [1968] A.C. 997.

150. *British Airways Board* v. *Laker Airways* [1985] A.C. 58, especially Lord Diplock.

151. See R. Errera's discussion of *Ministre Des Affaires Sociales* etc. (1987) *Public Law* 119.

152. With modifications in the field of social security administration, see J. Mashaw, *Bureaucratic Justice* (1983) and *Due Process In the Administrative State* (1985).

153. M. Garland (1985) 98 *Harv. L.R.* 507; Morrison (1986) 99 *Harv. L.R.* 1059.

154. E.g. Denning, *Freedom Under the Law* (1949), pp. 91–2.

155. Note 133 above.

156. *Bushell* v. *Secretary of State* [1981] A.C. 75; cf. Lord Diplock at p. 96 C–D.

157. See Purdue *et al.* (1985) *Public Law* 475.

158. Bushell, op. cit.; Franks, note 125 above, paras. 273 and 288. Nb. the use of a Standing Committee of MPs to hear objections into the proposed Channel Tunnel.

159. Cf. Franks, op. cit., para. 317.

160. Purdue *et al.*, note 157, op. cit. at 477, and (1987) *Public Law* 162.

161. Ibid., p. 487.

162. Note 156 above, and Birkinshaw: *Grievances, Remedies and the State*, Chapter 2.

163. *R.* v. *Secretary of State etc. ex p. Gwent C.C.* [1986] 2 All E.R. 18.

164. Making users pay would reduce the overall level of Government subsidy, reducing the PSBR and taxation.

165. In *Bushell*, the court accepted, the Minister would not have been assisted by a discussion of traffic-flow predictions and the inspector's recommendations thereon.

166. Again in *Bushell*, the commitment to motorway interconnections. On issues that were relevant for discussion the Minister must not have precluded alternatives, as this would run the risk of being an unlawful fettering of his discretion.

167. [1987] 1 All E.R. 161.

168. A Department is unlikely to do anything other than confirm its own policy or inclination. Without testing of their position, how fair is their review likely to be?

169. E.g. Town and Country Planning (Inquiries Procedure) Rules, S.I.419, 1974. In *Bushell*, the Minister *accepted* the inspector's recommendations.

170. But not where he disagrees on a matter of policy and its application: *Lord Luke* v. *M.H.L.G.* [1968] 1 Q.B. 172. See Cm. 43 (1986) and Government observations on major inquiries; and see the Energy Committee's criticism of draft rules restricting objectors' rights at inquiries into proposed electricity stations (H.C. 310 1987–8).

171. *R.* v. *Secretary of State, J. Mowlem and L.D.D.C. ex p. G.L.C.* (1986) J.P.L. 32. Informal meetings and discussions did take place.

172. The Chairman was subsequently not re-appointed in March 1987.
173. *R.* v. *London Regional Passengers Committee ex p. Brent L.B.C. and Others* (1983) *Financial Times*, 20 November.
174. An estimated 20,000. See *Pearce* v. *Secretary of State for Defence* (1986) *The Times*, December 31 and the interpretation, in the servicemen's favour, of s.10, Crown Proceedings Act 1947. According to *The Guardian*, the Crown sought an assurance that its witnesses would not be proceeded against for perjury after the Royal Commission's hearings, 6 December 1985. A Royal Commission does not have power to take evidence on oath. Cf. Crown Proceedings (Armed Forces) Act 1987.
175. *The Judge* (1979), p. 54. See *Mahon* v. *N.Z. Airways* [1984] A.C. 808.
176. Though the very range of the exceptions to the hearsay rule, especially *res gestae*, testifies to the tensions between narrow formalism and a fuller procedural justice: *R.* v. *Andrews* [1987] 1 All E.R. 513.
177. See e.g. the Court of Appeal and majority judgment of the law lords in *Air Canada* v. *Secretary of State for Trade (No. 2)* [1983] 1 All E.R. 161 and [1983] 2 A.C. 394.
178. See e.g. pp. 174–6 above.
179. It operates on the basis that it is a 'drastic invasion of privacy', *per* Lord Diplock in *Harman* v. *Home Office*, above. For pre-action discovery, exchange of lists of documents and the general procedure, see *Supreme Court Practice* Order 24; and for pre-trial disclosure of expert reports, *Naylor* v. *Preston A.H.A.* [1987] 2 All E.R. 353. For the EEC, see *Epikhiriseon etc A.E.* v. *E.E.C. Council and Commission* [1987] 1 C.M.L.R. 57. Cf. *Rafidain Bank* v. *Agom U.S.T. Co. Ltd* (1987) *The Times*, 29 July.
180. *Anton Piller K.G.* v. *Manufacturing Processes* [1976] Ch. 55 (C.A.); and cf. *Columbia Picture Industries Inc.* v. *Robinson* [1986] 3 All E.R. 338; *E.M.I. Records* v. *Spillane* [1986] 1 W.L.R. 967.
181. *Lee* v. *South West Thames R.H.A.* [1985] 2 All E.R. 385; *Norwich Pharmacal*, above; *Wilden Pump* v. *Fusfield* [1985] F.S.R. 581 (C.A.); *Ricci* v. *Chow* [1987] 3 All E.R. 534 and attempted discovery from a mere witness; cf. Newspapers etc. Repeal Act 1869, Sched. 2.
182. *Davies* v. *Eli Lilly Co.* [1987] 1 All E.R. 801 (C.A.). Cf. *Blyth* v. *Bloomsbury H.A.* (1987) *The Times*, 11 February.
183. See M. Dockray (1986) *N.L.J.* 219 at 221.
184. *Lee*, above. *Ashburton* v. *Pape* [1913] 2 Ch. 469; *Goddard* v. *Nationwide Building Society* [1986] 3 All E.R. 264; *Guinness Peat Props. Ltd* v. *Fitzroy Robinson Partnership* [1987] 2 All E.R. 716.
185. *Stanfield Properties* v. *Nat. West. Bank* [1983] 2 All E.R. 249.
186. While it is clear that Public Interest Immunity may be invoked by bodies which are 'private' in a legal sense to protect the confidential aspects of work which they perform on the public health (*D.* v. *N.S.P.C.C.* [1978] A.C. 171), the courts will circumscribe the circumstances in which it may be invoked (*S.R.C.* v. *Nassé* [1980] A.C. 102B).

187. Insofar as the Minister, and court, are under a duty not to allow disclosure of information injurious to the public interest.
188. R.S.C. Ord. 24, r.15
189. R.S.C. Ord. 77, r.12(2).
190. *Duncan* v. *Cammell Laird* [1942] A.C. 624, *per* Viscount Simonds.
191. The *breadth* of the decision was not supported by previous authorities, and was not accepted totally in Scotland or the Commonwealth (for the US, see *U.S.* v. *Reynolds* 345 U.S. 1 (1953)). The 'contents' claim was used extensively after 1947, especially to protect inter- and intra-departmental communications and communications between outsiders and officials.
192. [1968] A.C. 910. A judicial reaction had already set in against the full impact of *Duncan*; see D.G.T. Williams, *Not In The Public Interest*. On statutory privileges for information, see I. Eagles (1983) *Camb. L.J.* 118; see *Sethia* v. *Stern* (1987) *The Guardian* 2 November.
193. Confidentiality by itself is not an adequate ground to prevent discovery: *Alfred Crompton etc.*, note 49 above, and cf. *S.R.C.* v. *Nassé*, note 186.
194. *Judicial Review of Administrative Action* (4th edn 1980), p. 40, note 57.
195. In *Burmah Oil*, below, Lord Wilberforce declared that 'it is not for the courts to assume the role of advocates for open government'.
196. *Burmah Oil Co.* v. *Bank of England* [1980] A.C. 1090.
197. And communications with the senior officials of the Bank of England.
198. They did examine but decided that they were of no assistance to Burmah Oil's claim for an unconscionable transaction.
199. *Sankey* v. *Whitlam* (1978) 142 C.L.R.I; *U.S.* v. *Nixon* 418 U.S. 683 (1974); *Env. Defence Soc.* v. *S.P.A. Ltd* [1981] NZLR 146; *Aud.-Gen. of Canada* v. *Minister of Energy etc.* (1986) 23 DLR (4d) 210. In the first two cases, evidence was required for criminal proceedings.
200. E.g. diplomatic and foreign affairs.
201. [1981] 1 All E.R. 1151; cf. *R.* v. *Secretary of State for the Home Department, ex p. Herbage (No. 2)* [1987] 2 W.L.R. 226 (C.A.).
202. The reaction in some quarters was not unlike the response to the education of the children of the masses in the nineteenth century: the expletives were now written closer to the ground!
203. Note 177 above.
204. Airports Authority Act 1975.
205. By setting strict financial targets for the British Airports Authority to meet.
206. Which takes place after the exchange of lists of relevant documents. The certificate was actually signed by a senior civil servant.
207. Lords Scarman and Templeman dissented.
208. See Lord Fraser in *Air Canada* for the majority. He referred to cases of 'serious misconduct'.
209. Lord Wilberforce in *Zamir* v. *Secretary of State* [1980] A.C. 930; Lord

Scarman in *IRC* v. *Nat. Fed. of Small Businesses* [1982] A.C. 617; Lord Diplock in *O'Reilly* v. *Mackman* [1983] 2 A.C. 237, and cf. *R.* v. *Liverpool City Council, ex p. Coade* (1986) *The Times*, 10 October.

210. (1985) *Public Law* at 582.

211. He concentrates upon the *G.C.H.Q.*, the *Guardian Newspapers* and the G.L.C. 'Fares Fair' litigation. See also *R.* v. *Secretary of State etc. ex p. Anderson Strathclyde* [1983] 2 All E.R. 233.

212. (1986) *Public Law* at 230.

213. Ibid., p. 231.

214. Cf. Widdicombe's proposals *vis-à-vis* the Commission for Local Administration: Chapter 3, note 153 above.

215. The Commissaire du Gouvernement is not restricted to judicial review cases, but also participates in what we would refer to as private actions involving public bodies. On public law litigation and constitutional issues in the USA, see Chayes (1982) 86 *Harv. L.R.* 4.

216. Ibid., p. 237.

217. And *post Datafin* those bodies of indeterminate legal status, see Chapter 4, note 115 above.

218. See Lord Diplock: *O'Reilly* v. *Mackman* [1983] 2 A.C. 237. Cross-examination was allowable on the same basis as a private action commenced by originating summons, *not by writ*.

219. *R.* v. *Governor of Pentonville Prison and Another ex p. Herbage (No. 2)* [1986] 3 W.L.R. 504 (Q.B.D.).

220. *R.* v. *Lancs. C.C. ex p. Huddleston* [1986] 2 All E.R. 941; and see *R.* v. *Secretary of State ex p. Sherrif and Sons Ltd* (1986) *The Times*, 18 December.

221. Not by discovery, but by a 'voluntary' explanation of events.

222. Cf. the inconsistencies in this approach and those in *Ex p. Swati* and *Puhlhofer* [1986] 1 All E.R. 717 and [1986] A.C. 484 respectively.

223. Note 221.

224. *Bromley L.B.C.* v. *G.L.C.* [1983] 1 A.C. 768.

225. Note 210 above.

226. [1982] 1 All E.R. at p. 147a.

227. E.g. *Tameside*, where the Minister did not have adequate information to be satisfied that the L.E.A. was acting 'unreasonably', and *R.* v. *Secretary of State ex p. Hackney L.B.C.* (1985) *The Times*, 11 May (C.A.), where the court held, in refusing to rule as unlawful the Rate Support Grant Report, that 'a disclosure of thinking behind the principles of the guidance in the Report was not required'.

228. *Neilson* v. *Laugharne* [1981] Q.B. 736; *Hehir* v. *Commissioner of Police* [1982] 2 All E.R. 335; cf. *Taylor* v. *Anderton* (1986) *The Times*, 21 October. Cf. *R.* v. *C.I.C.B. ex p. Brady* (1987) *The Times*, 11 March.

229. *Peach* v. *Commissioner of Police* [1986] 2 All E.R. 129. Cf. *Evans* v. *Chief Constable of Surrey* (1988) *The Guardian*, 21 January.

230. Especially where individuals apart from the police gave evidence.

231. *Conerney* v. *Jacklin* [1985] *Crim. L.R.* 234 (C.A.).

232. And have used the evidence publicly to discredit complainants. On various notorious cases the closing of ranks has prevented the Police Complaints Authority obtaining essential identity information of officers. See the comments of the Metropolitan Police Commissioner in *The Guardian*, 20 April 1987.

233. See H.C. 307 (1985–6).

234. *Argyll* v. *Argyll* [1967] Ch. 302.

235. Chapter 4, p. 99 above.

236. Though damages or an account of profits would then be appropriate if disclosure followed a breach of the obligation. The Wright episode led to some startling measures from the courts to protect information already in the public domain or public knowledge – see note 109 above and G. Jones (1970) *L.Q.R.* at 466–70.

237. An injunction was not sought to prevent publication of Volumes II and especially III.

238. *Att.-Gen.* v. *The Guardian and The Observer* (1986) *The Times*, 26 July. An injunction was upheld in England to prevent distribution of *One Girl's War* by former MI5 officer, Joan Miller, but was lifted in the Irish Republic on 2 December 1986.

239. See e.g. *Faccenda Chickens Ltd.* v. *Fowler* [1985] 1 All E.R. 724, and [1986] 1 All E.R. 617 (C.A.). See Jones (1970) *L.Q.R.* 463; and the Law Commission's Report note 2 above. In *Wright's* case, the Crown sought to vindicate a right *in personam* to the profits of his breach of confidentiality and a right *in rem* to the confidential information itself, above.

240. *Alfred Crompton*, above, note 49. See the curious decision in *Woodward* v. *Hutchins* [1977] 1 W.L.R. 760.

241. *S.R.C.* v. *Nassé* [1980] A.C. 1028; note *West Midlands P.T.E.* v. *Singh* (1987) *The Times*, 23 June.

242. *Lion Laboratories* v. *Evans* [1984] 3 W.L.R. 539 (C.A.). This was not a publication of a wrongdoing as such.

243. *Francombe* v. *Mirror Group Newspapers Ltd* [1984] 2 All E.R. 208.

244. Nb. the test on the defendants in *Att.-Gen.* v. *The Guardian and The Observer*, above, p. 190. Cf. *Schering Chemicals Ltd.* v. *Falkman Ltd* [1982] 1 Q.B. 1. See *Bonnard* v. *Perryman* [1891] 2 Ch. 269; *Gulf Oil (G.B.)* v. *Page* (1987) N.L.J. 408. See Cmnd. 8388 and remember that bribing employees is a crime, Prevention of Corruption Act 1906. See Supreme Court Act 1981, s.72, and self-incrimination in intellectual property cases.

245. J. Phillips, *Introduction To Intellectual Property Law* (1986).

246. The first copyright act was passed in 1709.

247. Cmnd. 9712.

248. See D.T. Bainbridge (1986) *Mod. L.R.* 214.

Chapter 7: Conclusion – How Nigh is the End?

1. A.F. Westin, *Privacy and Freedom* (1967), p. 7.
2. See e.g. Companies Act 1985, ss.366–383 on meetings and Financial Services Act 1986, Part I, Ch. V and Part VII, on Conduct of Business and Insider Dealing in the financial services sector, and Company Securities (Insider Dealing) Act 1985.
3. The duties relate to registers, accounts and reports.
4. I.e. wide exhortatory provisions affording maximum opportunity for self-created standards: Employment Act 1982, s.1; Employment Protection Act 1975, s.99; Health and Safety at Work Act 1974, s.2(4) and (6); Transfer of Undertakings Regs. 1981, Reg. 10, etc.
5. See C. Docksey (1986) *M.L.R.* 281 for a full account.
6. Ibid.
7. E.g. Chapter 4 above, pp. 123–4 and Chapter 5, pp. 153–6. For the duty of confidentiality owed by a bank to its customers, see *Tournier* v. *Nat. Prov. Bank etc.* [1924] K.B. 461 and *Bank of Tokyo* v. *Karoon* (1984) F.T. 12 July.
8. This coincides with reform of its complaints procedures for dissatisfied clients of solicitors.
9. The Accounts Standards Committee is not open to the public, but follows 'notice and comment procedures'. See Banking Act 1987, s.47.
10. The British Medical Association. The Royal College of Nursing has taken a different attitude: *The Guardian*, 10 April 1987. Cf. Access To Medical Records Bill, November 1987.
11. A grievance procedure for complaints of clinical judgment was agreed to, providing those cases which may go to litigation are weeded out: (DHSS) H.C. Circ. (81) 5 and Hospital Complaints Act 1985. For pre-trial discovery of medical opinions, see *Naylor* v. *Preston AHA* [1987] 2 All E.R. 353.
12. As the 1980 Education Act is drafted, universities would not be covered.
13. Numerous private information-collection agencies which peddle information on prospective employees and their 'political' leanings for their members will not be included.
13a. Requests had to be in writing – a discretion is to operate for informal requests. Confidential information on a child's welfare to a third party or from a third party is not accessible. The governing body is to make arrangements for the keeping and disclosure of records, and a charge for copies can be made.
14. A procedure for third-party notice was contained in the original Bill.
15. Unless the parties involved have consented to disclosure.
16. In the former case the record-holder may have required the applicant to be accompanied by a person nominated by the practitioner.
17. Not simply *written*, as the original Bill specified.

18. The original Bill also spelt out incorrect, incomplete or misleading.
19. Note 18.
20. And include provisions for review of decisions by authorities.
21. See: DHSS LAC (83) 14; nb. *Gaskin* v. *Liverpool City Council* [1980] 1 W.L.R. 1549.
22. R. Dingwell (1986) *Mod. L.R.* 489.
23. It is essentially a professional association and not a governing body. In July 1987, it voted to 'Aids test' patients without their consent where a doctor felt this to be necessary; the BMA's ruling council subsequently blocked this move.
24. Reversed in *Gillick* v. *West Norfolk etc A.H.A.* [1985] 3 All E.R. 402 (H.L.). Confidentiality for Aids victims must be maintained: *The Guardian*, 2 October 1985; but cf. note 23.
25. *The Guardian*, 13 February 1986. The case concerned the obstetrician Dr Wendy Savage. For alleged G.M.C. equivocation on this point, see W. Savage, *The Guardian*, 3 June 1987.
26. Dr Savage wanted an open inquiry to avoid a 'cover-up'. An internal report for the health authority said the inquiry should not have been held (*The Guardian*, 9 July 1987).
27. Tyra Henry: *The Guardian*, 10 January 1986.
28. Home Office Circular of 17 July 1986.
29. The use by private bodies of information on the political affiliations of prospective employees has been highlighted: H.C. Debs. vol. 110, col. 1176.
30. Cmnd. 3638 (1968).
31. See T. Barnes, *Open Up* (1980).
32. Cmnd. 7285 (1978). See also Cmnd. 7520 (1979) on freedom of information.
33. See Barnes, op. cit., p. 4.
34. It was suggested that the Bill would have prevented the publication of the Blunt affair. Blunt, an adviser to the Queen, had been a Russian spy.
35. Cmnd. 9916.
36. Ibid., para. 40.
37. Para. 42, and see H.C. 588 (1977–8), *First Report of Select Committee on Procedure*.
38. Select Committees are usually non-partisan in their inquiries.
39. As Head of the Home Civil Service and Secretary to the Cabinet.
40. H.C. 92 II, p. 7.
41. H.C. 100 (1986–7).
42. E.O. Guide, paras. 4129–32. *Per contra F.D.A. News*, December 1984 and its Code of Ethics: see Chapter 4 above, pp. 107–8.
43. Note 41, op. cit., p. 34.
44. Interview with F.D.A. official 30 January 1986.

45. And that date would seem to depend upon a new party Government. It is of course true that many Tory MPs dislike s.2, but FOI finds little support.

46. The point has been made that s.2 is now so unworkable that it is better to keep the devil you know, etc. As a matter of principle the section is objectionable in its scope and uncertainty. This does not justify a more draconian measure.

47. Would this cover Zircon? See Chapter 1.

48. E.g. *Gartside* v. *Outram* (1856) 26 L.J. Ch. 113; *Initial Services* v. *Putterill* [1968] 1 Q.B. 396; and Lord Wilberforce in *BSC* v. *Granada TV* [1981] A.C. 1096.

49. Cmnd. 8388. pp. 41–51. Nb. s.2 of the Race Relations Act 1976; s.4 of the Sex Discrimination Act 1975; s.2 of the Witnesses (Public Inquiries) Protection Act 1892.

50. Cripps (1985) *L.Q.R.* 506, and *The Legal Implications of Disclosure in the Public Interest* (1987).

51. *Laws* v. *London Chronicle (Indicator Newspapers) Ltd* [1959] 1 W.L.R. 698.

52. *Thornley* v. *Aircraft Research Association Ltd*, 11 May 1977 (E.A.T. 669/76), discussed in Cripps, op. cit.

53. The less scrupulous internal procedures are, the more likely a conscientious employee will invoke public means of ventilation.

54. See Part V of Employment Protection (Consolidation) Act 1978, as amended. Could this statutory protection be conducive to an altered position in common law so that a contract may be deemed to exist? See Woolf J. in *R.* v. *BBC ex p. Lavelle* [1983] 1 All E.R. 241.

55. *Council of Civil Servants Unions* v. *Minister for Civil Service Unions* [1984] 3 All E.R. 935 (H.L.); *R.* v. *Secretary of State etc ex p. Benwell* [1985] Q.B. 554; *R.* v. *Civil Service Appeal Board ex p. Bruce* (1987) *The Times*, 22 June.

56. The Circular accompanying the Local Government (Access To Information) Act 1985 envisaged that the Act would involve no additional expenditure for local authorities.

57. I am grateful to Maurice Frankel for this information. The FOIA was also used to obtain papers showing that Ronald Reagan narrowly escaped criminal indictment for his role in assisting the monopoly control of the US entertainment industry by the Musical Corporation of America: *The Guardian*, 13 January 1987.

58. See Chapter 2 above, pp. 48 *et seq*. It does not exempt reasons for decisions affecting an individual's rights, nor policy advice from outside consultants/advisers.

59. Opposition leaders claim that the Government has made an issue of personalities by promoting 'like-minded' civil servants with whom they would not be able to work and whose identities they already know.

60. See the former Civil Service Department's booklet, *Legal Entitlements and Administrative Practices* (HMSO 1979).

61. Nb. *Bushell's* case, Chapter 6 above, note 156.
62. C. Bennett and P. Hennessey, *The Consumer's Guide to Open Government* (Outer Circle Policy Unit, 1980).
63. Cf. restrictions on answers which Select Committees may require from civil servants and outsiders: Chapter 4 above, note 38.
64. The following leans heavily on a paper given by Sir D. Wass at a conference organised by the FOI Campaign on 1 July 1986.
65. Ibid.
66. Ibid. Presumably, he was not addressing Northern Ireland Departments.
67. But would still be subject to scrutiny in the court.
68. At Sizewell, the CEGB bought essential equipment for a PWR reactor long before Sir Frank Layfield reported. In his report Sir Frank asked for 'full and accurate' records of the plutonium produced in civil reactors.
69. *Government and the Governed* (1984).
70. *The Big Public Inquiry* (Justice O.C.P.U., 1979).
71. S. Zuckerman, *Star Wars In a Nuclear World* (1986).
72. E.g. Sir John Hoskyns and the views of the Institute of Directors, see K. Owen, *Information Technology and Public Policy* (1985), vol. 3, no. 3, p. 204; *Re-skilling Government*, I.O.D. Policy Unit, April 1987.
73. H.C. 92 (1985–6), vol. II; see H.C. 62 (1986–7); *First Report for the TCSC on Ministers and Civil Servants*.
74. See I. Harden and N. Lewis, *The Noble Lie* (1986), pp. 127–9.
75. See Chapter 4 above, pp. 102–3.
76. See R. Dingwell (1986) *Mod. L.R.* 489.
77. Harden and Lewis, op. cit., pp. 253–5, 282–3 and 305–6, place considerable faith in the example of the Social Security Advisory Committee established under the Social Security Act 1980. By s.9(4) it has the right 'to be provided with information reasonably necessary for the discharge of its functions' and the Secretary of State must consult with it on proposals for a wide range of regulations. The Secretary of State must consider their report on the former's proposals and a copy of such report must be laid with the draft regulations. S/he must state how far s/he has given effect to the Committee's recommendations and reasons must be given for not following the recommendations. They have commissioned their own studies better to inform Parliament of social security regulations and policies. Ministers have not always paid due respect to the position and duties of the Committee. The authors suggest a judicial rather than a Parliamentary oversight of the operation of these provisions.
78. *Open and Shut: Enhancing the Right to Know and the Right to Privacy*, Standing Committee on Justice and Solicitor General (Ottawa, 1987).

INDEX